SELECTED
TO
LIVE

by

JOHANNA-RUTH DOBSCHINER

Pickering & Inglis
LONDON — GLASGOW

Copyright © Johanna-Ruth Dobschiner 1969

ISBN 0 7208 0212 1
Cat. No. 01/1806

First published 1969
Reprinted 1970
Paperback Edition 1971
Reprinted 1972, 1972, 1972, 1972, 1973, 1973, 1974,
1974, 1975, 1976, 1977, 1978, 1979

Selected to Live

By the same author
LIVING IS GIVING
TWIXT SOUL AND THE SPIRIT

Also published in *Norwegian, French, German, Dutch, Finnish, Portuguese, Spanish, Italian, Swedish*

INTRODUCTION

The ruins of memory lay untouched year after year. Covered by event upon event, these ruins refused to die. The breath of life was in them. Right deep down to the bottom layer.

The ruins of memory breathed and sighed and were part, and always will be part of the modern, new society; they will be part of this present day with its joys and sorrows; they will be part of the approaching tomorrow with its events still veiled and hidden.

The ruins of memory begged to be always part of life. To be, to remain, to belong, to be treasured, to be acknowledged, to live for ever!

But why do they want to be part of the present? Why not remain covered by hawthorn, holly and spring blossom?

Because I live and always will live. Within me are those countless millions whose souls will never die; who lived, loved, hoped, feared, and trembled like myself . . . for myself and my own kith and kin. Their bodies were worth nothing, their blood as cheap as water, their feelings and pain but smoke and ashes.

You have decided to come and join me by digging through these ruins, to search and to find the reason for their breath of life and their right to live.

Then, let us use our discoveries from among those ruins.

JOHANNA-RUTH DOBSCHINER

1

ADOLF HITLER'S BIRTHDAY WAS A GREAT EVENT. IT was April 1933 and all schools were invited to take part in the great parade. Our school brought its own token of respect . . . gratitude, to such a leader.

We had planned and prepared a gift since autumn of the previous year. The senior boys had made a large frame and in it was placed a picture of the Fuhrer. The picture was full of little holes like peg-board. We were asked to bring threepence to school, threepence for one nail, black, white or red. Indeed, we were encouraged to bring many threepences to school, for it was fun to hammer nails into this picture peg-board, to see it taking shape, until, finally, a full colour portrait of the Fuhrer had been completed. All the money would go to the party as our contribution for all the Fuhrer was doing for the Fatherland and . . . the world!

Primary and senior classes assembled in the gymnasium. There on the platform, between flags and swastikas, was the portrait. We looked at it once more as we stood singing the National Anthem as well as the Party song. Quietly we filed into the school grounds and were drilled into rows. The flags were about to be distributed, small ones, medium and large, according to age groups. Each class was headed by a flagbearer. As their names rang out over the loud-speaker system, joyful 'oh's' and 'ah's' could be heard here and there; my six-year-old heart felt like bursting when I heard mine. I had been chosen to lead my class!

Having been thoroughly trained not to show signs of emotion on matters of religion or politics at school, I quickly stepped from my row and received a holder and a large flag. Would I be able to carry that weight in a dignified manner? My fellow classmates gave me looks of approval or jealousy. I had become their hero. Some-how I could not explain my teacher's face. She knew who I was. She must have felt for me, knowing how difficult it was to obey.

The procession was spectacular, full of colour, music and song.

Coming to the Reichstag, we met the Fuhrer. All right hands were stretched high with a fervent shout of 'Heil Hitler'. He greeted us with his 'Heil' and a broad smile. The portrait was handed over by the senior boys and the procession moved on. Bands and music surrounded us for hours.

Conversation that night dwelt mainly around the events of the day. What was in the hearts of all the parents of those children? I remember the atmosphere in our home. Fancy, our only daughter, chosen to carry that flag! The committee couldn't have known who she was, or had the decision been influenced by evil intentions. We would never know.

In the next few days all decorations and flags were removed from streets and buildings. The houses and roads looked bare once more. Those tall houses, the broad city roads, the clean stone fronts of flats and offices, they made our city look proud and fine. I loved the hometown of my youth!

On Sundays the roads looked broader still, the buildings fairer. When the sun added its magic touch one would marvel at the fine architecture.

Our home and shop were situated in the Ullstein House, the property of a large newspaper and printing firm. Beside the shop was a huge archway with two high double glass doors. Going through them you found yourself in a marble hallway from which you could reach the different floors and departments. We, however, walked across the marble hallway, and through another swing door to the backyard. Passing through yet another hallway the dwelling houses could be reached.

We children loved to play in this spacious labyrinth of passages. Coming in this way we would enter our home. Then, running along our hall and through our rooms we walked sedately through the shop and out to the street, to repeat the process until our parents would realise we were up to our favourite game once more. The one who was admonished was the recognised loser and the fun was over till next time.

Although we children were happy and content we were all older than our years. Responsibility was ours as far back as I can remember. We were not to air our opinions regarding the new reign in the country, not to mix with Gentiles apart from school hours and not to repeat home conversations. The innocent chatter of a child had already brought imprisonment and death to many a parent. Even teachers at school could be trusted no longer. They were compelled to question their pupils regarding the home attitudes towards the Fuhrer and his party.

Life became more strained as the days went by. I admire my parents for the way they shielded us from worry and fear as long as they could.

One Sunday morning I brought terror into our home. It was my habit to take my doll for a walk on Sunday before she was given her doll's dinner. She was greatly loved and cared for and mother always made her a dress and hat to match what she had made for me. This particular Sunday two tall policemen approached me. They asked the name of 'my child' and remarked on how well she looked and how well she behaved. They congratulated me, and said that I must be the best doll's mother in the city! It made me proud and I felt grateful to my admirers and asked them to accompany me to my home, as my parents ought to meet such nice policemen, I thought. On the way I promoted them 'police-daddy' and 'police uncle' and was very eager to introduce them to the doll's 'grandparents'. Not giving them the slightest chance to refuse, I marched them towards the large Ullstein building. The poor policemen must have been very embarrassed, but naughty me gave them no chance to back-out. Pressing the doll into 'police-daddy's' arm, I placed myself between them, reached out for their hands and walked them to our back-door. There I introduced them brightly to my frightened mother. Knowing her daughter only too well, she pulled herself quickly together and apologised to the amused constables for the impulsiveness of her youngest. My new friends thanked me for a lovely time and promised to meet me again. This last remark worried my poor parents for a long time to come, and when letters for the 'doll's-mummy' arrived, my father's blood pressure truly took a jump. I was supposed to answer these letters, but they would not let me. Very disappointed I took my precious letters to school, and asked my teacher to help me with a well-spelled reply. In some mysterious way our correspondence found itself in a national colour magazine. The editor sent me a postal order which thrilled me but made my parents furious.

After this incident they explained to me more fully the dangers which faced us and ours. We were still under the protection of the

Dutch Government and its Consul in Berlin, but which rascal or hooligan would possibly know that we were Dutch Jews! All over the city, shop windows of Jewish proprietors were smashed, and slogans painted on walls and dwelling houses. It could be our turn next. Why should I try to invite trouble when it would surely reach us in due course. This conversation made us all aware that lighthearted friendships could no longer be entered into.

A new era dawned during 1933.

Family ties grew stronger and relationships between in-laws strengthened. We saw more of each other and appreciated the worth of family and friends.

Yet, to a child, any show of kindness, irrespective of creed, colour or nation, triumphs in the end. For instance, I liked the kind gentleman who entered our shop one afternoon. He came to buy a handbag for his wife's birthday. It had to be of fine quality leather, and elegant to match her accessories. He discussed the details at great length with my mother and asked her to show him many designs and colours. Soon the counter became a mountain of bags. It must have exasperated my willing mother, for still he was not pleased. He wanted definitely 'that one in the window'! This was a difficult request as my father was not available to take it out of the window. But she would try.

As soon as mother had disappeared the kind gentleman spoke to me and asked if I wanted to play a little game till my mother came back. I liked the idea. He suggested hiding all the handbags on the counter inside one of the large cases on display. Then he would go and hide the case while I would try to find him. I was not very sure if such a game should be played in case some of the goods became damaged, yet I did not have the heart to disappoint him. Hesitantly my promise was forthcoming . . . I would not spoil the fun!

Another rascal had been aided by an innocent child. This time, however, my innocence landed my parents in a great loss.

My elder brothers sneered at and ridiculed their small sister. They would never do such silly things. When would I grow up? There was such a gap in our ages. Werner was six years older than I was. His twin, a girl, had died on August 30th, when only three months old. I was born on August 30th, six years later. Just a 'substitute' according to his boyish teasing. A 'treasured gift' in the eyes of my parents.

Werner was a fair boy, taller and thinner than Manfred in outward appearance; he also seemed more fragile, yet his strength was respected on the playground at school and also at sports. In nature, both boys were very similar. They were good friends, had many interests in common and were homeloving and quiet. Chess or draughts was a regular week-end activity in our home. During the better weather we could always be found in the park. The boys liked these walks and joined us as often as possible.

Manfred was a year younger, darker in appearance and, if anything quieter than Werner. When Werner, always technically-minded, wanted to have fun and experiment, Manfred withdrew to his music and study. He was specially gifted. Music was born into the very fibre of his boyish nature. He could pick up any instrument and, handling it for a short while, could play the tune of his choice. At twelve years old, when taking part in his first concert at High school, the programme read 'Manfred, the wonder boy'.

Gifted as he was, many were the offers which came our way regarding educational grants for a future career in music. The reply was firm and always the same, 'Our son must learn a trade, he shall work with his hands. Knowledge in his finger tips will see him through any crisis he may have to face in his future life'.

Manfred obeyed. I cannot remember any outward resentment. He studied and played his instruments in the spare time at his disposal. The musical section in our shop was his special hobby. He would go around tuning instruments, dusting, tidying and re-arranging shelves for display, and composing little tunes when his emotions were stirred.

At week-ends the boys spent their time together, showing interest in each other's hobbies and talents, or joining in experiments. The electric train set always needed to be modernised and often it absorbed them till late on Sunday night.

I loved to play outside. The park and lots of children were my delight, the freedom, fresh air, sunshine and laughter. There were long avenues and many hilly stretches. In winter we took our sledge and the fun was tremendous. There were ducks and swans; any stale bread or crusts were confiscated for them. My father took me to this paradise whenever time would permit. He was a wonderful man. I respected, loved, and admired him too.

My mother was one year older than my father. There was little she could not do. If we wanted something, she could always help. If she had not the time to do immediately we could rest assured that she would attend to the request at a later date.

I am glad I was born, and I am glad to recall my childhood. I treasure the memory of home and family life. I am grateful for the strict training and discipline that was mine during those early years. I am puzzled and bewildered by the experience which war and depravation pressed on us all, but I have learnt that a loving invisible hand held mine through it all and I am firmly convinced that neither death nor life, nor angels, nor principalities, nor things present, nor things to come, will be able to separate me from the love of God, which is revealed in Christ Jesus.

2

ANTI-SEMITISM IN GERMANY WAS ON THE INCREASE. Raids and unpleasant incidents were reported from all large cities. Men in prominent places of employment were informed that their services were no longer required. The intelligentsia in medicine, music, art and science disappeared from the public scene. Many emigrated or endeavoured to do so. Actions against Jews were stepped up sharply. To find whole families in gas-filled flats was a common occurrence. It seemed to them the best way out.

Our home and family life was still relatively safe, our Dutch Nationality the only security. Repeatedly, the Dutch consul in Berlin informed my father that he could not continue to be responsible for our safety. Youthful enthusiasts did not enquire about their target's nationality. Already at High school, my brothers had been molested. Headmasters no longer had any control. Party politics roared through schoolrooms and colleges. Normal study had an added flavour, a bitter taste for many. Children were invited to join the Hitler Jugend, to become primary, junior and senior party members. One was encouraged to gain awards and promotions. The rat race for power and status, at all costs, was on!

We had to make decisions. The Dutch consul advised early emigration to Holland to begin life anew in my father's hometown of Amsterdam. The next few months were a succession of events. The business which had been in our family since 1884 had to be wound up. All goods were sold off cheaply as time was short. The furniture left in a large van and soon our flat was empty. A taxi took us from the home, the only one I had ever known, to the station, the gateway to an unknown future for us all.

On the platform we met all our relations and their children. It was an emotional re-union and farewell. I, however, was too young to understand the anguish of such a moment. To me, adventure and the unknown future beckoned with excitement and thrill. I was looking forward to the journey and the new country ahead!

On April 10th, 1935 we arrived in Amsterdam. It was late and we were tired. How I wish now that I had been older and more understanding. Here we were, in our own country on a dark April evening, but none of us knew a word of Dutch and there were no relatives or friends to meet us. My parents were so weary, they must have felt lost and alone. Quietly we took our cases and awaited the arrival of a Jewish Community representative. We felt more like refugees than Dutch citizens. It had never entered my mind where we would live. It had never been discussed. Most probably my parents' thoughts ran on the same vein. No one raised the subject Come what may, we would accept any roof gratefully. One door had closed—the door of security; another one had opened—the door beyond which lay a blank. . . . Surely trust in the God of our fathers was all we could hold on to now.

A Jewish-looking gentleman approached us. In broken German he discussed the immediate future with my parents, and then he summoned a taxi. After a short ride, the taxi drew up before the main gate of our new 'home'.

Quite vividly I remember every detail of the next few hours and days. It was not a dream, but reality; they had placed us in an 'Asylum for the Homeless'. It was chilly and a drizzle added to the general feeling of malaise which now affected us all. We were tired, hungry and strained to breaking point.

The wooden gatehouse was lit by a single lamp shaded with a green bakelite cover. We had to show our papers. Having exchanged some remarks with the watchman, our representative took leave of us satisfied with another mission accomplished, while still another person took charge. He led us to a barely furnished hall with high walls and long narrow windows. The paint work was a uniform cream-like colour. The long windows were covered by dark green curtains which only just fulfilled their purpose. One inch more would have impressed a visitor with excess generosity on the part of the authorities in charge. Lighting was scarce. The atmosphere was in tune with our feelings that night.

Someone, probably the dining-room attendant, showed us to a table and told us to sit down. The wooden benches were hard and the tables long and bare. A waxcloth hid the whitewood—practical, but, oh, so unfriendly. It was not long before a simple but very welcome meal was set before us. The large mugs of tea and the white bread with jam was true luxury.

Revived and nourished we waited for the unfolding of scene number two. Mother and I were to be separated from my father and brothers who would spend their nights in the male section of the building. Mother was very composed, but I cried for our men. . . . Tears filled her eyes as she smiled down at me and I was somehow ashamed that I hadn't shown more courage. Suddenly a nurse came to take me away. I could not understand her and resisted strongly, then they let mother come as well. We were taken to a large bathroom with shower cubicles and tub baths. Nurse showed me where my mother would wash, and tried to explain that she would bath me in the adjoining cubicle. Not wanting to bother my tired mother by any more remonstrations, I followed indignantly but quietly. The nurse washed and dried me, then finished with an inspection of my hair. Within half-an-hour a humiliated, tired and clean girl joined her mother in the already dimmed dormitory. I saw many beds. Some ladies sat up straight when we tiptoed in, looking curiously at us and forming their own opinions of the newcomers. Our beds were side by side in the centre of a row. It was a comfort to be together. Mother talked with me for a little, assuring me that the men would be all right and with us again in the morning. Soon we were asleep.

At breakfast next morning, everything seemed much brighter. We were able to laugh and joke about our experience of the previous night and compared this dining-room with that depicted in Oliver Twist. We all agreed it must have been the same, the only difference being that we were offered a second helping. After such a generous and nourishing breakfast we felt ready to face another day. The arrangement was that we would live in the Asylum on a bed-and-breakfast basis until a suitable flat could be found.

That day we set out to see something of Amsterdam and to find the Jewish Community buildings and its offices. In a fortnight it would be the annual celebration of the Jewish passover, and we would like to have a solid roof above our heads for this feast with its intricate ceremonies and special food laws. Officials advised us not to worry, all would be settled by then.

During our wanderings we ate snacks of herring, cucumbers and onions from the favourite Dutch herring barrows, and drank cups

17

of lemon tea in street cafes. We were free from persecution, although strangers in our own land, but we were content and thankful. Soon a settled homelife would unite the family again.

Rented houses could be found, but were they within our means? What were our means? I'll never know. Father was out of work, my brothers still had to find a trade and be accepted as apprentices. I had to go to school. The Jewish Board of Guardians and Assistance came to our aid. Visits to the National Assistance Board and the Labour Exchange were daily routine. I became used to this trekking around town, but did my parents? The humiliation and strain of this period in our lives aged them considerably—even I could notice that. They were short-tempered and very serious. We had escaped the Jewish persecution in Germany, but would we ever be secure again? It seemed that we could not have our personal possessions with us until a flat had been found. We had to make-do! That also burdened us, as we were used to regular changes of clothes. We coped as best we could.

After some months the lease for our first home was signed. The house was in a nice bright street in the east end of Amsterdam near a lovely park, the Zuider Zee and the open air swimming baths. All houses in this district were comparatively new council flats, each building housing four families. Each house had an outer closed door, and on it a plate with the names of the residents and a personal bell, giving each flat a sense of privacy. If you wanted to visit the family in the top flat, you pressed their bell. Presently the outer door, which your friend had touched by 'remote control', would open. This was done by a cord attached to the door-lock and to her landing above. In modern houses the cord was replaced by an electric push button and a loudspeaker system. We had to shout down 'Who's there?' and wait for a reply.

Another interesting feature intrigued us: at the top of the building there was a flat of attic rooms. Each tenant owned one of the rooms as a storage place. If need be, it could be transformed into a spare room for an unexpected guest. Outside the front attic window you would find a strong iron bar with a hook at the end. All houses and factories had one. It was a clever device to help the furniture removals to proceed with speed and efficiency. Nothing was carried up the stairs, all articles were 'hooked' in the van and pulled up to the flat in question.

Removals are a treat to children of all ages. Even their parents love to peep from behind curtain-draped windows to admire, or otherwise, the furniture of their new neighbours. Who could blame the curiosity of all and sundry when our contractor opened the van doors? These foreigners had such different furniture . . . their heads followed each article as it flew through the air to the first floor window. Look at the size of the wardrobe, sideboards, chairs and beds! True it all looked far too big for these little rooms, yet to sell it and buy new furniture would have been equally as odd in view of our circumstances.

Soon we had settled into our new Dutch home. 'Masselltoff' was the good wish of relatives and friends, but our road was to be rocky and steep.

My brothers became apprentices with local businessmen. Manfred, to an optician, and Werner to a tailor. I cannot remember them ever grumbling. They truly were good boys to my parents, considerate and helpful in every way. Wherever they went, they were liked for their good manners and their courtesy to the older generation.

I was enrolled in the local school, a fine building, matching the modern district. It was airy and bright and had a large playground. The classrooms were spacious, allowing the light and sun to penetrate throughout. Here I began my Dutch education in the autumn of 1935. It was a strange experience, a class full of Dutch speaking children and a Dutch teacher. I could not follow a word at first. Yet, somehow, language becomes part of one's life and soon I chatted and laughed in Dutch with the other children. After four o'clock, the games on the street in front of our homes taught me a great deal. The 'dutch-foreign-girl' had settled down. The slate, the squeaking slate-pencil, sponge and cloth were my daily companions. We all used them at school. I liked this method. In Germany we had used pencil and exercise book only: it hadn't the fun of the screeching slate-pencil! When underlining a word you could make the slate-pencil screech extra loud, bringing those who hated it out in goose flesh. We went to the local open air swimming baths with our teachers, and even in rather cold and rainy weather we enjoyed ourselves thoroughly.

Soon I, too, learned to swim and was very proud of my progress. On Saturdays I did not need to attend school and during the winter months I was allowed to leave early on Friday afternoons as it was then we Jewish children prepared ourselves for the Sabbath day. My brothers arrived home early from work. Every detail was important. The scrubbing of the wooden staircase to our flat, the laying-out of clean clothes for the Sabbath, the polishing of our shoes, the shopping, the preparing of meals, the setting of the table with the starched white cloth. The silver had to be polished and the candlesticks especially had to look their best. The poppy seed loaves were a regular order. They were placed at the head of the table together with the bread knife. Then a beautiful red velvet cover would protect these loaves till the ceremonial blessing after the synagogue service. This cover, fringed with gold thread, was likewise embroidered, displaying the two tables of stone with its ten commandments. This special setting of the table was again done on Saturday morning when new loaves were cut and new wine poured. This breaking of bread and the drinking of the wine when blessed, has always been the most impressive act of worship in the Jewish home. Each member of the family partook of these elements in strict rotation, from the Father of the house to the Mother and then to the children, one by one. Once this act of worship was performed, my father placed his dear hands on each of our heads. His blessing for the boys contained a plea to the Almighty, to bless them and let them grow in wisdom and become like Abraham, Isaac and Jacob. The girls were blessed, to become like Sarah and Rachel, and be fruitful and multiply.

At last the men sat down, while we women, mother and I, served the meal. Frequently we commenced the meal with traditional cold fish, stuffed and very tasty. Then came the hot chicken soup which we ate with brocks of poppy seed loaf. The meals were eaten leisurely, adding to the harmony and pleasant conversation all round. We complimented our mother for yet another fine Sabbath meal. Smiling happily she would leave the room to bring in the next course. After the chicken, vegetables and potatoes, we lingered over a large glass of hot lemon tea. Everyone would reach freely for the biscuits, peanuts and other homely delights.

On Sunday mornings and twice during the week after school hours, I went to Jewish classes in order to continue my religious education. I loved every minute of these and was first in all subjects. The Rabbis always regretted the fact that I wasn't born a boy! The lessons seemed to come easier to me than to most of my classmates. Mine was a good orthodox home. The example there was the best teacher in the subjects others had to be taught from a book. I read and wrote Hebrew fluently, knew my prayers off by heart and could recite sections only to be said by boys, for I heard them each morning during prayers at home. These quiet times were observed strictly by my father and brothers alike as soon as each was washed and dressed and before they came to breakfast.

According to the command and custom of the Fathers, they bared their left arm and applied the black straps of the Tefillin. Around their forehead they laid the black box with God's words. They worshipped Him and thanked Him, and prayed the words of the prayer book and Deuteronomy 6. 4-9. Mother and I, being females, had our own special duties and prayers, but the words of Deuteronomy 6. 4-9 were repeated twice a day by us all in our private prayers.

On Saturday morning we went to the small local synagogue. Saturday *is* the finest day in my memory. Warmth, love, unity, homeliness and holiness was the theme pervading and uniting us all. I treasure this day and all the Jewish festivals. The weekdays with their strain and worry could be set aside and forgotten. At the week-end we were refreshed to face another week and all that was in store.

My father was still looking for a steady job. The stumbling blocks were age and language problems. Having left Holland at the age of four, few accepted him as a Dutchman and just smiled at his treasured passport. It made me sad to see him enter the house some nights, a beaten, tired human being. It was so unlike how I had known him in the years gone by. Often he had temporary jobs as a representative, but that would not keep our heads above water. Mother accepted piecework. Our sewing-machine had never been used as much before. We all helped with the finishing touches of her stacks of wallets. They were made of thin artificial leather, and we enjoyed working with them.

As a matter of course, my brothers handed their weekly wages to my parents, who in turn gave them a small amount of pocket money. Although I would never admit this openly, secretly I admired the unselfishness and consideration my brothers showed towards my parents.

Once a year we received a special voucher from the National

Assistance Board. Then my mother took me to the Central Corporation Clothing Department. There I was fitted with a red and black checked woollen dress, brown woollen stockings, black shoes with a clasp, white flannel underwear and a navy blue rain-cape made of smooth felt. All these items had standard designs and regulation colours, but I did not mind wearing them. I was too young to realise that they marked the wearer. They were new and warm and I loved them. It must, however, have hurt my parents to allow me to be clothed by the State, when in Germany only the finest quality and styles were good enough for me. In Germany several of my uncles were in the clothing industry and as the only girl in the family they had always sent me presents of model garments. These were memories of the past.

Yet we were never heard to complain. How could we, when such sad and worrying news reached us from relations left behind in Germany? The raids continued and business was on a steady decline. Life was restricted in every way. The same news reached us from my father's relations in Poland. Persecution, persecution everywhere. Cries of help came from all directions. How could we help? We who were strangers ourselves. We were free, but not at liberty to invite others into the country. We would have to be responsible for their maintenance, and this we could not do. Father's brother had been thrown into Buchenwald Concentration Camp, and his wife and children pleaded with us to do all in our power to get him out and over to England. Could the Dutch Queen not intervene on his behalf? Surely he, too, had some Dutch blood in his veins.

How and what happened is not known to me, but Queen Wilhelmina was, in some way, instrumental in getting him out of Buchenwald and into Britain. All trace of his wife and children lost and as far as we know they did not survive those years. Now he lives, or rather exists, a stunned, broken, sad and disheartened human being, his mind dwelling upon the past.

Other cries for help came from my father's sisters in Poland. What could we do for his aged mother? Surely we could not stand by idly and see her molested in her ripe old age? No we could not. It meant a major reorganisation of our homelife. First we arranged that some method of transport would be made available for her. The Dutch Government gave permission as long as we would guarantee her maintenance. This we did gladly, althought it meant an even tougher way of life for us. While the machinery of red tape worked in that direction, we started getting busy with house hunting once more as an extra room for grandma was essential. We had been able to grant the wish of the sister in Ludwigshaven am Rhein in preparing a welcome for this aged and lone traveller.

Soon after we had moved into the larger flat a short distance from our first home, grandma arrived. We could not understand how she had endured that journey at the age of 82. She was extremely emaciated and in poor health. We loved her, nursed her, spoiled her. My father was a most devoted son. No wonder my brothers also possessed these characteristics. It was a treat to see my father and grandmother together. Their re-union was not to last long. She died two months after her 82nd birthday, three months after entering our home. Peacefully she slept away in her son's arms but in a free country, to be buried with dignity and respect on free soil and in a Jewish cemetery.

Once more our homelife fell into a regular routine allowing us to enjoy two normal years. I emphasise NORMAL years—so strange and yet so true. In this period I passed through the last year of primary and the first year of secondary school, the only true study I have ever known, although I remember practically nothing about it today. Yet they were normal years to me, with normal events and normal friends.

During these 'normal' years I was privileged to enjoy the one and only holiday of my childhood. It was more than a holiday to me. What I learned in those three weeks was to become part of my life as a growing girl. Independence was born!

My parents had booked this holiday to help me forget the stress and strain of the past years and the death of my grandmother. They thought it important that I should meet and have fun with children of my own age and religion.

At the end of a dark green, tree-lined avenue, on the top of a hill, the Friedmannstichting was situated. It was a large white building surrounded by lovely grounds. There were fields for games and adventure corners for the younger children. The tiny tots had all they could wish for, sandpit, swings, chute, etc. My favourite game was football. I cherished the boys' title for me, their 'best goalkeeper' of the season. These were very happy weeks. There, my desire to become a nurse was born; there the true spirit of friendship was born, the value of true team spirit and the love for many people. There I also met the nurse who was to become my heroine during a difficult period in my life. There I matured and became more self-reliant and independent. All this within the short period of three whole weeks! Impressionable and most valuable! It had to last for a long, long time, and still today I treasure its memory.

'There shall be wars and rumour of wars' was a prophecy entirely unknown to me in those days. Yet the rumours were with us all the time.

Pleading letters from relations reached us almost daily. What could we do? They were not Dutch and the Government could not accept immigrants in great numbers unless their resident relatives would guarantee their full financial support.

Events, however, caused a change in this policy. From sheer desperation, members of mother's family left all they had, to find a place on an immigrant ship on its way to Cuba, Havana. There were thousands of people on board, people from varied backgrounds, but they could pay for this journey as most of them had sold their ALL, just to get enough cash for this journey to freedom, to establish a new life. It was this hope that kept them happy and cheerful during the long weeks at sea. This hope helped them brave sea-sickness and storm. It kept them strong when mental and physical strength was ebbing. At last they approached the land of their adoption. The city of refuge, gleaming in the bright sunlight, beckoned her welcome.

Then, without any explanation, the blow fell—Cuba had decided to refuse admittance to the refugees. The captain was forbidden to enter the harbour! Although radio messages were sent to land explaining the desperate situation; the shortage of fresh food; the sudden drop in morale; the impossibility of return as a certain death awaited all aboard—nothing availed, the government had made its decision. The ship had to turn! Some jumped into the sea in a suicide bid, yet were just as quickly recovered by their equally desperate relatives. After lying anchored for days outside the harbour, action was imperative.

'Whither pilgrims are you going?' Yes, where? The Captain tried other ports en route, but none would have this shipload of Jews. It sailed the seas. Stores ran out, the food shortage became critical. Several European Governments discussed the situation from a humane point of view. At last, France, Belgium, Holland and Britain decided each to take a share of those desperate refugees. Anyone with relatives in a guest country stated their preference. Thus it happened that after some weeks the large ship with its sad load sailed into Amsterdam harbour. Our seven relatives were among its passengers.

Freedom to mix among the population would not be their right for a long time to come. They were interned until suitable accommodation could be found. A seaman's hostel was cleared and prepared to receive those worn out people, while the Dutch Government and its Jewish community welcomed them most heartily. They could eat to repletion, sleep or relax to their hearts content, leaving their immediate future in the hands of their benefactors.

We visited them once the 'all clear' was given. Mixed feelings filled us all. To see those people who had known comparative ease and luxury with only the barest essentials of life was indeed a pathetic sight, and yet, they were still together, they had the gift of life.

The Lloyd Hotel was a large place. Each family was allotted the use of a cubicle with beds and some chairs. The walls did not reach the ceiling and it can be imagined how the chatter, or the whimpering of children, became at times unbearable and nerve wracking.

I enjoyed the weekly visits to my cousins. It was a great place for games such as hide-and-seek. The labyrinth of corridors and passages was the delight of all the children, who, needless to say, made the best use of this spacious playground. The authorities did their utmost to integrate those refugees into the normal life of the city. It was a slow, but rewarding task.

At long last it was time for our people to leave the Lloyd Hotel. Two small houses were allocated to them while the Jewish community gifted furniture and household necessities.

Yet their, and our, freedom was of short duration.

3

HOLLAND IS WORLD RENOWNED FOR HER CLEANLINESS in home and street. Everyone knows the spirit of the Dutch house-wife. Her day starts early, the washing fluttering in the morning breeze long before her family rises for breakfast. Neighbours join to beat their carpets in unison and one can hear the sharp banging as blankets are cleaned with a special twist of the hands. During spring-time, this banging is a familiar sound in most gardens. Housewives begin early and help each other with the heavier part of the cleaning.

On the 10th of May 1940 I awakened early, hearing these familiar sharp banging sounds as I thought. . . . Not feeling sleepy any longer I listened to the almost rhythmic sounds. They seemed to mingle with voices which increased in quantity and quality. Leaving my bed, I drew the curtains aside noticing that other neighbours were doing the same. Everyone was looking at the sky. It was an unbelievable sight. The heavens were dotted with black objects. The 'bangs' were white hazy puffs in between some black objects. The dotted sky developed within minutes into men dangling from parachutes. Some were hit by our machinegun fire and fell like fragments of dust to the ground, but most of them descended un-harmed. An army of German soldiers had come into our country— quite literally 'out of the blue'.

Holland had been invaded by Germany without declaration of war. . . . We had been overrun!

Everyone dressed in a hurry. No one went to school or office that morning. The war had begun! Fighting was fierce. The Dutch forces fought with great courage but it was of no avail. Within days, we had to surrender. The enemy had cleverly planned his attack and succeeded. Before long, the German soldiers were everywhere. It was a strange atmosphere. The Dutch people lost hope. This was not to last however. Almost at once, the loyal Dutch banded them-selves into resistance groups. Fearlessly they fought their own cold war. Many acts of sabotage, successfully committed all over the country were never traced. Resistance workers obeyed a constantly moving headquarters.

Probably the enemy welcomed these acts of hostility. It was a good excuse to torture further his arch-enemy, the Jew.

Publicity directed by the invaders swamped placards, newspapers and entered the homes by radio—'acts of sabotage were the work of the Jew and his friends. They must be curbed. The Dutch people were invited to co-operate and make the invasion and temporary occupation a pleasant event. Do not be influenced by Jewish propaganda, Germany has good intentions towards Holland'.

Having escaped the claws of the advancing bear for five years, it had now caught up with us. We knew ourselves to be in a trap. From now on, every day had its own unpleasant surprises. New rules and regulations were almost daily to be found in the headlines of press and radio. Most of these were directed towards Dutch Jewry. We were compelled to say farewell to many personal possessions, while much of our freedom and social life was curtailed as well. Jewish people had to hand over their bicycles, cars, radios, etc. In industry, Jewish businessmen had to leave the work to their Gentile partners. Posters outside shops stated bluntly 'Forbidden to Jews'. Theatres, cinemas and hotels had now closed their doors to us, compelled to do so by the occupying authority.

A wave of anti-semitism swept across Holland. When Dutch citizens refused to obey, they themselves were treated as Jews. There was no way out, we had to live with it.

More rules and regulations came into being. We were forbidden to use public transport of any description. Jewish children, having been compelled by the new regulation to leave their present form of education, were placed in an entirely Jewish day school. It was a long walk each day for my friends and myself. In all kinds of weather, that hour's walk had to be undertaken. After school, the same walk home again. Sometimes I wonder if this enforced exercise and the strange way of schooling did depress us children in any way. I cannot recall this. We were as happy and contented as we could be, learning day by day to become wise as serpents and harmless as doves.

The winter of 1940/41 was wetter and colder than previous years. Could this be true or was it sheer imagination? Was it because the enforced walks made us notice the elements more acutely? Whatever

27

the reason, my parents decided it was time to move once more—now, and for all time to the Jewish quarter of the city! Here we could enter shops freely. Here we were near the Synagogue, the school, friends and a Jewish doctor. We searched once more for a convenient flat. Satisfied with our choice, we moved in during those cold winter months.

When the midnight bells rang through the city welcoming in 1941, people shouted their 'Happy New Year' to each other, we listened and wondered and waited. What would the new year bring for us Jews? No one knew. In the mind of the adults among us, a picture was being built up, but we children were ignorant of all this.

Decisions had to be made constantly. The first one of 1941 was that I would have to leave school and learn a trade in order to equip myself for whatever life held in store for me. One should know how to earn a daily living! This was my parents' firm belief.

With mixed feelings I entered upon this new phase in my life, not in the slightest interested in the trade my parents had chosen for me. To be a tailoress—what could be more dull and boring! I imagined myself holding a needle, and with a thimble on the middle finger of the right hand! It seemed a must, yet to me it looked more like a carnival hat, ironically trying to make a fool of me. This could not be MY life. How absurd! I couldn't imagine myself sweeping the floors, sorting materials into rag-bags, sewing endless seams by hand, making countless cups of tea, delivering orders to the rich and the not-so-rich among Amsterdam's inhabitants.

This picture, which I built up in my imagination since that first interview and during the early days at work, I had to learn to live with. I hated every day, but somehow I learned as well. I must confess, it was a thrill to bring a wage packet home on Friday nights especially when half a crown became my own proud possession as pocket money. I felt I had worked for it and it was my true reward. The rest of the money joined the household budget for food and clothing. This seemed natural to me. My brothers had set this example and still handed their wage packet over, receiving back their respective pocket money.

Soon I was used to this new routine. I knew what my daily task was to be and was gradually taught to accomplish it. Quite naturally my stitching was not neat at first, but my employer was pleased with my progress. When goods had to be delivered, I welcomed the break from constant concentration. I loved meeting people, getting to know new clients, and re-visiting the older ones. My work-bench saw many different types of sewing. I was even taught to assemble fur. This was hard work, but amazingly satisfying. As a contrast, we were also taught how to re-foot socks and stockings. It gave a new lease of life to the old and worn ones. Mr. and Mrs. Ding-Dong, as we called them, managed their business together. She attended to the finer work, while Mr. Ding-Dong was left to manage the re-footing and the financial side of the business.

He was a very nervous person, always moving around, restlessly looking for matching materials, then, bending his pale, freckled face, he would push his gold-rimmed glasses once more into their proper position before furiously pedalling his machine. He was an expert in this re-footing process! Does anyone do this today? I wonder! He also had a special way of folding them for delivery. They looked nice, all the different colours and materials folded the same way. This art has remained with me to this present day.

It was a special treat to deliver a garment which I had helped to make. A house which had special attraction for me as a youngster, faced one of Amsterdam's many canals. It was an old mercantile building. The brass door handles were always shining, the maid was always kind and efficient in the way she invited me into the parlour. Here a table was always in readiness whatever time of the day you happened to call. The silver always gleamed and the grand-father clock always ticked in regular rhythm. It was always quiet in that house. It gave me a chance to listen for the footsteps of the lady herself. Politely I delivered my message and carefully laid the parcel before her. She then would reward me with a smile, a calm 'thank-you' and a small piece of silver. I accepted it gratefully as a reward for my part in the sewing. Walking across the thick carpeted hallway, I would bid her good-bye, emerging into the constant flow of bicycles on the road in front of her house. Usually I remained on the pavement till I came to the corner. There I crossed the canal bridge and made my way through a labyrinth of small streets to the main road. Back at the Ding-Dongs, I felt really refreshed after my little outing. The rest of the day was not so severe as it had been before that errand.

Had I occasion to deliver goods in the late afternoon, it was permissible to go straight home and not return to work for the remaining hour. This was the sweetest treat to grace any working day. It meant, I could go home in a round-about-way. Crossing several canal bridges, I would make straight for the hospital on the Nw. Keizersgracht. It was the largest Jewish hospital and had very high standards. Among the greatest thrills of my young days was this walk along the canal bank. Here I could loiter a little in front of the main entrance hall, I could sniff the smell which all hospitals and clinics hold in common. How I envied those uniformed girls, those veiled sisters, those white coated doctors. They had achieved their ambition while I had to sit day in day out sewing dumb seams, brushing lifeless materials into rag-bags and extending the usefulness of worn socks.

Each time I passed my beloved building I was more determined than ever to become one of the staff; I would equip myself secretly in my own way. That week-end I spent my pocket money on a bottle of methylated spirits. Hiding it in my room, it became my inspiration when depression would want to take hold. A little sniff of that bottle would remind me of my dreams for the future and encourage a drooping heart to keep aiming towards that goal.

As time went on I collected several medical instruments: not for use, just to have and to caress. I also fitted out a first aid box and kept all my treasures beautifully together in a black leather case, which, incidentally, I still cherish to this very day.

When would my parents allow me to train as a nurse? They would not even discuss the matter. Times were too serious, they would say, to think of such nonsense. It would be too hard work and would not get me anywhere in life. A sensible trade would see me through. Such was their decision.

At night, by torchlight, I would read through second-hand medical books. Subjects far too difficult for me would capture my attention. While trying to master them I would fall asleep, and often awaken long after midnight with the torch still burning in my hand.

The urge to be among ill people grew stronger with each passing day. I wanted so much to be at their bedside, to learn to nurse and treat their wounds, comfort and cheer the fearful, to love little children. When would I be able to do this?

We were not allowed to sing at our workbench. Too much chatter was frowned upon as well. I loved both and in consequence was frequently reprimanded by freckled Mr. Ding-Dong. I felt that if only I could smell that bottle of methylated spirits more often, it would convince me that dressmaking was not to be my ultimate future.

Sister Henny, who had befriended me during my holiday in Hilversum's Children's Home, had achieved her ambition. She had left child care and was now working among the sick in our large city hospital. She was my heroine, my example. I wanted to become a nurse like her. Sometimes, when off duty, she would arrange to meet me. It made me feel grown up and wanted. These were precious moments. She allowed me to ask questions by the dozen, and I took full advantage of the opportunity. She was able also to put me in my place and I would take it from her without offence. After all, it was Sister Henny who had said so!

No wonder, therefore, that I turned to her when frightened or perplexed.

4

THE RUMOUR OF YET ANOTHER NEW LAW AND regulation became reality overnight—all Jews were compelled to purchase bright yellow stars, five inches in diameter, outlined in black and inscribed with the word JEW in capital letters. These stars had to be sewn firmly on outdoor clothing, dresses and suits. No Jew was allowed to leave his or her home without this notable insignia on the left breast pocket.

Now we were outlawed indeed—seen and known of all men, especially by those who sought to destroy us. Day by day, as it had happened years ago in Germany, people disappeared mysteriously. Round the clock arrests were the order of the day. Those who had means and connections would often find an underground hiding-place. It was risky and a big step to take. Once you had taken this course, you had to stay underground, and remain illegal till the war ended . . . favourably!

Whole families disappeared by other means. They wanted to keep the Honour to themselves, not wishing to face the future of slow, but certain extermination. The gas taps were the easiest way out. It did not frighten the children. They would never know, they would never suffer. Only God knew what agony many a parent had to endure before reaching such a decision.

Suffering draws people together. It creates a false sense of security, yet the comfort of union is sweet. Father's brother, a widower, and his young teenage daughters wrote from Belgium asking if they could come to stay with us as a temporary measure, until things would blow over in Belgium. There, too, the iron grip of the enemy had tightened and daily life became more burdensome. My parents' reply, of course, was 'Come over as soon as you can'!

Uncle Michael was a jolly man and cheerful in any situation. Our cousins, Edith and Ruth, were almost strangers to us. We had not met since we were small. It would be very exciting to have all these real cousins in our midst.

Early in February 1941, father's relations arrived in Amsterdam and we walked them to our city home. It was good to be together and enjoy the relationship missing for so long. My brothers and cousins were of the same age group. They had a lot in common and enjoyed long walks and talks. Being six years younger they looked on me as a tail-piece, someone who wasn't-old-enough-to-understand!

Saturday, February 21st, 1941 was a pleasant day, yet still cold. A brisk walk after dinner would do us all the world of good—this was my father's suggestion. Would I be willing to show the girls a little piece of Amsterdam's historic beauty? It did not please me. I had a previous arrangement with my girl friend from the orphanage around the corner, we loved our window shopping expeditions on Saturday afternoons. After some whispered discussion with my father my brothers took up the suggestion and obligingly offered to take the girls around Amsterdam.

Once the dishes were clean and in the side-board, the table reset for teatime, we divided up for the afternoon programme. My parents and uncle set out to visit the local Rabbi, a personal friend of the family. My cousins were soon on their way to get acquainted with their new home town under the able guidance of their male escorts. I, too, was on my way to the orphanage. It was a pleasure to go there. The girls, so well behaved, appealed to me. Everything, even their clothing, seemed so tidy. Could they possibly be happy in these clothes? During gym, at school, one could see their underwear, it was pure white and well starched. No frills or fancy embroidery. They would turn up each morning in that multi-coloured flannelette blouse, partly covered by the navy blue gym-tunic which always had its broad pleats perfectly pressed. They seemed like straight arrows pointing to the thick, black woollen stockings which reached right up to the suspender mark. They also wore high laced black boots! In cold weather a navy gaberdine coat with matching beret completed their uniform. One could single out these girls in any company.

Yes, I did like my friends there. Even now, my thoughts were with them as I walked with my parents and uncle to the corner of our street. With a casual 'cheerio' we parted company. 'See you later' were the words which followed me. 'See you later!' We hesitantly used those words. Who could guarantee their truth? Our destiny lay in other hands.

33

Rita was waiting for me in the hall. Having exchanged the latest news of the day, we decided to embark on our usual expedition along the windows of the city stores. Happily, we admired the new spring fashions for the teenager, already in the shops. Gradually we became conscious of gloomy and frightened looks around us. Some people started running. We looked at one another enquiringly, what was it all about? Had something happened again? We overheard snippets of conversation which aroused our curiosity even more. At last someone bothered to answer our question. Their reply made me go cold and stiff inside. 'They are pulling up the bridges and are going to raid the whole city centre.'

The blow had fallen.

Screams of frightened women were heard all around. Brutal and cruel shouts of soldiers endeavoured to drown the cries of frightened humanity. Little children, perplexed by the sudden panic, ran from their homes and wandered whimpering along the streets. Suddenly, there, on the other side of the bridge, we saw the cause of the terrorised atmosphere. Dozens of Gestapo had pounced from their lorries on men and boys within reach. All who wore the yellow star were seized and pulled in one direction. The man-handling was terrible to witness. We were frightened and started to run as well. We ran and ran until we were out of sight of those helpless victims.

Even here, the atmosphere had been affected by the human explosion across the bridges. The streets were empty, except for a few, like us, who were looking for refuge.

We were shocked, our voices sounded shaky. Where could we go? Neither of us knew. Walking steadily away from the troubled area, we came to the Weesperplein. The people here seemed unaware to a great extent of what was happening across the bridge. Seeing the J.I., the large skyscraperlike building, I had an idea! The Matron of this home for elderly Jewish people was my own dear former Matron of the children's home in Hilversum. We could go there. She would take us in and advise us alright.

The porter allowed us through at once, since he knew me so well. Hardly a Saturday passed without a visit from me to this building. Today, however, seemed different. The porter must have known about the raid: he, too, looked frightened and did not take time to chat as usual. He just made sure we would go up to Matron's flat at once and wait in her sitting-room if she was not in. We promised.

She was not in. It gave us ample time to sit and think. We dared not put our feelings into words. Only rarely did we glance at one another's faces. Desperately attempting to avoid thinking of the horror, I thought of the calm personality of MY Matron. She was the most mother-like person one could imagine. She had a lovely skin, bright blue eyes and her reddish cheeks completed the beauty of this cheerful person. People remarked on her early silvery-grey hair. I adored it. Her white coat was always immaculate, surely changed many times a day. She was well-liked and respected. How fortunate that I was so close to her; it made me glad and proud to know that Matron liked me!

It seemed like eternity, but at last my dear Matron arrived. She stood as though rooted to the ground, then slowly made her way towards us. Her face was expressionless, ours probably fearful. I almost felt guilty for having come to the home, but what else could I have done? No one spoke, but our eyes met, then I began to cry and Rita joined in. On her way to the kitchenette Matron's hand rested for a moment, on my shoulder, then she proceeded to make tea leaving us to cry. It relieved us a little and on her return with the tray, I was ready with the question, 'Can we stay with you, at least until the soldiers have left again?'

Matron assured us that we were welcome to stay in the home as long as we needed its safety.

While she went on her rounds again, we sat by the window, not speaking but thinking along the same lines. Our eyes searched the streets to identify a familiar face. When would life down there return to normal?

At 6 p.m. after another session of tea, sandwiches and fruit, Matron suggested we try to make our way home. She had made enquiries, and it seemed all clear again. We thanked her, but left hesitantly and with heavy hearts. How could young girls be so suddenly cowed and grow years and years older? Never again would we be the lighthearted youngsters we had been prior to this incident.

That fifteen minute walk home was an eerie and nauseating experience. The streets remained quiet and forsaken, but from houses along the route, sobbing, shouting and hysterical anguish reached our ears. Mothers were sorrowing for sons and husbands.

The toll of arrests must have been heavy for the anguish was great.

Crossing the bridge over our canal, we parted company. Rita went back to the orphanage and I walked along the water's edge towards our house. In the distance I could see two people on the steps in front of the flat. Getting closer, I recognised my cousins. Running the last few yards, I saw that something was far wrong. Their red swollen faces, their wet eyes, their sobbing told me enough. "Where are the boys?" I demanded. "Where are Werner and Manfred?" They cried even more loudly and put their arms about me. Shaking myself free, I repeated my question more urgently. Sobbing heavily they told me what I had suspected all along: the boys had been arrested during a demand for 8,000 men between the ages of 18 and 40. They had been dragged away from Edith and Ruth, pushed and kicked towards the Jonas Daniel Meyer Plein. There the thousands of men were herded together. They had been told to kneel down on the bare cobbled stones, raise their hands high above their heads and remain in that position until the order was withdrawn. Those who were weak or could not comply with the command were soon made to do so by a blow from a rubber truncheon.

My cousins continued their sobbing. I had had my turn some hours before, now I was still and cold. My mind worked doubly fast. Dear Werner and Manfred, so young to die so cruel a death. To be arrested and treated as outlaws just because they were Jews—God's chosen people, persecuted throughout the ages. God, have mercy and save us!

We unlocked the front door and wearily climbed the stairs to our flat. The fire in the stove was still warm and bright. Yet I shivered and couldn't stop. Only then did Edith and Ruth take over. They quickly produced three tumblers of Russian tea. With both hands around my tumbler I tried hard to think straight. It was unbelievable. My brothers gone! How could they endure the hard prison life. Where would they be taken? Would they be allowed home again? I groaned within myself—home again! Who would ever come home again? Once in the lion's den there would be no escape. No, the future looked dark, very dark indeed. Secretly, I hoped they would die very soon; better dead, I reasoned, than to be tortured and starved. They had been such quiet and sheltered boys; they had never had opportunity to rough it.

The voices of my cousins roused me from my frightened thoughts. How would we tell my parents when they returned home? Would father be all right? In deadly silence we stayed together, waiting, thinking and drinking tea.

Within the hour my parents arrived. Who would tell them? There was no need to do so. My father ran first into the flat. "Where are the boys?" Rumours about the raid had spread like wildfire throughout the city. "Where are the boys?" he shouted again, his eyes staring at us fearfully. Meanwhile my mother had reached the flat. She was grief stricken. My uncle stood beside her, trying to comfort her a little, and assuring her we would find out whatever we could before the night curfew. My cousins had been sobbing again, and my father, completely beside himself, paced up and down the living-room repeating again and again, "Oh, the boys, the boys, the poor boys, oh, Werner, Manfred, ah, the poor, poor boys."

I still was dry-eyed and completely stunned by all that had happened and also somewhat frightened by all the commotion in the room—the crying, the questioning, my father's anguish. Uncle Michael was the only one in control of himself.

Then, after a short silence, my father rounded on me. "Of course, it is all your fault, naughty, disobedient child. Had you taken your cousins around Amsterdam instead of going out with your friend, your brothers would have been at home tonight. They were home-loving boys. They did not want to go out, but they went to oblige. They were always being helpful. You have driven your brothers to their destruction. Oh, my dear boys, my boys, where are you?"

However much my uncle endeavoured to halt my father during his heartbroken accusations, the more violent he became. This, together with my mother's grief, broke my tension and shock at last and kneeling beside my mother, I wept uncontrollably, seeking her comfort. It is difficult to recall just when we went to bed. We waited, wept and discussed what to do, whom to contact, to try to obtain the boys' freedom.

No one slept much that night. One dozed off and then wakened with a fearful feeling of shock, time and time again. We still heard shouts outside and the revving of car engines. All knew what this meant—more arrests! Our thoughts were with our boys. What had they endured already, what lay before them? They would be so homesick, so alone. The hard and sudden enforced labour would tell on their health. How long could they stand it? Would they be flogged, ill treated, starved? Would they be warm enough? They had no change of clothing. All had been arrested so suddenly. Our thoughts were with them. 'Poor, poor boys, if only we could get in touch with you. If only you knew how hopeless we feel. In spirit we are close to you. Be brave boys! Stay together if you can and encourage each other!'

How could they possibly stay together? Their fate wasn't in their own hands. Werner, always the weaker of the two, was at once sent to another labour camp. This, we did not learn until much later. Weeks of waiting and worrying had to pass before this official notification was found in our letterbox.

'Buchenwald', this dreaded and most familiar name was once more connected with our family. Father's brother, Jacob, had been arrested and spent several months there. Since then his health had been ruined for life. While he was there, the enemy arrested and murdered his wife and children. When at last he was set free, thanks to the Dutch authorities, who had worked very hard with some British Organisations on his behalf, his life's work was shattered, his home looted to the last article, and his nearest and dearest dead and buried in mass graves.

Now our Werner was in the claws of these self same sadists. My parents were demented. They cried and wailed, painfully imagining the passing of day and night in a concentration camp. Now the boys were separated. They had nothing to hold on to, they were alone among a host of men of all ages and backgrounds.

Our homelife had changed entirely. Even my cheerful uncle was unable to encourage my parents. The silence around the house became even more noticeable once our relations had found a flat, leaving us alone with our grief, although we still met at week-ends and exchanged all our news. All we knew was through rumours and from hear-say. There was no real news direct from the camps. If news did leak through by some illegal means, it was fearful and frightening and we tried very hard not to believe it. Undoubtedly there was some truth in the rumours, and, like a jig saw puzzle, we pieced together a picture of life out there in the dark unknown.

The arrests continued day and night and all of us had inwardly accepted the fact that we were looked upon as outlaws and that arrest was imminent at any time. Did we get used to the idea, and the mental and physical sufferings which accompanied such an atmosphere? I'm not sure. Danger was interwoven within the pattern of daily life. From a practical point of view we would discuss the situation: the struggle for survival was on—we would endeavour to keep alive, even if it meant separation. Better to be united after the war than stay together to be put to death. Naturally, however, we would try to stay together as long as possible; this was our arrangement. Meanwhile, we prepared in other ways. Each of us acquired a rucksack and filled it with bare essentials and official papers, some tinned food and toilet accessories. With marking ink, name, address and date of birth was written across each. Soon, most Jewish people had such a bundle in the hall of their home. Everyone was prepared!

Three months after the arrest of my brothers, word reached us by some stranger, that Uncle Michael, Edith and Ruth had been arrested overnight and were on their way to the unknown. Once more we could do nothing. We were helpless in the claws of the invader.

Many children had become orphans suddenly. Coming home from school, no parents were there to welcome them. Sometimes families were separated. Parents were arrested, children were left. The Jewish Board of Guardians accepted responsibility for such and placed them in the care of willing foster parents. No one could guarantee their safety, but at least they were looked after.

Each night when I returned from work, my mind was filled with anxious thoughts for these orphans, these frightened children, these baffled and perplexed little human beings. Inwardly, my longing grew stronger day by day to mother some of them in our home. I discussed it with my parents, who at first had many objections. Yet, my brothers' room remained empty. The aching void was always with them, and at last they realised this would be the best action under the circumstances, but the final decision remained a dream until the terrible news reached us that Werner, my oldest brother, had died! Officially we were informed to forward a stated amount of money which would cover packing and postage of his ashes and some personal belongings.

Oh, how hard and cruel the written word can be!

The clothes and the ashes came, and all the sadness and suffering with them. How would we ever know if these were really his ashes?

We had our doubts, but accepted the ashes as such and buried them respectfully.

Although, according to records, Manfred was still supposed to be alive in Mauthausen, we were not at all sure. We did not hear from him for months. When the final word about his death came, we knew it to be true. We had lost our boys. Life had been cruel to us and to them for so long, but they had so far carried the heaviest burden. Now we knew they were free of their fear and physical suffering. Could we have wished it otherwise for their sakes?

At sixteen and a half years of age I was old enough to realise that my parents needed something to take up their attention and time. With the death of my brothers, the constant arrests around us and the uncertainty about other relatives abroad, their courage and hope deteriorated from day to day. They had become entirely different people. The suffering had broken their life and spirit.

Leaving them alone all day while at work, worried me continually. I saw no point in sewing at the Ding-Dong's any longer for a pound a week, while I could mother some orphaned children in our home instead. Having formulated these plans in my own mind, I explained the idea to my parents. After some persuasion we were all agreed it would indeed by a very good idea.

My father contacted the Board of Guardians. They inspected our house, and promised to get in touch with us before long. Father would do all the shopping, mother the housekeeping, and I would see to their needs morning and night. My parents insisted that I should continue to learn the tailoring trade while the children attended school. I accepted their decision.

Two extra beds were sent to our house, and thus we were able to foster four children. From then on my brothers' room was re-named the 'children's room'.

It was a great day, when seven, instead of three people, sat down to an evening meal. All of a sudden the war rations did not seem so severe.

The children needed time to settle. They were frightened, shocked and very sad indeed. Can we ever understand how a little one feels when its love and security are suddenly lost? What can we say or do to be an adequate substitute? One does not want them to forget their parents. We suffered with them, all sharing the same loss. They knew about our boys. It was a link between us and helped to make us into a new family. There were no blood ties, but ties of race, circumstance and deep personal loss. They began to feel a sense of 'belonging' once more.

At first there were Susan and Mirli, aged twelve and nine, then Hermann who was ten. Eva, Merli's sister, also found a welcome when she needed accommodation. Margaret, aged three, was placed last and was delightfully spoiled by her older 'brothers and sisters'. We felt so proud of our new family! Now that new life had entered our home, it was extra hard to sew those long seams and attend mechanically to the tedious jobs detailed by my employer. Only a few weeks after the children had come, my patience came to an abrupt end. Without counting the cost or visualising the consequences, I put the needle into the blouse under my care and left it there. Then I sheepishly, yet determinedly, asked for my books. No persuading could make me stay one day longer.

Thus I left my first job, walking the long miles back home. Soon I realised the full brunt of my impetuous action. How could I find the courage to meet my parents? How could I have deprived them so abruptly of this weekly income? Instead of approaching our house, I made for the hospital.

At the reception I asked for Sister Henny. She was in theatre and not available for at least an hour. I had permission to wait. An incredible long wait! Once again I learned the value of this friendship. It was only two years since I had admired her as 'nurse' Henny in the children's home, now she seemed so much more important as 'Sister' Henny. Everyone liked her, patients and staff alike. She was straight-forward, honest, and yet kind, understanding and gentle. I counted it a real privilege to be numbered as one of her friends. Youthful, lightfooted and yet poised, she walked towards me down a long flight of stairs. Smiling as usual, she greeted me with a cheerful 'hallo'.

"And what are you doing here at this time of day?" She searched my face and repeated her question. She had noticed that 'all was not well'! Once I had told her all my problems and the immediate worry of going home to explain the situation to my parents, she became very serious. "Wait here," she ordered, "I'll get my coat and we'll go for a walk. I have got to talk to you." We went for a walk, a long walk. During that walk I learned a lesson I would not forget as long as I lived.

Having set the fuse alight, I dreaded the moment of explosion. Yet it was inevitable. How to face it? This walk, this talk, was to be my God-given lesson for this and other faults.

Were the streets busy, was it raining or was the sun shining? None of those details registered on my mind. Reality had to be faced, I had to grow up.

When I left Sister Henny at the hospital gate an hour and a half later, I was wiser and more mature. One more step had been taken in the school of life. 'CONSIDER OTHER PEOPLE'S FEELINGS, CONSIDER OTHERS!'

"Hansie," Sister Henny had said, "you want to be a nurse when you grow up . . . you want to care for people and help them . . . you can hardly wait for the day when you are old enough to put on uniform and be called 'nurse'. If you want to be a *real* nurse you can begin to train right now. Go home, look at your parents, look at them, long and deep, think about them and realise that they are broken and sick. Their own flesh and blood has been torn from them. Boys they have loved and cared for throughout childhood and youth, through illness and problems of adolescence, their pride and their hope, these boys have been taken from them suddenly. Try to realise the pain and suffering they have endured, the agony of mind and loneliness and the utter finality of death. Hansie, don't be hurt if your parents seem unfair and unreasonable to you. Dismiss all seeming unfairness, forget it, train to be a nurse . . . now! Go home, be a good and kind nurse to those two broken people. Tell them you've come home to be with them, to help with the children. At the same time, get a job near home, just a few hours morning and afternoon, to bridge the financial gap. Go home, Hansie! Be a nurse!"

It was the usual time when I entered the house. I could choose the time when to drop the bomb, time to brace myself for the inevitable explosion. After dinner I ventured to explain. I was bombarded by a burst of words from both father and mother. I tried to be understanding and calm, I so wanted to be a nurse. I did not even cry when the silence of the night at last came to our home. The ordeal was over. No more tailoring for me. I was free!

News travels fast, and I soon heard that the local schoolteacher and his wife wanted a young girl to take care of their two small sons while they were at work. No time was to be lost. The very next day

I called at the house, a few minutes distance from our own. I was welcomed by a very nice young couple.

It was a thrill to experience the unreserved trust they seemed to place in a complete stranger like myself. Experience with children? It never gave me a thought. My love and desire to look after those small boys was uppermost. The parents sensed this and asked when I could come. The next day was the earliest and I remember that I rang that bell long before the agreed time. The whole care and feeding of the little ones, the choice of clothing for each day, when to visit the barber, when to go for a walk, all these were to be my responsibility. Each day I passed my home with them, collecting my mother's shopping list on the way. The boys grew to love her and she looked forward to this daily break from housekeeping and strain.

These were wonderful weeks and months. Knowing oneself to be needed and loved gave such an added zest to life. It made one grow inwardly, resulting in outward contentment, joy and happiness. This in turn passed on to others, brought happiness. Nothing is so infectious as happiness! Yet, life's crossroads had been reached once more. From the street of contentment and happiness, a sharp bend was in sight.

With the falling of autumn leaves, many people around our neighbourhood disappeared mysteriously. Like those who had gone before, they were never heard of again. Whole families were seen no more. We all knew where they had gone but no one spoke the word 'underground'.

The Dutch Resistance Movement was very active, and their 'around-the-clock-watch-and-work' can never be overestimated. Much is known but very much more can never be known, for these heroes died in helping the persecuted.

Everyone wanted the chance to go 'underground', but not everyone could afford such safety. It was an expensive business to live for months, perhaps years separated from society, family and friends—to live and depend for your life and safety on the love and kindness of fellow human beings, who endangered their life by saving yours.

It was a situation which needed careful planning and much thought. Families had to be approached and questioned. Would they be willing to accept a human being? A man, a woman, a boy or

43

even a little baby? Families often had to be split up. Their whereabouts could not be discussed, the Resistance movement alone had the information. My first remote encounter with a situation such as this took place in the summer of 1942.

Having rung the bell several times at the fine canal house where I came each morning to take charge of my little ones, I understood at once what this sudden 'not at home' meant. Arrest, or underground? The neighbours enlightened me. No raid had taken place during the past night. This to me, meant 'underground'. As I turned from the house where I had experienced so much happiness, I hoped, fervently, that this lovely family would survive.

Without a job once more, we decided it would be better if I stayed at home and helped my parents. This I enjoyed . . . but not for long.

The days and nights proved a strain at times, almost too great to be borne. The continual fear of the 'knock at the door', the excessive ringing of bells, hung over our heads. One learned to listen for the stopping of heavy lorries outside the house, the opening and shutting of car doors, the rough voices, all those familiar horrible noises one had grown accustomed to, the result of which always proved so fatal in the end.

Each Jewish mind worked overtime, desperately endeavouring to produce a situation in which one would be at least comparatively safe. Often it could become the very trap which the invader had cleverly set for a mass deportation. One had to be wise as serpents and harmless as doves.

Daily more people disappeared. The time had come when both day and night were equally dangerous for man, woman and child. Many families, guided by illegal organisations, were rescued from the fate of millions, and lived. They hid in attics, cellars or on farms. Other families would build secret cupboards for their charges, or create double-walled rooms. Endless were the ideas born in the minds of our well-wishers. Sometimes it was possible to dodge the authorities for some time by 'legal' means.

Hearing about the comparative safety which the hospital staff and their patients enjoyed, I was keen to find a place among them. Still my parents would not grant me permission to take this step. If not as a nurse, I reasoned, then I would endeavour to become a patient. If I only could lie under the coveted hospital roof, my home would at least be safe while I was away. It was worth a trial.

Sister Henny had to be contacted. Surely she would do her best to help. I depended on the satisfactory outcome of my secret plan. At once I made my way to the big hospital at the Nieuwe Keizersgracht in Amsterdam. Yes, Sister Henny was in and would see me. "But my dear," she insisted over and over again, "we can't admit you if there is nothing wrong with you. It would endanger the lives of Matron and all of us if it were known that a fraud was in our midst." I pleaded that she should use all possible influence to take me in before the curfew that night. Reluctantly she told me to be at the main gate at 7.45 p.m. precisely. Gratefully I left.

The day continued normally enough. It was Friday and mother prepared the dinner of the week. We always had lots of extras on Friday nights and a lovely homely atmosphere into the bargain. I could not refuse any food during dinner in case my parents would suspect anything. Then, during tea, I told them of my plan.

"Mother, Sister Henny is allowing me to sleep in hospital tonight. Father, just in case they ring the bell tonight, tell them your daughter is very ill in hospital and has to undergo an operation."

"Good gracious, child, have you lost your senses? We don't want to lose you as well." My mother added her objections, "You can't go to the hospital if you are fit and well. What are you up to?" The stream of words had to be stopped somehow.

Quietly I interrupted: "I'll be all right, Father. I'll go to sleep there, and you sleep here at home, and we will have tricked the angel of death once more. Don't worry, Mother, I'll be all right." I collected my comb, towel and facecloth and left the house with a casual, "Cheerio, everybody, don't worry".

Success! They had not suspected the truth of the matter. I was on my way to the hospital; the 'play' had begun.

At the appointed place Sister Henny was waiting for me. Accompanying her, was a towering, broad-shouldered giant with bushy red hair. Although he was dressed in a doctor's white coat, I knew it was the radio control engineer. He would pull the strings and get me admitted illegally. I now had burned my boats, and could not turn back. It was 8 p.m.!

The next fifteen minutes passed as on a race track. I was hustled upstairs in a lift, thoroughly prepared for the operation to come, while Sister Henny for once talked non-stop. "Well, have you made up your mind? What would you like us to do? Amputate a toe, a finger, break your leg and set it? Make a scar and stitch it?" We discussed my anatomy in record time. The bargain was made—my appendix for a fortnight's safety!

One obstacle, however, could not be removed—the heavy dinner in my stomach. The risk had to be taken, we would commence with a local anaesthetic plus the extra large incision for possible inspection purposes. But it did not work. Soon I became very breathless and restless and the surgeon ordered a general anaesthetic. Drifting happily over green fields, I spent the best part of an hour in absolute freedom without a care in the world.

It must have been well after midnight when I wakened in the ward. A kind, middle-aged nurse watched over and comforted me. It was so sore, and the continual bouts of sickness ripped the pain in my wound. "When you feel sick, put your hands on your stomach" she advised me, "it's not so sore that way. There now, try it, hold very tight!" Not till she was sure that I knew how to overcome the sickness-pain, did she take leave of me. I shall never forget that ministering angel, nor her helpful words that first night. In the years to come I repeated them often to my own patients when the need arose.

Mercifully that night had an end, and when morning light entered the ward, my stomach was truly empty and at peace . . . and so was I! These few hours had performed a miracle and I felt much better by the time the day staff took over.

One ordeal was over and the next just around the corner—visiting hour at 3 p.m. Would my parents come? Had they expected me home after breakfast? Had the plan worked? Were they still in the house? If they came to look for me here, the truth would have to be told.

There was my father. Cheerfully he entered the ward and spotted me at once. Nodding here and there politely, he made his way towards my bed. As he sat down, his chair bumped against my bed, making me flinch just a little. Quickly I covered my error by asking for mother and the children. He chatted, lightheartedly, for less than three minutes, then told me to get ready as soon as possible as he wanted me to help him with some messages that afternoon. No one had called that night in our street, but shouting and screams had been heard from neighbouring houses. No one knew when they would reach our door. Suspense, always suspense.

There was no easy way out. Plucking up what courage I still had left, I told him the truth. "Father, I've had my appendix removed, I can stay here for a fortnight. No more worries until then." At first he was speechless: the silence was most embarrassing. Then a torrent of words poured over me. It was shocking and disrespectful to act in such a manner. It was inconsiderate and typical of the youth of today. He told me he was speechless; how I wished he were! Not once did he take into consideration the true reason for my action. He would go home and tell my mother. This made me cry bitterly. I did not want to hurt her, or to make my parents lonely in any way. I only wanted us to live, to live together, and this was just a means to an end.

After leaving a bag of yellow plums with me, he departed most unhappily. At the door he exchanged a few words with the ward sister. She, not knowing the true position, was bewildered by my father's remonstrations and his anger. Suddenly he was gone.

My head spun like a spinning top. I wanted to sleep, to be sick, to talk to someone nice, to drink, to do anything than just lie there. I felt oh, so lonesome.

It seemed an eternity before Sister Henny came to see me that night. It was good to have her with me at last. She just listened to all I had to say. She nodded and smiled at me, stroked my head and held my hand. Her comfort was a heavenly balm to me.

Soon the ward settled down for the night. Nurses performed their regular duties, dressings had been changed, medicines given, beds remade and the suppers served, when two Sisters with another lady entered the ward. They spoke to my night nurse, who was preparing herself to go on duty. She looked very upset when the two Sisters left, leaving the lady behind. No one liked to see distressed faces those days. They made you wonder. Yet for some reason, I seemed to be the cause of the trouble. Night nurse came over to me and explained that I had to be moved to another smaller ward. This did not worry me, I had not made friends with anyone so far and was glad to give my place in the ward to a new patient, if it was needed. I had no reason to be suspicious.

My bed was wheeled along many corridors, up in a lift and along more corridors, until we reached the swing door of a small ward. It had already been darkened for the night, but by the shimmer of the duty lamp I saw one window at the end of this narrow small ward. My bed was nearest to the door and I noticed three more beds. The patients must have been sleeping, for no one said 'hallo'. A lady sat beside the duty lamp, but did not even come over to welcome me. There and then I took a dislike to her, whoever she was. The ward had a strange unhealthy atmosphere, I thought. It amused me, when the orderlies left me with a final 'good luck'. After reviewing my new surroundings for a short while, I fell asleep. It had been a heavy day, physically as well as emotionally.

Very early next morning I received the foretaste of yet another ordeal. When fully awake, I raised myself for a drink from my locker and that lady stood beside me! Where had she come from so suddenly? Looking at her pleasantly I smiled a 'good morning', but a short and sharp reply was all she managed to produce. I could not understand it. What was she doing here? Soon a nurse arrived with a bright 'good morning, ladies'. She had entered with another person who exchanged places with that 'stranger-of-the-night'. The other patients had made no attempt to converse so far. Sheepishly I glanced at them. It distressed me. They looked very depressed and I assumed that their illnesses must be of a very serious nature. I was sorry for them. Little did I know that they were only meant to speak when absolutely necessary. While nurse served the breakfast, my curiosity had reached its limit. I asked her about this strange ward with its exchange of 'ladies'. Her information chilled me through and through. "You realise, my dear, that this is the official sick-bay of The Theatre. When you are better, you must go back again. The ladies are the official warders, they are responsible for you until you join the deportations once more. We are only permitted to nurse you."

My wound was forgotten, I sat right up, "Nurse, it's a mistake!" My voice rose steadily. "I've never been in The Theatre. I did not come from there. Please get me out of here." I started crying and the new lady came over to me. She was more kindly than her predecessor.

"Please lie down and do not cause any trouble for us. Do as you are told, and you will soon be out of here."

"Yes, I know," I interrupted her, "I will be out of here, but I don't belong to The Theatre; I don't belong to The Theatre,

I've nothing to do with The Theatre. I want to go home."

My distress was beyond reason and it upset me to such an extent that nurse administered a sedation, which calmed me just a little. Still sobbing I tried to visualise what had happened.

Near my home, a large theatre had been taken over by the occupying forces. After removing all seats and other furnishings, arrested people were herded together in this large hall; male and female, old and young. Old mattresses and blankets were all over the floor. The rucksack, their only possession, was their company while they waited for the dreadful moment of deportation. Evidently some people fell sick and developed complications. To avoid panic, they were sent to this hospital to be nursed and guarded until they could resume their journey to the land of no-return.

But where did *I* fit into this muddle? I had never been arrested. Or could it be that my parents had been caught after all? Had they explained that I was here and were they being allowed to remain at The Theatre until I was able to join them? It could not be! If only someone would tell me, if only someone would speak. Who would have predicted two days ago that my own arrest would take place in the very building where I had sought safety for us all?

The day seemed like a nightmare in an abysmal cave. I could neither eat nor drink. I refused treatment and medicine. I cried and demanded my doctor. No one came near me except the nurse on duty. Her only information was equally depressing: the doctor was too busy, Sister Henny had a day off and was not in the building, and, lastly, there was no visiting hour. No one, no one to turn to, and the continual presence of the 'silent-lady' and the even more depressing ladies in their beds. I now understood them fully. They had nothing to live for, nothing to think about, we were all going the same way.

By late afternoon I was beside myself. I hadn't stopped demanding the doctor, crying and protesting that a mistake had been made. If my parents had not been arrested, what would become of them if I were taken away? I had walked into this trap and plunged us all into misery! In near hysterics I rose from my bed, the stitches forgotten, I wanted to get out and away from here. The lady stood beside me once more. She literally saved me from a nasty fall. Exhausted, lightheaded and speechless, I was laid on my bed. Someone rang for the nurse. "*My* doctor, *my* doctor," was all I could demand at that stage. An injection did the rest. . . . When I came round, *my* doctor stood smiling beside me. His hand on my shoulder, he spoke reassuringly: "Put your belongings on top of your bed, and we'll go back to where you belong!" Now I sobbed with joy and relief. A sharp twinge went through me, however, as I left my silent and sad fellow sufferers. I knew I would never see them again.

Within ten minutes I was back in my former ward. Word had spread about the mix-up in index cards. The strange and sudden manner of my admission had been mixed up with other strange and sudden admissions. Who had been responsible we would never know, but I was back where I had come from, and that was all that mattered. I had left the ward as a stranger, but returned to a warmhearted and friendly welcome. Flowers were all around my bed and everyone clapped their hands while I was wheeled to my former position at the window.

How I needed the following twelve days for recuperation in *my* ward, under the care of *my* doctor!

When at last I was able to walk out of the hospital on the 31st of October 1942, it was to a new life and freedom. Yet my parents never knew till very much later the cost of that little appendix.

My arrival was comparable with that of a fairy godmother. It was Mirli's birthday and I was able to present her and all the others with lots of small luxuries, farewell gifts from my well-wishers in the ward. I had fruit and chocolates and raisins and half a bottle of orange juice. Besides, before nightfall I would be able to finish the dress I had promised her. It was practically completed, but some embroidery around the neck would add that extra touch to make it 'special'.

We spent a most happy evening together. That night I turned around in my bed with a heart full to overflowing. Free and home! No, I would not listen tonight, surely nothing would happen this particular night. 'Please, let nothing happen this happy night of reunion', I prayed. 'Let us all sleep without worry, just this once'. We all *did* sleep that night and nothing happened.

5

NEXT MORNING I AWAKENED RATHER EARLY AND
remained quietly under the blankets. Judging from the comparative
silence in the flat and down below in the street, it was early yet.

Yes, I was home! I'd experienced a lot in the past few weeks and
felt much older. I'd seen and heard so much, I'd learned to respect
other people's feelings just a little more. I would never behave like
a child again. Little did I know that I would never have the chance.
The road ahead required thought and planning. I had to be ready
for anything.

After breakfast I helped the older children to get ready for school.
Nothing had to be left behind for the road was too long to return
for anything forgotten. If a play-piece was left behind, the unfor-
tunate one had to go hungry until dinner at night.

Soon the house was quiet and mother made another cup of coffee
which we drank silently together. Somehow, there was little talk
between us these days. We just enjoyed the luxury of being together.
I knew myself to be helpless to suggest any subject or begin a
worthwhile discussion. As always, actions had to speak louder and
more directly than words. I began to help my parents devotedly
in a way which they would never have experienced in other circumstances. Did I, unconsciously, endeavour to justify my life and
freedom? What right had I to live and not to give? Give what, and
to whom? I had to give myself and that to anyone, until the end
would come for me as well. Just now it was my parents and the
orphans.

Marijke, next door, knowing about our children, gave me her
large and most loved doll. She looked very sad and thoughtful when
she placed the doll in my arms. "Love her for me till we come
back, will you?" she almost pleaded. Should I ask any questions?
It was quite plain, they had received a call-up with the morning
post. "Of course we'll treasure her," I assured Marijke. "Give my
love to your parents . . . see you soon." It sounded most
casual, but then, we all knew what to expect. Any good wishes

would sound artificial, it was better to say little than sound insincere.

Often I wondered about our other neighbours in The Convent. They seemed to live in a different world altogether. What did our life mean to them? They had to adhere to a routine. The deadly silence in the building after the sound of a gong was so contrary to the chatter and laughter in the backyard during their free time. They skipped and ran, played ball and told stories, they were happy and gay whenever I looked down. I was told they prayed a lot and for very long at times. Oh, well, everyone had to make their own choice. I could not see or think any further. Their very existence was a distraction from our dismal thoughts and prospects.

Gradually the days closed in, the signs of autumn were all around us. The trees in the park across the canal were quite bare. Winter clothes came out sooner than in previous years. The winter gales had arrived and with them the colds, sore throats and flu. Not having had proper nourishment for a long time, our resistance was lowered more rapidly. Personally, I had never felt quite right since my operation. Had it taken more out of me than one would normally expect? Emotionally it practically ruined me. I had thought it was the end for us all when I was lying in that prison ward. No, I'd felt washed out for weeks now. My eyes were burning and my throat felt so dry. It pained me more from day to day. One day I noticed a glorious red glow all over my skin. Thumbing through my medical book, my heart leapt for joy. Could it be true? Scarlet fever!

Not wishing to raise my parents' hopes too high, I did not mention my discovery, I only told them that I felt terribly ill and needed a doctor. They realised that I spoke the truth. The doctor called later that morning and changed the atmosphere in our home into triumphant joy: he confirmed it was scarlet fever!

Six weeks of absolute freedom, no worries, no cares! We were compelled to attach a sign outside our door 'DANGER. NO ENTRY, SCARLET FEVER'. This and this only would hold the invader at bay. Complete security, such bliss!

Our home-life developed a new routine. The children were prohibited from attending school, so each one was allotted a small duty in the running of our home. We had nothing to grumble about. We were safe behind closed doors. It inspired us to prepare for a happy Channuka feast. This feast of dedication in the Jewish home is celebrated about the same time as Christmas. We, too, give presents, sing songs and burn candles. We celebrate the victory of the Jews after yet another battle, and the rededication of the Holy Temple made possible after finding the famous cruisken of oil. Judas, the Maccabee, with his servant, searched frantically for oil to obey God's command to keep the altar light burning at all times. But everything had been destroyed. No oil could be found. Great joy echoed throughout the camp when just one drop was found. Wonderful, oh wonderful, this one drop burned for eight days and nights, lasting until new oil could be brought to replenish the stock.

Since then, each year, for eight days duration, this lovely feast of liberty, dedication and victory is celebrated. Each day, one more candle is lit, until on the eighth day eight candles plus the servant-candle are brightly cheering all who recited the ceremonial blessings and thanksgivings. Songs are sung, presents distributed, fruits, nuts and sweets are there for the taking throughout the duration of the feast.

That year we celebrated with very grateful hearts, for we had at least each other plus the safety of scarlet fever.

We made presents for each other, such presents as were possible during these years of restriction and deprivation. Our gifts were usually practical, with the occasional luxury of some specially baked delicacy.

Being a good deal on my own and still in bed, my thoughts travelled far and wide and my mind was acutely active. The last five years had passed in a whirlpool. So much had happened, but what lay ahead? It was a sobering thought. We were safe for the time being, but for how long would we be able to stay together? It was a fact which had to be faced. How would we react to separation? I could not imagine my parents' lot, they were so dependent upon one another . . . and where would I finish up?

My room was upstairs. From the window I could watch ceaselessly the activity in the convent gardens below. There it was so peaceful, the only distracting noises coming from the front of the house, made by the horns of tugs or other boats. I enjoyed my illness with the security and rest which it brought for us all—a blessing to be grateful for.

It was at this time that I became 'God-conscious' for the first time in my life.

If one has been raised in a happy Jewish home, religious life is a joy and a tie which binds all members with cords of mutual trust and understanding. Traditional observances, burdensome to the eye of the outsiders, are natural, and full of delightful privileges to the Jewish family. We were orthodox and quite strict in the observance of our religion, and the synagogue services were never missed although we had to walk a great distance to get there. But . . . in how far was Almighty God part of our everyday lives?

It suddenly shook me deeply to realise that He was so badly ignored, never considered and mentioned at all except in prayers during private and public services. Was He a reality at all, or just a memory from the ancient days of our patriarchs? Was He interested in us or just a negative vague spirit? Could He, and would He, if called upon, hear and answer any requests? These and such-like questions went round and round in my head. If He was real, if He could be contacted, and if He could hear . . . yes, that would be a tremendous help at this time, I reasoned. But why did He seem so remote? Whose fault was it? He had been close enough to Moses and other great people in our history.

It was there in that bedroom, while blessed with scarlet fever, that a mighty truth suddenly penetrated my whole being. It was like a message from on high, a strange experience indeed. I was awed and full of joy and gratitude. The experience expressed itself in three words. These gave me strength, depth of life and a determination which had to last me for the next two years. Through the wildest and most dreadful events, these three words were to be my reality and assurance. Over and over I repeated them in thought, even whispering them aloud. In December, 1942, this remote person the Almighty God had allowed me a glimpse of Himself . . . I now knew that He was and is and would come again. Three words now stood rock-like in my life . . . 'GOD . . . WITH . . . US!'

Where had they come from so suddenly? It did not worry me. I felt rich and full and wanted just to bubble over and tell this great truth to all. But where to begin? Well, right there at home. Now or never, I had to share it with my parents, I had to tell them before it was too late. Once they knew it, too, they also would be able to face the future with courage whatever it had in store.

I started to get busy, I told the family not to disturb me as the Channuka presents had still to be finished. This was an easy way to be left alone and it was the truth. From this moment onward I worked constantly and very hard at the finest presents ever and the most practical too.

But first the decoration of my room had to be finished. Having to stay in bed, the candles would be lit in my room and the evening would also be spent there. Three large sheets of writing paper were to carry my three words, decorating the wall above my bed. There they were on view to each and everyone. I drew the words with the loveliest, curliest letters I could possibly manufacture. A lovely border surrounded each word and all was coloured in bright blending shades. Admiring my handiwork, I pinned them in place.

Now to work on the presents. Searching in my drawer, I picked the whitest handkerchiefs I could find. On each one I embroidered the words 'God with us'. While working and planning the evening, I thought deeply about what I could say to my people. What I *could* say? No, what I *had* to say! Since that moment of revelation I was *compelled* to tell them about it. I could and must not withhold this truth from anyone. It was a gift, a free gift. It had to be shared. As if I belonged to an invisible someone, I acted as under orders. I felt privileged to have this responsibility and set to work, and soon a little talk came into being.

The afternoon had slipped by so quickly, that it was evening before I realised. After dinner, I had still to wrap the presents. The handkerchiefs in tissue paper and my father's bookmark, also embroidered, lay on top of the little heap. While awaiting the arrival of my 'guests', I just lay there still, very still, looking at the three sheets of writing paper on the wall and absorbing the truth of its meaning: 'God With Us'. Each word separate and the three together, this was a volume of riches to treasure!

Yes, it was a command. I had to get this message of assurance through to my parents and the children. It was strange indeed for me to speak to my own parents on such a matter. I knew myself close to God that evening, and that He wanted me to tell them. His request had to be obeyed.

As usual, Mother had been preparing the meal all afternoon, planning to be free for the celebrations that night. Inwardly, I dreaded the moment when she would open my door to bring me the evening meal. But the unavoidable moment came and . . . "hope you like your di . . . what is that? Did you make these?" Mother pointed to my display. "Yes," I nodded, "do you like them?" "Very nicely done," she replied. "How on earth did you think of it?" I said that I would tell her later, hoping that some curiosity had at least been aroused. So far I had, at least, been successful. All the same, she must have realised that something was brewing, because I heard broken sentences to that effect reaching me from the kitchen downstairs.

While the family continued with their dinner and the clearing and washing of dishes, the newness of this revelation continued to burn itself into my being. GOD WITH US.

Soon it was time to begin the evening's festivities. I received the 'oh's' and 'ah's' at the sight of my drawings with real delight. At least they liked them. What else could I do at that stage? Just smile and acknowledge their surprised recognition with a grateful 'Thank-you'.

The table was covered with a tasteful embroidered tablecloth. The freshly polished brass Menorah (nine armed candle holder) was adorned with just one white candle and the servant candle, which would have the privilege to light the candles each day till at last eight candles would burn brightly on the eighth day. Satisfied, this servant candle would join them for the last time. We were handed our prayer books and we turned to the section for Channuka. Father began by reciting the blessing, the thanksgiving, and then lit this one lonely candle with the shammos, the servant. Now the time had come to join in the singing of the Moautzur, the song of Channuka. A beautiful song. A lovely melody. A memory and tradition many thousands of years old. A rich treasure was ours, to be part of God's people, the children of Israel.

Our eyes met while singing this song of triumph, and my voice faltered. We all knew that our thoughts were the same. Oh, our boys, our poor boys Why all this suffering? This unnecessary suffering! Continuing the final verses of our triumph song in a weak voice I looked longingly at my God-given verse. "Oh, heavenly Father," my soul sighed, "please keep your promise! Do not leave us, don't forsake us!" My sighs were fervent prayers, and frantically I held on to these words. The invisible Almighty surely would not leave us to be destroyed altogether!

The song was finished. We all shook hands and kissed one another with tears in our eyes. The children smiled shyly and we

56

smiled through our tears. I stroked my father's hair over and over again. No words could express our feelings. He just shook his head and tears rolled down his cheeks. He remained motionless. Poor father, he suffered so much more than mother. She would sob, relaxing the tension, but father could not do that.

Clearing my throat and taking a deep breath, I realised that the greatest moment of my life had come—to encourage my parents, because the Creator wished it so.

"Mother and Father, and you children, too, I want to speak to you and give you a few words which have come to me while lying in bed. We should not be sad or serious at Channuka, but we should face reality, not just celebrate the liberty of our forefathers. We, too, want to be glad. We want to find comfort and hope during our days of Channuka in this difficult year. There *can* be comfort and hope if we take Almighty God at His word. Mother and Father, we know what has happened so far, but we don't know what will happen in the days to come. We are still together, but we don't know if we will be in the near future. . . ."

"Don't talk such utter rubbish," my father interrupted, then mother chimed in: "Let her talk, Leo, and afterwards I'll make the tea."

"Whatever happens," I continued, "and should we get separated, wherever we are, let us never forget that. . . ." and I pointed to the words, 'God with us'. "He will be with each one of us, all the time, everywhere. Please don't let us ever forget it. It will be our strength and comfort until we meet again. That's all, I just wanted you all to know this and to remember it! Always! There is only a little present for each of you this year, but it will be all the easier to keep it with you. Never forget its truth and its comfort."

It was all over. I handed them their presents. First my parents, then the children theirs. They unwrapped them and quietly looked at the words. Each one said a quiet 'thank you' and I felt very uncomfortable. Yet my mission was completed, and I hoped, very sincerely, that the words would have the same effect on them as they had had on me.

"You are only a child, you have no need to talk so depressingly. We are together and we will remain so." With this statement, my mother slammed the bedroom door and stepped towards the kitchen to make the tea. We were still quiet when she returned with the

57

cups and saucers. I had no desire to cheer the atmosphere in an artificial manner. Reality had to be faced and as devout Jews it was high time to think of the promises of Almighty God and take Him at his word.

How He would be with us, I did not know, but *HE* knew, and I believed!

Into early February we managed to maintain the smell of Dettol on our landing and keep the sign 'Danger, infectious disease' on show. Yet, these good days had, inevitably, to end one day. Braving the storm once more, life returned to its usual cat and mouse game with the enemy in our midst. Strangely, we felt that the Sword of Damocles really hung on a very thin thread. We lived quietly, solemnly, earnestly from day to day. We were extraordinarily kind and patient with one another. Did we unconsciously number our days? Had the Gestapo noticed the long duration of our 'danger' notice? Had it made them alert to their neglect of No. 107 in that street? From March 1943 onward, the dagger pointed unmistakably to its neglected prey.

One of the greatest heartbreaks was the general call-up of the pupils from the secondary schools. Boys and girls alike received these call-ups by early morning post. On a given date a week later, they had to assemble at midnight in the Central Station in Amsterdam. They were needed for 'practical work' at some labour camp. They had to take their rucksack and a blanket. Midnight—during the normal curfew hours—how cunning! This ensured that they had to come alone. No parents, no scenes. Total separation at once. None of these children ever returned!

I still remember, today, the bitter cries of despair one could clearly hear towards the midnight hour as parents opened their doors to let their children go. May God have mercy on all who caused such dreadful agony to parents' hearts, and such suffering of mind and body to all these youngsters and those who remain to face loneliness, loss and bewilderment for the rest of their lives.

One morning late in March, the Gestapo stood at our door. Inwardly shaking, we made haste to open. They gave us no time to think or imagine the reason for their visit. With calm assurance they made their request: they had come for nine-year-old Hermann. He, hearing his name, endeavoured to make a quick getaway, but the soldiers grabbed him and left as suddenly as they had come. We

58

were stunned and speechless. Poor boy. Was it not enough to have taken his parents and the other members of his family? Could they not have left this child in peace, to survive, and to grow up within our fairly secure family circle? Poor Hermann, where would he be now? What would they do to him? Would he be very frightened? Would he be hungry? It was a sad day for us all. We only thought of our little charge whom we were unable to protect.

At 8 p.m., as curfew was about to begin, a loud banging on the front door shook us to the core. Yet, one always hastened to open at once. It was an inbred reflex action. The children stood as though rooted to the ground, mother sat stunned at the table and father was right behind me when I opened the door. He almost fell in . . . a dirty little boy. With all his weight he had leaned against the door to get in as quickly as possible. Our Hermann was home! "I got away, I got away!" was all he murmured over and over again. We did not ask him any questions, we just looked at his grin and were thankful to have him home again. He rubbed and scratched himself continually and mother urged me to get the water ready for a nice steaming bath. He did so need it. Only one day from home and such was the result. I shuddered to think of the future! Clean and tired he went to bed. There he ate every bit of hot supper which mother, in the meantime, had been able to prepare. How he had escaped we'll never know, all he would reveal was centred around the fact that he had climbed over roof tops and down the stairs of another house.

After such an eventful day we all slept soundly that night, only to awaken to an even more horrifying day. They were back by 10 o'clock to look for their prey once more! That was the end of our little boy.

One morning, soon after the departure of Hermann, I returned from shopping to find the children in tears. Father and mother had been collected and taken to The Theatre for questioning; the rucksacks were gone. Fear gripped me. Was this it? Had the end come at last? The oldest girl assured me that they would be home by nightfall. Whoever did come home? A wry smile covered my face. Who could count on such a promise? Of what importance were two creatures among millions? I tried hard to think straight, then putting Susan in charge I told them I would soon be back. I had to go to The Theatre to assess the situation. Just ten minutes from our house stood this building of terror. Would they allow me to see them? I ran all the way arriving their breathless but determined. Heiner, yes, Heiner, he was my hope. This far-off relation of my father's, a person we never saw around the house, surely he would not refuse my earnest plea. In some way he worked for the enemy. Or did he? I could not understand the complicated situation, but I did not care, I wanted to free my parents and I had to use this means.

When I had control of myself, I casually approached the Gestapo on duty. Being unmistakably in the lions' den I had to think and act fast. "Sir, I wish to see my uncle, Herr Heiner, please put me in touch with him." Not wishing to hear the answer in case it would be in the negative, I stepped back and gave my attention to an undone shoe-lace. Once this imaginary mishap was rectified, I rose and looked into the most kindly face I'd seen for a long, long time. Karl was a very sincere and helpful man. He took me to a little room. On the way, I passed a weeping crowd of unfortunates and a muddle of rucksacks and blankets. There was no need to tell him anything. He had seen my parents on arrival and had since been in touch with the authorities on their behalf. I pleaded with him to make sure of their release. We had not to look excited or worried: it would endanger his and our position. He looked at me for a long time, then slowly, and emphatically, he said: "Go home, and get the dinner ready, they'll need it!" I got the message, shook his hand firmly and gratefully, and walked with him past the guard. We parted with a smile to avoid betraying the real object of my visit.

This surely was an act of faith, for I *did* prepare the dinner and set the table with the finest tablecloth and the Sabbath cutlery.

As promised, they arrived home by dinner time. What a re-union . . . we laughed and cried and remained very close together all that evening. Yet, I have never discovered just why they had been arrested. Was it meant as a foretaste of things to come? They had been greatly surprised to hear their name over the loudspeaker system that afternoon—to them their freedom was a miracle. They were upset and broken after the sudden arrest and we all took a sedative and went to bed before curfew. We would, at least try to get some hours of sleep should the arrests be repeated. It turned out to be another sleepless night and then another bleak day faced us all. We all realised that safety was ebbing away. Only a miracle could keep us together.

I dared not mention my 'Channuka-encouragement', I only asked rather hesitantly if they had packed their handkerchiefs and their bookmarks. We did not shun reality any longer. Sitting together like condemned slaves, we discussed certain essentials. Father impressed on us that it had to be 'every man for himself and God for us all', and not to make the mistake of trying to stay together. If one was arrested, that one must go and the rest seek safety, anywhere. We understood only too well, we sensed our days were numbered and inwardly we prepared for the parting. Father put our thoughts into words 'We must be strong and accept a possible parting until the war is over!' No one replied, a sense of depression descended on us and remained with us from that day on.

We addressed each other in terms of endearment and went out of our way to be kind towards each other, from morning till night. It was an altogether frightening and very unhealthy atmosphere. When would the incident of Hermann's re-arrest repeat itself for us as a family? Every new day was a burden, every night a ghastly experience. We lay awake, listening for the heavy army lorries. Would they stop tonight, or pass on once more? When heavy army boots sounded on the pavement, we automatically held our breath. Often we heard that determined hammering on someone's door. Whose? Oh, God, help us, send deliverance, somehow, from somewhere. Give us courage and strength. Be with us!

'Every man for himself' my father had ordered. Could we do it? Would we, when the time came?

Drearily April made its entrance. The dismal grey weather was a true reflection of our attitude to each hour of our lives. Even the hands of the clock seemed to drag themselves wearily over their prescribed course. Was there no way out? No one to help? We kept our thoughts and fears to ourselves. Shopping, eating and sleeping became a mechanical exercise. The nights continued to be a nerve-wracking experience. It was good to meet over breakfast every morning, we treated it as a gift. We learned to look long at one another desperately trying to imprint each other's features on our memory. A heavy sigh to Almighty God was heard frequently in these days. Our prayers had no words, our whole beings craved for freedom and security.

6

ON THE 9TH OF APRIL 1943 AT 10 P.M. OUR BELL RANG loud, long and continuous. We knew at once that this was it! My heart thumped! I buried my head in my pillow and burst into a flood of tears, sobbing and frantically beating my bed with my fist. No, Lord, no! Please, please let us stay! The children, in their bedroom next door, were disturbed by now. The heavy boots of the soldiers came nearer and nearer up the stairs. The children cried and called for me. Susie, the oldest, quietened them and warned them not to mention my name. They wouldn't stop and I couldn't either. I cried, tore my sheet and shook all over. Why did no miracle come our way? Now, this minute! Please, Lord, come and help! 'God with us', I couldn't feel it now. I had told my parents to believe it and hold on to it. Oh, mother! I could hear her crying with pain. Had they hit her? "Get out of that bed this minute or a bucket of water will bring you to your senses!" Father appeared to be trying to protect her and to calm the soldiers. I could hear him reasoning with them. Poor father, he was a broken reed himself. Suddenly all was quiet. Was mother dressing hurriedly, or had something horrible happened in that bedroom? Someone came upstairs. "Come on, children, hurry!" It was father. "Good girl, Susan, bring the children into the sitting-room. Are you warmly dressed?" The little ones still cried for me. Then my door opened slowly and quietly. It was my father: "Bleib gesund mein Kind!" (Keep well my child!) A quick kiss on my hot wet face, and he was gone.

Oh, no, the soldiers were on their way up. A hard voice said "Hurry up, everyone, we haven't got all night!" I kept perfectly still as I heard him moving about in the children's side of this large partitioned room. I expected the dividing door to be flung open at any moment. But at last, his footsteps faded away, as he went downstairs.

Mother's voice had regained its normal tone. She asked permission to see if the gas and electricity had been turned off at the main. Her quick steps came nearer . . . passed the kitchen, the switches and made for my door. I knew it, I knew she'd come. "Oh Muttie." She embraced and kissed me warmly: "Mein liebes Kind, bleib gesund, halt Mut!" (My dear child, keep well, be courageous!).

They shouted for her. A last hug. She was gone. The door banged and I heard them all tramping down those wooden stairs. Then the starting of the heavy engine as the lorry drove away from the house.

A ghostly silence enfolded the building. I dared not move, yet my brain worked at double speed. It was a frightful night. Listening to every sound, I wondered if the house would be looted before morning. It was still curfew time, but looters knew quite well where arrests had taken place, and the seals would not be applied until the next day. If they found me, would they notify the police? I'd heard of assaults and rape and the bribery of silence for consenting victims. Weak with shock and the realisation of the danger of my position, I remained motionless for a long time.

When at last I was able to relax I knew I had to act quickly. This would be my last night in our home and I had to use the time wisely and well. In pitch darkness I dressed, putting on as many garments as possible. Every movement, every step, had to be watched to avoid the creaking of floor-boards, the stumbling over a shoe, the knocking over of a chair. Although my movements were as quiet as possible, my plans almost perfect, someone must have heard me when I used the toilet later on, for I heard heavy footsteps on the landing. They stopped outside our front door, and there was silence, as if someone was listening intently. Then followed knocking on the door, over and over again. I was petrified, but I was determined no one would get me to open that door. If they wanted me, they would have to break it down and find me. I stayed in the toilet till I heard the steps fading away. I was almost certain that they went higher up in the building. It surely couldn't have been a neighbour? I would never know. I would play safe.

Once the silence had returned, I planned the next few hours. My rucksack could not be taken from the house. That would be fatal. I would take some essentials from it and re-pack them into a very small case. Although I looked everywhere, however, no rucksack could be found. Had father hidden it to avoid suspicion? There was no time to think or worry about the matter. Replacements had to be found—toilet articles, some cutlery, an unbreakable cup, a change of underwear and a few sugar lumps, important papers, addresses, and writing material. This had to suffice as my little black case was full.

Fully dressed with hat and coat, and my little black case beside me, I spent the last night in my home. It was the longest night I have ever spent; it seemed as if six o'clock would never come. Silence, darkness and fear surrounded me. I said a mental farewell to all our belongings, knowing full well that I would never return. The lovely large furniture, the clock with the brass pendant and especially our beautiful cuckoo clock—never again would I see any of them. The empty beds, the untidy rooms, the photographs of my brothers, my father's own oil paintings of which he was so proud, the large built-in bookcase, full to overflowing with fine books in special bindings. All, all had to be left.

Mother, like most Jewish mothers, had gathered a trousseau for her only daughter. Linen of every description could be found in that hamper—table linen, materials, silver, and most probably many things I will never know of. Mother had kept an iron cross bar through the two hooks on the lid, and this was padlocked. I used to think it funny, and often curiosity drove me to touch it, yet an unspoken rule prevented me from ever asking any question connected with the subject of my future. It all seemed so unimportant now; I would never use any of the things my mother had so lovingly planned and prepared. Everything would be taken over by the enemy.

It had been a lovely flat, the sitting-room windows allowing a fine view of the canal below, the barges going to and fro all day long, their horns sounding as they approached the bridge. When you opened the window and looked to the right, you could see the gates close slowly. The traffic would come to a halt, the men begin to turn a handle in the middle of the bridge, and it would then leave the sides and slide towards the middle of the canal. Then the barges would slowly glide past, paying their dues into a wooden shoe which dangled down from a fishing rod . . . hupsedesee . . . with a fine swing it could be hauled up, and the bridge opened once more to the stream of traffic.

A few houses to the left, past the doctor's surgery, and right beside the warehouse, was a small but homely picture house. On Saturday and Wednesday afternoons the long queue of school children made a colourful picture against the grey stone canal houses. I, too, used to join the queue before it was 'Forbidden for Jews' We saw the most exciting cowboy films, and plenty of love stories. I had enjoyed those hours. After all, it was *my* picture house and on *my* canal.

I recalled my adventure in the Convent. Curiosity had got the better of me, and I had to find out what went on inside. My mind had been made up, I'd investigate. It had to be planned carefully so that I could slip into the building unnoticed. I had decided I would wait for the ringing of that bell, and the sounding of the gong. Often I saw people climb those terrace steps. Surely they were joining the sisters inside, so why shouldn't I? I would, at the very next opportunity! Sooner than anticipated, I found myself in the long dark corridor. Following the other people I found myself in the chapel. Each person selected a pew of their choice and knelt down folding their hands in pious reverence. Oh, dear, what now? I, too, selected my pew, the last one, staying beside the door. No one could see me there, but I could see everything from where I sat in my seat. I'd never knelt in my life; it was a sin and foreign to the Jewish religion. It was most beautiful. There were artistic statues of holy people, stained glass windows depicting Biblical scenes, and golden crosses in many of the corners. The most important feature seemed to be the altar. Everyone faced it and bowed down reverently, saying prayers in the process. Lots of flowers in exquisite vases adorned the building. Then the sisters entered, two by two, singing a Latin song and holding their prayer books in front of them, precisely at the same angle. They did not look like the bright sisters one could see at work and play in the back garden. They looked solemn, intent and very holy. The Mother Superior took her place near the altar and a young priest began the service proper.

Sitting there in the back row, I had prayed in my own way in my own language: 'Dear God, please don't mind me coming into this place. I just want to see what it is like.' Although I had no idea to whom the sisters directed their prayers, they certainly were very reverent and submissive. The atmosphere was awe inspiring.

I smiled, ironically, recalling as many memories as could be crammed into these last hours. I awoke from my day-dreams as I noticed that dawn had found its way through some small cracks in the black-out paper. It was close to 6 a.m. My head began to spin again, but I had to be strong. This was no time for sentiment. Clear thinking was of the utmost importance. Had I attended to everything? Would I be able to get a glimpse of my parents during the days to come? What would I do if they asked for belongings of a personal nature? I would not be able to help. They must not know that I had left for good the place we called home. Once more I went through the rooms which I would never enter again and silently bade final farewell to all the memories they held for me. My people would be wiped out, and in some ways I hoped it might be soon, for in my imagination the mental and physical suffering they would be undergoing burned itself deeply into my innermost being.

The crucial moment had to be faced . . . very quietly I edged myself through our front door, trying to avoid the inevitable squeak if it was opened too wide. I did not want the neighbours to know that I had been left behind. If I had not been missed, I might be free a little longer. In time lay hope, hope for survival, hope for a future. Holding my breath, I raced down the two flights of stairs, realising that practically every one of these wooden steps was certain to creak. At last I stood in the cool morning air and stepped out briskly, as if filled with a definite purpose and aim.

The streets were quiet. Here and there was a cyclist on his way to work, a milk lorry, a van returning from market and the inevitable fearsome green lorry, perhaps on its way 'off duty'.

Only ten minutes from here was The Theatre to which my people must have been taken. So near and yet out of reach. It would be suicidal to go near the lion's den. Oh, how I longed to see them!

Opposite The Theatre was the day nursery where I had just begun a new career a few days ago. Strange as it may seem this 'day' nursery needed more and more staff to act on *night* duty, as each day fewer children were collected at closing time. Where their parents had gone, one had only to surmise. Just another family would never be united again! The little ones seemed to understand what had happened when a parent failed to collect them in the evening. This once so happy place became a valley of tears. Almost continually, day and night, there was somewhere the pathetic cry of a toddler or baby, crying for the arms which meant security and

66

mother love. The nurses were at it constantly, off-duty hours ceased to exist. They worked calmly, endeavouring to ignore the terrors across the road. An extra job was the caring for babies of arrested mothers residing in The Theatre. Most of them would be deported after midnight. It was our duty to look after the little ones during the day and make them clean and comfortable for their long journey . . . so ridiculous!

On my way to the day nursery that morning my mind was a blank. Hesitantly, yet deliberately, I reached the main door at last. Not daring to look across the road, my eyes fixed themselves on the bell, listening sharply for steps in the corridor. Yes, someone was coming. The bolt and lock rattled, then clicked, assistant Matron looked in amazement at my expressionless face. "You are early, my child, come in." She obviously looked for an explanation, yet wanted to avoid hearing the inevitable story.

"They called last night . . . the whole family," was all I needed to say. She did not even reply, but put her arm gently round my shoulders and led me to the office. After a short silence I had to ask the vital question: "Did you hear any trams last night?"

She nodded. 'Oh dear, that could well have been the moment of departure for the new arrivals as well.' Endless streams of trams arrived after midnight, passing the main doors of The Theatre. People were driven inside by shouting and excited soldiers. 'Hurry, hurry, hurry', was all one could hear. Old and young, male and female, some carrying babies, others leading toddlers, and all laden with rucksacks, disappeared one by one into the unending line of trams. It could last for hours some nights, as the transports left the Plantage Middellaan. No one dared to lift a curtain and wave a last farewell to a friend or relative. A soldier seeing you would simply point, you were arrested and joined the one to whom you had so lovingly waved a farewell. Oh! the sheer delight to play with human misery.

Had my people indeed been among last night's transport? No one knew. How long I sat with matron in that office is not clear to me today. No one spoke, it was cold and I was just existing. After some time, I simply rose and left indicating my intention to go on duty. No one attempted to stop me. Did my face betray the whole story?

It was early yet. Some of the children had just wakened and were drinking their warm milk; the others who still slept were allowed to do so. Sleep obliterated much misery. Routine had long been relaxed and one endeavoured to give freedom, love and comfort in as many ways as possible.

One of the nurses, trying to be kind, pointed to the general mending basket in the centre of the ward. Would I like to give her a hand later on? Forcing a smile, I nodded and passed on. I had to get to that window. Through it I could see The Theatre doors. I had to keep well back. No one must see my curiosity from the other side of the road. Only soldiers on patrol now. How many thousands had left these exits during the night? Who was still inside? For some time I watched each door. What did I hope for? Just desperately wanting to see the dear faces and yet . . . perhaps not . . . for if I saw them, it would mean . . . transport!

In a very short time all the staff were acquainted with my parents' fate, all knew that they could not count on my help today. I just stood there and kept watch. How long would I be able to keep it up before the soldiers spotted my presence? Could I possibly hide continually from those ever searching eyes? Did they not constantly look for more arrests? Suddenly the assistant Matron stood silently behind me. After a while she enquired if they could do anything for me when they went across to serve the children's dinner. This offer certainly wakened me up from the trance into which I had settled. I thought desperately and asked if she could find out if my parents were still inside. I asked her to tell them that I would be all right till they returned. I told her to impress on them to be brave and courageous. I asked her to give them my warmest love. . . .

She left and I continued my depressing vigil. The minutes and hours ticked by. The morning rush hour had begun. Cars and people, lorries and trams were speeding on their daily tasks. Was it an extra dull day? An air of misery seemed to hover around and over us all, or was it just over me? Cups of tea and coffee were handed to me from time to time, but my eyes would not leave these doors. Every move of officials and soldiers was weighed in my judgement. No one attempted words of comfort. Everyone knew why I was there and who had been arrested, and they left me in peace. All at once, something shook me from my state of semi-shock. The sudden revving and roaring of engines made everyone in the building take notice. What we saw turned many a face ashen pale. My blood ran cold, I was unable to utter a word. An extra transport had began. Biting my nails, I experienced the most helpless and hopeless hour of my entire life.

More than a dozen army lorries were lined-up outside The Theatre. A sorry stream of people left the building heavily laden with bundles and rucksacks. The children who only a short time before had been fed by us were now carried outside by their mothers, or a nurse who handed them to their fathers. Short, harsh orders intermingled with the despairing cries of the unfortunates. Helplessly they disappeared into the steel-plated army lorries, up two steps and another broken heart and tear-stained face was on its way to. . . . I could see them no more, the windowless body of the trucks hid all its misery from view. As each one was filled to the brim, the living load was secured by the flap being lifted into place and the iron pegs clicked into their holes. As lorry after lorry moved off another empty one took its place. Could it continue much longer? At last the flow diminished. Only two vehicles were left and they filled up rather slowly. Was this the end for today? Had I missed them, or had they been spared just a little longer. Where there is life there is certainly hope as well.

A gasp escaped me . . . there they were! My mother came first, white-faced but tidily dressed even after the ordeal of arrest and a night in The Theatre. Hesitantly, still hoping for a miracle, I suppose, she struggled up the few steps into the army lorry. Directly behind her was father. He looked so strange and so different. He was ashen-faced, his eyes stared without expression before him as if he did not care where he was going, and his very movements gave the appearance of a mechanical robot. His mind was obviously elsewhere. In seconds, he, too, had disappeared. This is my memory of our last farewell. Mother had turned her head towards the nursery. Had she hoped that our eyes would meet just once more? It was too dangerous. It was not to be. Barely a minute, and the heavy revving of the engine set the lorry in motion. It also brought me back to reality, my mind was a blank. Numb, tearless and speechless I stared at the place where moments ago a living burial had taken place.

It was all over!

Calmly and slowly I left the window where I had watched and waited the last few hours of this dreary April morning.

What next?

I made my way to the staff bathroom. Here, no one would seek to follow me, I could be still, to think, to plan and to visualise the future. Here I could be alone with my God.

A sudden weakness came over me. The coldness within me began to melt slowly, I could no longer control myself ... the breaking point had been reached. Fumbling for father's large handkerchief in my uniform apron, I began to sob: at last I could let go, I had no power to control it and did not care. Hot, exhausted, but also wonderfully relieved, I contemplated the present situation. The safety and solitude of this bathroom became the springboard from which I would enter an entirely new world. Situations and experiences hitherto unknown would unfold themselves hour by hour. Determined to be courageous, alert and useful in the complex battle of self-preservation, I left the bathroom and entered a crazy world.

7

SLOWLY I MADE MY WAY DOWN THE LANDING. AS WITH Abraham, it was true also with me that day, I went, not knowing where I was going (Hebrews 11.8). The babies played happily on the floor, the toddlers enjoyed fun at their tables or in the indoor sandpit. Little groups were taken to the washroom in preparation for lunch. They returned most beautifully washed, combed and wearing our aprons and bibs. It all seemed a normal kind of day, life going on as usual in our nursery in spite of the disasters across the road.

A young nurse approached me with the news that matron wished to see me in the office. Indifferent to any decision likely to be made, I knocked at the office door. Mechanically, almost, I entered her room and was asked to sit down. Without the slightest reference to the events of the past hours, matron told me I was to go off duty that afternoon and use the time available to report to the Board of Guardians at the central headquarters in town. Being under age, the community was responsible for my movements and maintenance. A sudden thought flashed across my mind . . . the children, our children, they too had been fostered due to the arrest of their parents. Before tonight I, too, would be fostered out. . . . I now was one of them.

Thanking matron for her help, I made to leave. "Nurse Dobschiner," she called after me, "would you wish to continue your employment with us, we will be happy to have you. Please let me know once you are settled and do keep in touch."

Thanking her once more, I left the office, and collected my coat and black leather case. I walked the streets for hours, having deliberately refused to glance across at The Theatre when leaving the nursery: Psychologically, it was the best antidote for the turmoil of my mind. The long walk relieved the inner tension and helped me to come to terms and accept what had to be!

The streets were crowded, the vendors noisily shouted their wares, cars and trams rattled their way through the old narrow streets. I fought my way passed them all, almost in a dream. I knew I had to waken up and face reality sometime and reach a decision as to what I was going to do. Would I ever grasp it fully?

An empty stomach reminded me that even I in my present condition still required to eat to meet the needs of the body. How extraordinary that one could forget a regular habit like eating, when other more important matters predominated. Caressing the little slip of paper my mother had managed to slip to one of the children's nurses at lunch time, I meditated on its meaning. She had advised me to look well after myself; to take care, and abstain no more from non-kosher foods, to eat anything which would nourish me and on which I could lay my hands during the lean years. Dear mother, she meant so well. It must have been a great battle of conscience to advise me to break our strict habit of orthodoxy. Yet, this I could not and would not do! Somehow, the Lord would provide me with enough to keep myself from 'unclean' foods. I knew one or two Jewish butchers in the centre of our ghetto, one who also served tea and rolls. The thought of Russian tea and rolls with sausage made my mouth water indeed, and automatically I walked faster.

The shop was warm and people stood around the counter or sat on stools facing the narrow marble ledge along the wall. Everyone discussed the recent arrests, everyone seemed to have lost someone. They sympathised with each other, giving such comfort as was possible under the circumstances. Being alone, I ordered my rolls and tea, and at last relaxed in a small corner. How wonderful to be able to rest. How good to eat and drink and feel warm. I ate slowly and sipped my tea even more slowly, spinning out what time I had left. I ordered more rolls and tea and then began to count the money I still possessed. My parents had left me a little purse with loose change, but this I had to ration carefully as it would be my last privately owned riches for a long time to come. I needed no experience to realise that it would not take me far, let alone through the rest of the week. There seemed no other way out but to report, as soon as possible, to the Board of Guardians if I wanted a reasonably respectable bed for the night ahead. But another plate of rolls would do no harm. It was even more appreciated than the first, and a second glass of lemon tea was put before me as a matter of course. I cupped both my hands around it and sipped the scalding hot stimulant, obtaining at the same time as much heat as possible from the glass itself. Dreamily I gorged myself, I was shivery, sleepy and not quite myself.

How long I used the hospitality of that butcher's shop I really do not know, but looks from the other customers made me feel I had outstayed my welcome. Their conversation continued on a slightly lower key. Why did they mention continually the subject of 'safety and escapes'? How pointless! Who would want to be hunted continually? Perhaps they still had relatives to consider. Perhaps they still wanted to live. Perhaps someone was waiting for them somewhere. Someone to love and care for. Oh, well, who could blame them! Did they suspect me as an informer? All right, I would go! I was not in the slightest interested in their conversation. I had my own business to attend to.

Gripping my black case firmly I prepared to leave, since to stay any longer would only postpone the events which inevitably were awaiting me somewhere. At the counter I asked for more rolls with salami and liver sausage, these would be my stand-by for the rest of the day. Having paid all my debts, I left.

The weather reflected my exact feelings. It was a dull, cool and uninterestingly quiet day. I, too, was indifferent to everything around me. I felt strangely quiet and cool and rather dazed. These exact sensations were to return to me most frequently in times of danger or in perplexity. Thus I walked street after street, on and on, barely noticing the traffic speeding past.

The Board of Guardians was a good bit away yet, but I was used to walking, and I did not spare it a second thought. It had been years since I had last used public transport in any form, or even cars or bicycles. One had to keep on walking, walking, walking! Stop, and then you felt how really tired your body was.

As evening was approaching I reached the familiar building. There seemed to be people everywhere. Again all these worried faces, these eyes red from sleeplessness and frequent crying. Children of all ages were mingling with the grown-ups. In all their faces one could read the story of fear and bewilderment. Here and there pleading little voices cried for 'Mummy'. This sight of misery and despair once more brought home to me my own situation. It was difficult to be brave, but I did my best. One had to. 'Every obstacle conquered will make you stronger for the next one', Sister Henny used to say. So I did not cry, just swallowed very hard and soon I, too, felt strong again. Just the same, did I look forlorn? An official approached me. "Can I help you?" he asked in a most matter-of-fact tone. Not knowing if he really could, I told him all that had happened in the past twenty-four hours. Without the slightest sign of surprise, he was ready with the mechanical instructions: "Along the corridor, Room Three, please!"

Rather startled at his detached attitude, I made my way along the 'sausage-machine' to which I was now destined. The reality of a saying I had heard somewhere, long ago, came to the front of my memory: 'Everyone for oneself and God for us all'. A strange saying, surely such as would only spell disaster in the end! Yet, looking around at this distressed mass of humanity, old and young, rich and poor, I wondered, 'Who cared for them?' Even the man at reception, what did we matter to him? He was only interested in his job at the desk which, in the meantime, ensured him exemption from deportation. Thinking these thoughts I made my way to Room Three. Another official asked the obvious questions and then handed me a card with details of my new foster parents. He smiled and wished me good luck.

Having a fairly long walk ahead of me to the southern part of the city, I set out at a steady pace in order to be there before curfew at eight o'clock. That day I learned the true meaning of taking just one step at a time. At last I reached my destination. The building contained four flats or dwelling apartments. The whole structure had a modern appearance and looked bright and inviting. All the houses on both sides of the boulevard were built in the same style, with balconies on alternative storeys.

This was to be my new home. Rather pleased I climbed the broad, stone outside stairway, then rang the bell beside the nameplate 'Rennie'. An electric buzzer sounded and the door opened automatically. I entered, closed the door securely and climbed the carpeted stairway to the Rennie's flat. A kindly lady in her midforties invited me to enter. The private house door shut behind me. At last, I had reached the end of the road, I thought to myself, it would be safer here than in the centre of the town where most arrests took place.

Mrs. Rennie made coffee for us both while I told her all she wanted to know. At last she showed me my room. Incredible! I'd never had a room like this. It even had a balcony. If only my parents could have seen me here, their mind would have been at ease. Mrs. Rennie left me to settle in. The other members of the family would not be home till later and I would meet her husband and two grown-up daughters at dinner time.

Carefully I folded the luxurious eiderdown and laid it across the chair by the window. Such pretty curtains, in fact, all the furnishings had a general pattern of unity. They radiated calm and peace to my still turbulent soul. I stretched out on the bed and fell asleep before I could think or worry any more. When I eventually wakened, the room light was on and the curtains drawn to hide the gloomy black-out material. A young girl, known to me later as Mirjam, stood beside the bed with a hot cup of tea. Yes, I was ready for it. We chatted about absolutely nothing and were almost relieved when Mrs. Rennie called us for dinner. A quick wash in the beautiful bathroom, and I was ready for more introductions.

Without any fuss I was accepted into this home, as one of the family. No one fussed over me, I was allowed all the freedom I could possibly enjoy under the circumstances. The conversation on this and other nights centred on the new arrests of the day, what news had been received from Westerborg, the central collecting camp, speculations about the immediate future and discussion about rumours and gossip in general. Somehow I could not feel really interested, I lived in a sort of detached fashion from day to day.

Each morning I left after breakfast to start the long walk to the city centre and my work in the nursery. Each day I gazed at the large glass swing-doors of The Theatre from which I had seen my parents depart for the last time. Each day the roll call of the little ones became smaller as more and more were collected during the night. Each night, also, the volume of traffic increased. Each new day had its revelations of human misery and innocent suffering.

When off-duty for an hour or two, I would walk along the Plantage Middelaan over the swing-bridge and along the canal towards my old home. It became my daily pilgrimage. The occupants of the barge outside our house greeted me always with that same serious, but understanding nod of the head. Often I felt tempted to speak to these, our former friendly neighbours, but not wishing to endanger their safety, I held my peace. The house looked forsaken, so dead and quiet. Not once did I see any of the other tenants of the building. But did they see me through their curtains and were they frightened to speak to me? Who could blame them, there were always so many informers around. It was wiser to keep to yourself and not put anyone under unnecessary suspicion.

One day, at the end of April, while on my usual pilgrimage, my heart thumped with shock and anger as I glanced towards our windows. I stood stock still, frozen with horror as I realised what had happened. Everything, yes, all that was ours was gone. No curtains at the windows, the glass panes gaped a horrible bleakness at my staring, questioning gaze.

The gangway of the old barge squeaked . . . the son, Mr. Boran, came towards me and placed a hand on my shoulder, nodding his head repeatedly. "It happened this morning, they came with two vans, it took them all morning." I wasn't surprised. I did not want to cry anymore. Forcing a thank-you smile, I bade him good-bye.

As I walked away I visualised all that was gone. Quite impossible, and yet so true, it was a hard reality to accept. How ridiculous! I thought about my old doll. She had been given to me when I left Berlin. She was then 35 years old . . . I'd grown to love her. She had such human features, such real black wavy hair. A fine wardrobe of fashion and underwear made it fun to play with her, even at my age. I conveniently called it a hobby to train for my profession. Probably she had been smashed by now, or damaged during the removal, I couldn't imagine anyone taking care of just a doll. What about our unique cuckoo clock? Would I ever see one like it again? Impossible! It was an heirloom and it pained me to know it had gone for ever. One could get deeply attached to objects which made home the personal place of one's own creation. The solid oak sideboard, the large box of easter crockery and cutlery. My mother's personal 'treasures'. Everything was irreplaceable. The family albums. There was no end to this train of thought.

When I described these happenings to the Rennies that evening their sympathy was with me during the first course of dinner, but soon the conversation resumed its normal trend; the arrests, the possibility of escape, the news from camps. My sorrow had not really touched them, my loss wasn't theirs, my interests unimportant where life was concerned. Perhaps they were right, all would be dust in the end.

8

DURING THE NEXT FEW WEEKS, LIFE SETTLED DOWN TO a normal pattern. The days became almost monotonous. I left the house each morning early and worked quiet unrestricted hours at the nursery, leaving well after six in the evening. The long walk enabled me to reach home just before curfew. After all cages were shut, one just had to wait for the nightly hunters. Strangely enough, however, I slept soundly, very tired after the long days. Working all day at the nursery caring for the little ones, until they too, were deported, participating in all their joys and sorrows, and sharing their meals, made me look on this place more like a home than my foster home out there in the South of Amsterdam. Here I was close to The Theatre, close to my canal home, close to so many memories. When I arrived at night for dinner at the Rennies, the talk seemed so superficial, always the same subjects. I made it a point to retire early. In my luxurious room, so lovingly given to me by the Rennies, I could be alone with my thoughts and my memories. I became content in these new ways and surroundings. Yet, it was too good to last for long.

Another mental and nervous explosion had to be faced. One morning as usual, I walked smartly towards the nursery, when passers by close to the building stopped me, recognising my uniform. I was advised, strongly, not to proceed in that direction, but to change course and return to the place I had come from. They did not give me much information, but what I did hear was sufficient to make me thank them gratefully . . . once more I had been spared. Incredible, how could they have done it! Those little children and all those young nurses who had worked so sacrificially day and night, the matron, the doctor, all the staff. Information leaked through soon enough, they had emptied the nursery during the night and commanded the staff to bring all the children into the lorries. Who could argue? Who could or would plead? Poor little ones! I hoped, as usual, that their fear and suffering wouldn't last for long.

77

I returned to the Rennies. Mrs. Rennie was surprised to see me but took the news calmly. I crept to my room, my refuge, my heavenly solitude. Through the curtained windows I observed the hustle and bustle down below. These were free people, the people in trams and private cars, the daily shoppers, the little children holding their mother's hands or those still in prams. Where were our toddlers and babies? My Amsterdam, my dear city, my country, oh, Europe, how many humans would you have to sacrifice before the final end? 'God with us', of course I realised this, but we needed strength, oh, how we needed strength, and enduring faith as well.

The days were much longer now, the nights too. I couldn't sleep, having no long walks and hard work to engage in. Oh, yes, to help at home was a privilege I was now able to discharge fully, it paid some of the debt I owed this family. The payment from the Board of Guardians would never make up for the freedom I had enjoyed in their home. Yet having more time to think and contemplate my own situation did not encourage my spirits. At times I was filled with fear of the unknown, yet at other times I imagined myself to be able to face just anything . . . with courage. Oh, how silly . . . roll on events and show your colours boldly!

There was no need to wait long. Monotony did not belong to our day and age. Sunday, the 20th of June, became yet another terrible day for our people. Around nine o'clock in the morning one felt an uneasiness. The atmosphere was not quite right for a Sunday morning. One could hear noises, familiar, but uncommon in this area. It surely couldn't be true, not here in Amsterdam South? I did not dare to rise from my bed, I just listened to the sounds I had come to know so well. The roaring of army lorries, the screeching brakes of trams, many trams, the harsh and almost hoarse voices of army officials who tramped backwards and forwards in their nail-studded boots. Did they need all that activity, all that noise to pluck up courage for their evil deeds? I just *had* to peep, just to get a glimpse of what was happening out there. What I saw, dispelled any doubt regarding what was happening. This was it! It was action-proper for Amsterdam South!

At each corner and other strategic points along the boulevard one could see the familiar green lorries, but there were also rows and rows of trams, all now standing motionless ready for their cargo of human misery. I could see from dozens of houses the emerging groups of men, women and children, the sight I knew so well. It was strange to see it happening in daylight, to have sorrow and misery exposed to all the neighbours, to become a spectacle, almost an entertainment, to those who delighted in our suffering. There were few, very few, like this, but they did exist, everywhere. All their faces looked shocked as they were driven towards lorry or tram. Many cried hysterically, others wiped their tears silently, but the children were so frightened. Parents tried to comfort them, but what for; these little ones had to accept their lot in the same way as their parents. For them, too, there was no way out. I saw some youths trying to escape, they always did. What was the use, the soldiers were everywhere, they saw to it that no one escaped so that the final annihilation might be postponed. If, and they always were, captured, their punishment was too severe. Torture was worse than death . . . this heavenly gift, this freedom from suffering and loss.

I felt cold and shivery this morning in June.

In some strange way I realised that this day would be *my* day of arrest. Having no luggage it was easy to be ready for whatever lay ahead. My small black case was always near; it only needed the addition of a few toilet articles.

While collecting these in the bathroom and studying my face in the mirror, the door bell rang. I ran to the living-room. My heart was pounding. All the Rennies were assembled there along with two Gestapo and a Dutch black-shirt who assisted the Germans with 'language problems' or rather obstreperous victims.

The shout of 'Alles mit' assured me of their errand. Mr. Rennie talked in German, showed them many documents, and unsuccessfully tried to humour them. Somehow his papers must have had a valid stamp which at last pacified the hunters; a stamp which would prolong the struggle for life a little longer.

They pointed to me: "And what about her? Who is she? What is she doing here?" They paused, waiting for Mr. Rennie's reply. He could do nothing. "She only lives here. Her parents have already been arrested. . . ."

'Sie . . . mit.' I knew it. It was all over now.

With a strange sigh of relief I said good-bye to the Rennies, thanking them for their kind hospitality. It seemed that for the first time in years, I walked in complete freedom. The strain and stress which went together with the fight for survival were no longer needed.

Quiet, relaxed, and at ease, I began to talk to my escorts as they led me down the two flights of stairs.

"Could I do anything to help you? I love children; would you like me to look after them?"

They still did not answer, but looked in amazement at one another and at me. So I tried again. "Just as well it has stayed dry today. Have you been at it for a long time?" And once more looking at the children: "Would you please speak to your Oberste and obtain permission to let me look after the children until we get to the station, then they can join their parents once more. There is a lot of confusion and unnecessary hardship for both parents and children during the journey."

No reply was given. By this time we were downstairs and I joined the stream of misery which made its way along the Boulevard to the trams and lorries.

Soldiers were everywhere: a voice from a loudspeaker was shouting orders at random. Then in glad surprise I heard: "Any parents who want their children to reach the station in comfort may hand them over to the nurse who is waiting in front of the tram wagon No. 24. You will be reunited again before entering the station."

That nurse was me. I could do it! They had listened after all! Already little ones near me looked hopefully into my face. What could I offer them? A smile and plenty of kind words; a little time of warmth and security. They came, and as they came I loved each one and lifted them into my tram. Just enough to handle I thought.

I looked and marvelled. It seemed like a day's outing if one could only disregard their faces. Most of the children were over six years of age and wore the large yellow star, and all had big labels tied to coats or jackets with full identity details.

Moving around in the tram, I talked to the little ones and smiled many a tear away. But, oh how bewildered was the atmosphere. However, they had a chance to revive a little before the major ordeal in the station. One particular boy about eight years of age attracted me strangely. He just stood on the platform and stared unseeingly before him. Not a tear on his face: unaware of anyone around him.

After my second round of the children, I ventured near him, and stood quietly beside him for a minute or two. Even my arm around his shoulder did not have any effect. My questions were left unanswered. I loved him.

As some children became restless I left him, only to return to that lonely little statue as quickly as I could.

He had to be made to talk: he had to! He was evidently under high tension and unable to relax. I took his little hand saying, "We'll stay close together, shall we?" Contact had been established without a word from him, but his eyes had softened: they were wet.

I began to sing, and some of the little ones smiled and joined in. We sang nursery rhymes, popular folklore and school songs.

The steady stream of people passing our tram had not stopped. It was the same picture all the time—misery and utter hopelessness. Some looked up in sheer amazement as they heard our singing: others couldn't help smiling for a moment and we smiled back, yet every now and then a little one broke down and wept again. Thus smiles and tears, songs and chatter intermingled. Meanwhile, the little boy had joined us, and I held his hand whenever I could.

The lorries, revving their engines, began their deportation.

"All set?" A soldier asked. "Yes, all set!" I replied. He jumped on the platform and gave a sign to the driver. Shaking and shuddering, the tram began to move slowly. Not being used to such a long train of wagons filled to capacity, the driver had to cope with problems of control and speed.

Rolling along, my mind was with the present only. The fact of being part of this very large consignment destined to an uncertain-certainty, gave me strength and courage to bear up to the very end. The trip was slow and uneventful. Everywhere was the shuffle of people with small baggage and rucksacks. Everywhere there were lorries. Before and behind us were wagons and wagons of trams.

My children were silent now. They listened to the voices from outside. Harry sat beside me, still unnaturally quiet. By now we had left the more familiar streets and were heading towards the station. We could see the platform from our tram. How was it possible? It was already jammed with people and baggage. Where had they come from? The raid must have started very early indeed: or had they been sent from The Theatre?

We stopped, and slowly filed out, assisted by our soldier escorts. We all stood silently awaiting the next order. Meanwhile, the children left me one by one to rejoin their parents. Harry and I stayed together. His parents had evidently been arrested some days before while he had been out playing, and he just could not tell anyone where his brothers had got to; they had lost each other that morning during the arrest. Poor Harry; he was too frightened to be worried.

Soon we became part of a massive, seemingly endless, stream of people, all pushing their way through the vestibule doors of the station. This unforgettable sight impressed itself deeply into my being. Men, women, children, babies, prams, luggage, headscarves, bowler hats, caps, tears, unnatural grins, eyes filled with fear, stony expressions; and everywhere the glaring bright yellow star. How strange and extraordinary a situation to be in! How could thousands of people of all walks of life, age and sex, be subjected to such a dehumanising experience: and accept it so meekly without resistance.

The stairway was very wide and the upward surge of people tightly packed it. I could see it all from the roadway. Soon my turn would come. I looked at the faces around me, mostly stony and unseeing now. Only the children's faces hurt me. I noticed one such face inside a fully packed pram. There it was, as red as a beetroot, and bathed in perspiration. A tiny round face, perhaps six months old, amidst sacks and bundles of all descriptions. The mother pushed the pram, while father walked alongside holding the hand of another child and carrying a toddler. Being in the same part of the queue, I kept close to that pram. After all, I was alone, and I could help them up the stairway if need be.

"Harry, don't get lost," I urged him. "Keep close to me!"

We reached the stairs. Making my way to the front of the pram I gripped the bodywork and walked backwards up the stairs. One felt drawn to the mother; she was a woman who had to accept the deprivation and extermination of her little ones without a sound of protest. These were parents who had left their all: everything they had worked and aimed for. All their hopes and plans were in ruins.

The little one holding the father's hand was almost crushed amongst all those silent adults, and whined to go home. Wet, but tearless eyes gazed in bewilderment towards the daylight of the platform. Although the father held her hand, he too looked beaten and finished.

During this short climb we seemed to realise we were meant to stay together, yet none of us knew just how this was to be managed. Harry also held on to the handle of the pram and made himself one of us.

The platform. Could it be compared with a holiday peak travel period? No, it could not compare with any sight I had ever encountered before or since. It was jammed to capacity, and everybody was standing around looking hopeless and helpless. The few platform seats, more than adequate under normal conditions, were invisible. Everywhere one saw the green uniforms of our oppressors. Their wild gestures made up for the inability to speak our language. They were seen, and heard, and one obeyed. Now and then someone tried to argue or reason against transportation. Would they listen? They cared for no one. We were all alike, prisoners in order to be destroyed.

After only a short wait a great stir moved the crowd. Their voices swelled to a continual hum. This soon was drowned by the rattle of many wagon wheels on the rails beside our platform. It was a long goods train; I could not even see the last wagon. The full length of the platform was now filled by the gaping bleakness of each wagon, sliding doors wide open to receive their load. The iron bars hung from their joints, soon to be used to secure us inside.

Unconsciously we endeavoured to stay in the open a little longer. We fussed about the pram; we attended to the now bitterly crying baby; we fastened the shoes of the little one. We busied ourselves with ourselves as the voices of the soldiers thundered through the crowd 'Einsteigen, schnell-einsteigen'. Without the slightest resistance the crowd moved forward. It seemed as if these goods wagons swallowed human after human into their gaping space. Almost fifty in one wagon is a good guess. Then the heavy sliding doors rolled shut and the iron bars were clicked into position. Fresh air to meet the needs of all these people filtered through the five inch gap at the centre of each door. Although many hundreds had left the platform, it still seemed to be as crowded as ever.

Still the cattle trucks remained on the platform. Why, oh why didn't they leave? The wailing began and one could hear the cries of fear from those locked inside. Children's voices, shouts of men, intermingled with requests for water, could be heard clearly by us on the platform. The degradation had begun. No sanitary arrangements, no care for the elderly or, for that matter, for anyone. No seating accommodation, sardines packed in a tin. So my people faced their journey.

An intense sadness, loneliness and depression mastered my already bewildered mind. Thank God it was only momentary. Events occurred in an ever-changing pattern that one had to keep alert or go under. Those who did go under became a problem to themselves and affected those around them by the melancholy or hysteria which had overtaken them.

Louder orders echoed along the platform, then the wagons rattled away. Sobbing and crying were everywhere as people saw their loved ones disappear, for many had been separated by the disorderly pushing into the wagons.

More and more people came up the broad stairway to the long platform of the Amstelstation. There always seemed to be room for a few hundred more. Hearing the clatter and chatter below I realised that thousands were still thronging the entrances of the station, and even the streets. From where we stood we could see the approach roads, and still more trams and lorries were arriving with their load of desperate people.

The little family which Harry and I had joined barely forty-five minutes ago, handed me a sandwich and a drink of warm coffee from their flask. Harry did not want anything. He seemed too frightened and shocked to have the will to live. He just stared and stared and stared.

Another wild movement throughout the crowd. Another goods train had arrived. All the wagons had their sliding doors wide open. My eye fastened itself once more on the iron bars which soon would secure us. They chilled my blood! The pushing and shoving began once more. 'Einsteigen, alle einsteigen.' The orders echoed again through the loudspeakers along the platform. We just stepped into the nearest wagon. People groped for their loved ones; they wanted to stay together as long as possible. Wives and husbands literally would not let go of one another. Mothers and children had their faces screwed into fearful agonising expressions. Did not we all hope for a miracle? Childish hopes, not to be fulfilled.

Oh my God, why hast Thou forsaken us? Hast Thou forsaken us? God Almighty, do deliver us! Silence; no reply. Nothing happened. Well then, Thou Almighty God, be with us. Emmanuel!

Be with us and give us the needed strength, moment by moment.

It was our turn! Harry jumped in ahead of us. We lifted the little ones in and he held their hands. The father followed, then the mother, and we both lifted the pram into the cattle truck. Oh dear, it was packed inside. We all stood, as it were, to attention. Around us the sobbing, and calm encouraging words of husbands. Our little ones started their crying once more. The baby seemed to be heart-broken and sensed fear. Wildly she looked around her, twisting her chubby little head back and forth with edgy jerks. I would take care of her, but could see little of her in the fully-loaded pram. While I loosened her woolly knitted bonnet, the sliding doors rammed shut plunging us all into momentary darkness, then slowly the five inches of daylight penetrated through the gloom. I thought of the iron bar in position on the outside.

The poor baby was soaking with perspiration and pimply-red where her bonnet had been. Heat spots? Flea bites? A sudden strange impulse flooded my whole being. Even recalling these moments I cannot explain how events could take such a split-second turning point. Spots! Cupping my hands I shouted at the top of my voice through the few inches available to me, "Attention, attention. Infectious disease. Open the doors at once. Danger! Highly infectious family in this wagon. Hurry! Hurry!"

The voices of the crowd outside swelled as a result and shouts of surprise or fear reached us. We all quietened down. I was fully relaxed now and ready for action. By the commotion outside I knew that officials were on their way. Moments later fresh air and light were with us once more.

As the officials faced me I ordered them to "stand aside please, gangway, please, Scarlet Fever!" Winking to the baffled parents, I lifted the pram and stepped backward on to the platform. The family followed and Harry too.

"Over to the waiting room!" a high official pointed to a glass sectional cubicle at the far end of the platform. "Nurse, you are in charge and responsible for that family."

Suddenly we were alone, for the first time that day. We looked at one another and smiled wryly. We could not speak for a long time. I placed the bonnet back on the baby's head in order to retain 'the spots'.

Soon a doctor arrived—one of us.

Showing him my patient I said questioningly, seeking for confirmation, "Scarlet Fever?" He asked if I was alone, and if I was willing to work with him. My desire had at last been granted. I was a nurse in action.

"Have you any instruments?" he asked. Proudly I opened my little black case where my treasures were hidden—my own private medical case and first-aid box. He smiled. "Right Nurse, busy yourself. Take the baby's temperature. I'll be back shortly."

For the first time I lifted the little girl from her mountain of clothes, luggage and packages. She felt hot and damp. I cuddled her against me, talking and laughing: she soon smiled as well. So did her father and mother, but not my poor wee Harry. We felt like goldfish in a bowl: we were stared at from all sides. Too many smiles would awaken jealousy and even betrayal. We had to pretend worry and fear.

So far the parents had not spoken a single word but looked on, dumbfounded, as I began 'working' with our little saviour and her 'Scarlet Fever'. Laying her gently on the bench I removed her wet leggings and nappy, while her mother handed me some dry clothes. I had to remember the part I was to play—'nurse in action' until further notice. Where to begin? Just there in that room.

As I took the baby's temperature, in the proper way of course, holding her legs with my left hand and the thermometer in the rectum with my right hand, the doctor returned and showed his approval with a smile. "How is she?" he asked. Without checking the mercury I replied, "101.2, poor little lamb". He looked on for a moment as I quickly dressed her before handing the baby back to the parents.

He then called me to the other part of the waiting room to 'discuss my duties' for the day. "Bring into this place anyone you can find, anyone who, in your opinion, is 'ill'. Be careful and judge aright. See what you can do, Nurse. I'll look along every now and then. Perhaps we can get some folk out of this, but be careful."

We were to work hand in hand that day. Having left the waiting-room we went in different directions, looking to see what our hands could do; to help just where we were needed. Incredible and unforgettable was our patrolling along that platform. One felt so helpless to answer the many cries such as, "Nurse, my mother, please look at her. Oh, what can we do?"

Or, an elderly man would faint and lie ashen pale among the crowd. I would revive him just to be 'fit' once more for . . . deportation. There were the many unhappy and fearful children who needed smiles, confidence and comfort to be brave . . . for deportation. There were the hysterical ones who could no longer control themselves after the long years of tension and depression. I took them to the doctor, and he gave them an injection to calm them . . . for deportation.

Although I was called here, there and everywhere, my eyes scanned the crowds for the quiet ones, those who had given-in to fate and yet were in real need of help and protection. Even in this category there were far too many to attend to. One had to be cautious or the enemy would get suspicious.

Making my way along the stairway I saw another family huddled together for comfort. "Hullo," I addressed a little one, who immediately turned away from yet another uniform. Uniforms must have frightened her before. Her parents were obviously beaten as well. What could possibly count for an excuse to keep this family out of the train? No apparent reason. Patting the head of the little girl, and pushing the damp hair off her hot forehead, I noticed pimples once more, watery eyes and a running red nose. Could this be the real thing? Either chickenpox or measles? Hurrah, this seemed a worth-while catch.

"Come along this way; you will be more comfortable where I take you." Following me without a word, we found our way through the dense crowd until we reached the waiting-room.

Dr. van Ebo was there attending to other true casualties.

As we walked in, I announced 'another infection'. "Over there, Nurse." He pointed to the still unoccupied part of the waiting-room. As soon as he was free he came over to inspect my latest patient. "Yes, Nurse, that's measles all right. Well done."

Delighted with the compliment I attempted to go fishing once more, but a sudden stir made me stop. Cries of despair and fear arose from the crowd, as if in reply to the cries from within the cattle trucks as the long trail of wagons left the station.

O my God, how dreadful. How many thousands will have left from here before nightfall?

While the crying was still at its height and the last wagon still within sight, I left the waiting-room with a decisive purpose: to rescue at all costs whoever seemed a deserving case. Humanly, who could decide? We had to be quick and move fast: this would be our last chance. The next lot of wagons would surely clear the platform.

I searched among the crowds. There was a woman heavy with child. "What are *you* doing here?" I shouted. "you are almost due. You should have proper care! Come this way, please."

She replied calmly and with a smile, "Oh no, I'm only seven months."

"No, you're nine," I objected.

"What about my brother?" Pathetically she pointed to the man at her side.

"Your husband," I emphasised. "He must come with you at a time like this. Come quickly."

Once more we wound our way through the dense crowd, as more and more arrests climbed those broad stairways. It seemed as if no one had left; the platform filled up continually.

Dr. van Ebo was busy when I arrived. I explained about my latest catch, and we then went into fresh consultation.

He explained his plans simply, step by step. We hoped and prayed in our hearts that all would go well and safety would be the portion of those we had rescued, and for ourselves.

"I've asked for an ambulance to transfer the people to our hospital. We must go with them, then return and collect the rest. They won't allow us more than one ambulance. Until it arrives we must make ourselves useful, but we can't rescue any more or suspicion will be aroused.

"Try to leave the station. Be resolute, be quick, be determined. Look busy at all times. Keep your aim in mind, as you will have to deal with many roadblocks and soldiers. Your job is to mislead.

"Make for the hospital, get strong disinfectant, and return to the station. Explain that you want this place clean and safe for normal service tomorrow. That is to be your explanation during your journey. Will you try?

"Now, good-luck. We'll meet again, I hope!"

As he turned to his work and I to mine, I wondered why he chose me to pass into freedom. Did he want me to stay out, or did he want a peg on which to hang genuine excuses to questioning officials?

Running downstairs, two at a time, I was confronted by my first 'roadblock'. "Halt!" he shouted.

Speaking in German I told him I was very sorry but I couldn't wait as I had important business to attend to. "Don't you realise," I explained "that up on that platform we have various infectious diseases and not a drop of disinfectant. A shocking situation." I shocked him further by requesting transport for myself to the hospital and back. He was furious and told me to get out of his way, which I gladly did.

One barrier was passed.

Twice more I had to face such obstacles before I reached the street. Those five minutes became an unforgettable nightmare, yet once I marched along the deserted streets I felt strangely out of place. I felt I should be up on that platform; I ought to be under arrest. I felt I was sticking out, like a sore thumb.

On and on I walked, with my yellow star on view to soldiers everywhere. None approached me except at two large crossroads. Here my path was blocked, with rifles pointing at me as though I were a criminal. Again I told them, almost breathless, that I had no time to spare, that I was on a special mission, and that they should not keep me back. Wonder of wonders, they, too, believed me and sent me on my way without a word of comment.

I reached the hospital at last. No one could be bothered to listen to my story. It sounded too fantastic. Apart from that, everyone was too busy: there was so much consternation and chaos. Most of the people talked among themselves, and discussing the arrest of loved ones. Eventually guided by a hall porter I got hold of a can of disinfectant and left as unnoticed as I had come. Once outside I had to adopt an official air again. No one tried to stop me going back to the station. Oh, how easy it would have been to escape, but where to? It wouldn't have been for long. The game had to be finished somehow. It might just as well be today.

After some hours it was ' home sweet home', but how dreadfully empty was our platform. Trains had come and gone, clearing the station of all the human misery of the early afternoon. My heart beat faster, and anxiety overcame me. What about Dr. van Ebo. How silly I looked on that empty platform with that large bottle of Lysol.

Almost mechanically, I walked the length of the platform towards our waiting-room. Thank God I saw figures. Yet, not all. Tired and worn out, Dr. van Ebo came out to me. Quickly he explained how matters stood.

"One ambulance has left. We must wait for its return, then busy ourselves in helping these people on stretchers and chairs down in the lift and into the ambulance. We must stay with them, Nurse, very close, or we'll have had it after all. Understand what I mean?" I understood indeed. We were aiming for 'united freedom'.

Meanwhile, I clung to my large bottle, not knowing what to do with it. There were no basins, no mops or cloths of any kind. But I held on to it, our mascot and means of salvation on that terrible day.

Thank goodness we did not have to wait too long for the ambulance. The men came towards us from the station lift carrying their stretchers. They viewed the situation in the waiting-room and had some quiet words with each other. Yes, they would disregard regulations and red tape. We all would have to go in that ambulance. It was too dangerous to leave anyone behind for they would surely be transferred to The Theatre to await the next deportation to the camps.

Leaving the large bottle of Lysol as a monument, we all descended in that lift, making our way to the ambulance watched by half-a-dozen soldiers who didn't speak one word.

Gratefully, we looked at one another when the doors were shut and the ambulance moved off on the beginning of our journey away from yet another nightmare.

9

IN THE RECEPTION HALL OF THE HOSPITAL, FORMALITIES took over once more. The sick and not so sick were split up into respective units for care and treatment. Soon Dr. van Ebo and myself were alone once more. It was the end of our adventure together and, thank God, it had been successful for some.

"Have you somewhere to go, Nurse?" he asked with concern.

"Not really, Doctor. I would love to stay here and be a *real* nurse, but I know it is not possible. Everyone seems to want a job here because we all think it is the safest place. Don't worry, Doctor, I'll be all right. I'll go to my friend's room and spend the night there. No one will object, I am sure."

"Well," he replied, "you go to your friend's room and tell her about our expectant mother." We had previously discovered that she was my friend's sister-in-law. Quite incredible, among all those thousands!

After shaking hands, we said good-bye. We felt as if we had worked together for months; we seemed to know each other so well.

While making my way to Sister Henny's room, I became once more aware of my situation. It was just an existence, a struggle for survival; and why?

No one replied to my knock. Hesitantly, I opened the door and ventured in. A mighty weariness came over me, I only wanted to sleep. Noticing some rugs, I wrapped them round me and stretched out on the floor. Sleep came very soon. It must have been well after midnight when my friend appeared. It roused me for a while. Evidently she must have known of my presence there, as she showed no surprise.

After a short argument regarding sleeping arrangements, I won and was allowed to remain where I was. I would not hear of me taking her bed. She needed the rest after her long hours in theatre. We did not talk of what had happened. We felt alike; no words were needed; and soon we both were sound asleep.

Next morning I wakened as Sister Henny knelt beside me with a fresh roll and a hot mug of tea. I didn't know it could taste so good. How thankful I was for such nourishment.

Incredibly, it was ten o'clock already. It had been a refreshing sleep and the previous day seemed just like a dream.

"You've got to tidy yourself and put on one of my aprons, Hansie. Matron wants you in her office by half-past ten!"

Searching her face, I could not discover the reason. Surely she wouldn't send me away today? After several questions I realised that no satisfactory answer was forthcoming; I gave up!

Having washed my face, tidied my clothes, combed my hair, and put on one of my friend's aprons, I looked fairly respectable. She nodded, with a smile of approval.

"Well then, Hansie, let's go. I'll show you Matron's office." Sister Henny led the way. It only seemed a moment or two before I faced *the* door. "Good luck!" she said, then I was alone.

I knocked politely and a voice said "Come in". So I went in. There then was the Queen of Hearts. She didn't look like a Matron to me: just like an ordinary woman with a uniform on. But, oh, once she opened her mouth, she was no ordinary woman. After I had wished her a "good morning" she answered with a reprimand in a none too quiet voice. "Since when have my nurses begun wearing ear-rings?"

Quietly I enlightened her that I was not 'one of her nurses' but belonged to the Creche across from The Theatre.

Her voice softened as she replied, and I could detect a faint smile. "Dr. van Ebo has spoken to me about you and has told me what you did yesterday. From today onwards you *are* one of my nurses!"

How could one hug such a woman? I was almost beside myself with happiness. A real nurse in a real hospital! I must have beamed all over, for Matron all of a sudden gave a big broad smile. "Please go now with my Assistant who will show you your quarters and then direct you to your ward. Sister Henny will answer any of your queries after duty tonight. Good-day, nurse."

"Thank you, thank you very much, Matron. I will do my very best." That was all I had time to say before walking along the corridor once more, this time with the Assistant Matron. I still had to behave, but no one could stop my happiness and my beaming smile. I was a nurse at the great Jewish City Hospital.

The Assistant Matron left me at the end of a long dark corridor with many doors. At once I checked my number. It had to be remembered. "Please report to 'infectious diseases' after lunch. You'll find your way to the dining-room and to the ward. Just keep asking." She was gone. Here was *my* room! I had to let off steam. I jumped, danced and bounced on the bed, throwing pillows ceiling ward and cuddling them against me a moment later. I was so very, very happy and grateful. If only my father and mother could see me now.

Now, off to the dining-room. I would follow my nose: the aroma indicated that it couldn't be far away! I heard the clatter of dishes and soon I was following other nurses who all seemed to be going purposefully in the same direction. Having reached the dining-room I watched the others and did exactly what they did, taking part in the general routine as if I'd lived there for years. A full dinner free of charge! I ate every bite and was thankful.

On the way out I asked directions to 'infectious diseases', and soon found my ward. The smell of Lysol was prominent, and the nurses behind the glass-walled cubicles wore masks. There were many male nurses on the other side of the corridor for these were the male wards. I walked into the female section and came to a halt in front of a Sister who said that she was expecting me; she explained I had to wear a special overall every time I entered my ward. She handed me one to put on, and tied the bows at the back. Then we walked over to the centre table where she kindly explained my work. This afternoon I would mainly observe my fellow nurses and lend a hand wherever it was needed. She introduced me to a girl around my own age, then left me with a kindly nod. I was among my people, my sick people, and I would help them whenever and wherever I could. Nothing appeared frightening or strange, no smells could nauseate or repel. It all seemed right. I was in the place of my dreams, dreams which had become reality. I was on duty to serve!

That night when thinking over the events of these last few days, everything seemed rather baffling. So much had happened since Sunday morning, yet tonight I felt so clean, so happy, so grateful. A nurse!

Next morning I was in the ward early, ready for anything. I was told to help with bedmaking, tidying, dusting, serving mid-morning drinks, giving medicines; and then I was shown how to give injections. On my first morning! Yes! And many more important duties had to be attended to by responsible juniors, for trained staff was now so scarce. It was great to be 'at it' all the time. To comfort the sad, to play with a lonely child, to soothe itching spots, to tidy the cupboards, to serve meals, to feed the babies, to help Sister wherever possible.

The next few weeks passed like a flash. One was scarely aware of unrest and war outside these walls.

The most noticeable thing about each patient, however, was that they had all something in common—'a broken heart'. Even the nursing staff, affected by this same symptom, showed a greater understanding and compassion to those around them than in normal times. Having a common bond, sharing a common loss, gave us a common desire to help one another with comfort and courage.

During these next few weeks I learned a great deal. Actually, I was undertaking responsibilities far beyond the realm of a trained nurse, but one learned to accept them gratefully and fulfil one's task efficiently, the only aim being the welfare of patient and community. Although war, unrest, raids and distress were outwith these walls, it could not be like that for ever. Yet, who wanted to face reality? Nobody, until it could be avoided no longer.

On the 5th of July another rumour of arrests sounded among the staff. Could it be true? One's heart beat faster, but the work went on in its usual manner. These rumours were confirmed by a voice over the loudspeaker system. "Attention, attention. Any members of the staff of this hospital who have been engaged in work of any kind under this roof for three months or less, are asked to assemble in the gardens for an important announcement. Please come immediately and without delay in order to avoid the disruption of daily routine."

I left the ward, but walked along dozens of corridors to give me time to think. Would this battle never end? There was that loud-speaker again: "Will the junior staff assemble in the gardens for a special announcement. Please make your way to the gardens."

Orderlies in white coats hurried alongside nurses—obviously married couples and lovers who had sought shelter and work in the hospital. Their faces bore the familiar expression of fear.

Oh well, I would go down to see what the Board had to announce.

The gardens were crowded. Couples and friends hand in hand

awaiting the inevitable. We all looked to the group of men from the Board who stood beside several high-ranking Gestapo. Each of them held books, papers or lists in their hands. At last they were ready for action.

"Ladies and gentlemen, due to over staffing here in this hospital and shortage of staff in the work camps, we are duty bound to alter this unequal situation. We have, therefore, decided to move the newer members of the staff. This seems only fair. We shall, therefore, read out in alphabetical order the names of those we require today. If your name is called please go to your room at once and return with your rucksack to the front of the building, where transport is awaiting you. We ask for your co-operation to carry out this transfer in a quick and efficient manner." Very cleverly explained, and how politely put! Everyone knew what was really behind all that talk; compulsory arrest!

I didn't need to wait very long. The letter D was soon reached and Hans Dobschiner's name was called. Following the other 'chosen labourers' I made for my room. The rucksack, which most of my people owned, I had lost long ago; but my little black case would go with me as it had done before. I saw no one I knew. Where could Sister Henny be? Was everyone keeping out of the way to make the parting easier? I didn't know and I didn't care any more. I walked down the stone flight of stairs without looking to the right or left. I walked out through the heavy wooden doors which were now open wide, as if for ambulance traffic. Two steps on the pavement and I was ushered into a lorry.

Around me were only elderly people, many with bandages or plasters. These rogues! They had not only rounded up staff in the back gardens: but elderly patients had been arrested too, probably from dayrooms or convalescing wards. Perhaps they had been told that the fresh country air would be beneficial for them.

But these people *knew*, as did everyone else, yet no one dared object. I sat down on the bench and looked around in order to fix my eyes on someone for just a little smile. Yes, it was possible. Several smiled back at 'nurse'. Did they perhaps feel a sense of security because a nurse was in their midst? Although we all were birds within a cage, wings securely clipped, yet one could always hope for deliverance.

The flag of the lorry clicked into position, pegs into bolts, and off we went. What would our destination be today? Where would we be unloaded? I felt quite hungry and wondered about my fellow-travellers. Some licked their lips, others sweets—a most treasured possession indeed. 'Give us this day our daily bread' was an unspoken thought.

The lorry did not travel too fast. One could look at streets, houses, people, and photograph the dear familiar city scenes on one's memory. After leaving the familiar streets, and the shopping centre, the journey became bumpy and the lorry jolted along faster over uneven cobbled roads. To my great surprise, we made for the dock area and its railway line which I had visited so frequently in the early years of the war, when my relations on their return from Cuba, lived as refugees in that large Sailors' Hostel.

As soon as we left the lorries we were directed to our part of the train. This time it consisted of carriages for human cargo, eight to one compartment. No crushing or discomfort. Recognising no one, I went where I was told to go. Only the elderly were with me. Not knowing just what to do, I smiled again. It wasn't long before we were conversing freely feeling as if we belonged to one another. It was a pleasant sensation.

Now and again someone would go to the window, and keep us informed of what was happening. A happy atmosphere developed; it could have been an outing of the Senior Citizens' Club! An elderly gentleman informed us that a soup trolley was on its way. The thought of hot soup made everyone's mouth water. How wonderful! It was not long till we received our share and we soon emptied the mugs to the last drop before wrapping them once more securely among our luggage. When would they be used again?

An elderly lady enquired in rather a loud voice in which ward had I been on duty. When I told her, she jumped in horror, pitifully pleading with me to leave them rather than 'pass anything on'. Her excitement, even hysteria, was the only infectious disease present, all my elderly companions became very frightened.

"Please, nurse, be understanding. It's not that we have anything against you personally; it is just that we could not face an infectious illness as we are so weak already. Please, nurse, leave our compartment. Please leave us."

A sure contradiction of all circumstances! I wasn't allowed out of that train, yet they wanted me to leave. We all had an idea of our immediate future, yet they worried about a nurse from the isolation unit being in their midst. It did not make sense!

They kept on pleading: "Please go; please leave us." Was this the Almighty's constraining command? Ought I to go? Out there, to face assault or even death for leaving the train? 'To be or not to be . . . that is the question'. "Yes, all right, I'll go," I told them.

Bidding them good luck and taking my case I opened the door and stepped on to the platform like a free woman. At once a soldier approached me, but I stepped towards him in a firm and determined manner as if *he* had been my aim from the very beginning. Ignoring the pointing rifle, I opened the conversation, smiling helplessly. "It's no use; they won't have me anywhere in the train. They are frightened you see, because I worked in the isolation unit with the infectious diseases. What on earth can we do? I think I'd better go back to the hospital. The trouble is it's so far away. Have you any transport going in that direction? I'd be most grateful for your help."

Rattling all this off in one breath with a flat Berlin accent must have taken him completely by surprise. He lowered his gun and turned to a passing soldier. "Are you going back to the city? Drop this nurse at the hospital, will you? Thanks."

Turning to me his only command was: "Follow that soldier, nurse." Trying not to show too much delight or surprise I stepped in a matter-of-fact way towards his friend, bidding my liberator a 'comradely' good-bye.

This time my journey was most remarkable, travelling solo with a soldier in an army truck to . . . freedom. Naturally, the only exchange of words was a short comment on the weather, a most useful subject when at a complete loss for words, yet feeling the certainty that one *must* speak.

He dropped me at the front entrance. I shudder to think what fear and consternation the sight of that lorry must have created in the imagination of those who noticed our arrival and heard the screech of the brakes. What rumours must have passed from mouth to mouth for the second time that day. Yet, only *I* stepped out!

Thanking my driver escort, I walked towards the door which at last was shut. All morning it had been wide open while people were carried out or speeded on their way to the unknown.

This time I only I, returned, and no one seemed surprised to see me or made any move to welcome me back. One was almost shy to be free or still alive, for it was always one more person to account for or get rid of. The enemy demanded a certain number of people; they had to be supplied. If they insisted that the staff should not be larger than a specified number, then this too had to be obeyed explicitly. Therefore, today I was the odd one out, an embarrassment to my hospital.

'Sorry, but I'd love to live a little longer," I thought; 'just a little while.' Self preservation, mixed with indifference, was a dangerous phenomena to be guarded against. At times one reached the low level of pure, aimless existence. Thank God, His invisible purposes and loving presence could break that deadening state of mind.

It seemed only proper to report to Matron first. This I did. Calmly she addressed me with the words, "Well, nurse, so you are back. Go to the kitchen and get something to eat and then go back to your ward."

"Thank you, Matron." No questions were asked; no feelings shown. I became part of the machinery once more.

Amid the hustle and bustle of the main kitchen's activity I enjoyed a good and peaceful meal. No one to talk to me; no one to question me. To eat and think all by myself. It was as invigorating as that last meal of rolls with salami which I had enjoyed in the little butcher's shop before I reported to the Board of Guardians.

My room had not been re-occupied, I therefore took possession of it as though nothing had happened. Perhaps I stayed longer than I should have, but one simply had to adjust again. Circumstances and events so piled on top of one another that it was essential that the brain and general system should have some brief moments of repose.

A little wash, a clean apron, and I reported for duty as if nothing special had happened that day.

The next few weeks were uneventful. No major raids, only sad little incidents but of great importance for those involved. Unconsciously, one settled to the 'safe' routine of hospital life, almost deleting from one's mind the thought of any possible upheaval.

One would not dream of leaving the grounds when off duty. One would not dream either of ever wearing anything else but uniform. The hospital and its uniform were still the only visible protection from the enemy.

Our city streets were the hunting ground for any soldier who wanted a game—the game of terrifying anyone who wore the compulsory bright yellow star of David. It would be so easy to pick on you, to find a reason for arrest. Being outlawed, you existed as a target for the enemy of our nation and people.

No wonder I felt stricken and almost at my wit's end when Matron called me to her office one morning and put me on district duty. She emphasised the great need for more staff for his type of work. They *did* want me out of hospital after all! They wanted perfect security for their older staff. Who could blame them? The hospital had a great percentage of sham sickness, made up of the people who had gone there to escape arrest at home or at work. Consequently, the really sick could not get the beds or care they needed, hence the team of district nurses required for this job.

Oh yes, Matron did explain it so well. It sounded perfectly logical, but I had felt so happy and secure inside. . . .

It was not long, however, before the vision of the ill folk at home gripped my imagination. They were really ill and needed nursing care twenty-four hours a day. They were in pain and in fear, and lonely too. Yes, I would go. Of course I would go.

Matron explained the condition of the female patient she had designated to my care. 'A young woman, acute pneumonia, needing careful attention and injections.' She was my responsibility. I in turn, would be responsible to her home physician.

Fear and disappointment left me altogether once I knew myself entrusted with that young life. I went back to my room, packed a few belongings, and reported to the district superintendent for detailed instructions. I was proud of my outdoor uniform, and the waist-length black veil to which I now had been promoted. The bright yellow star shone brighter still from the background of my dark blue garb; but I learned to walk tall! Twice a day I had to brave the danger of the streets to go on duty and return nightly to my hospital room. Twice a day!

Eagerly I made for the address given to me. They were a nice young couple. I would relieve the worry, pain, and the strain of nursing which up till now had rested on the husband. Mr. Sim showed me the house and my room, and before leaving for work we had a luncheon snack together over which we got better acquainted. I then attended to my duties. It was easy to roll up my sleeves and get the house in order; to do many a chore which, up till now, had to be left undone. It wasn't long before my patient and I became quite close and true friends.

I looked forward to meeting her each morning and she made steady progress. This new routine soon became part of my life. I enjoyed it. Their home was looked upon as my home, and they did all in their power to make me happy.

No one mentioned days off. One was not concerned with regular hours. One was on duty, and glad to be kept occupied There was this honest give-and-take, experienced only in times of stress. It made life worth living, even under present conditions.

Summer 1943: raids and rumours of raids, day and night. Always bad news reached our ears; never a let-up. The enemy steadily continued their programme of annihilation. Our numbers decreased hour by hour. Whenever Mr. Sim returned from work, he told us of raids and arrests. It became our main topic of conversation. Mrs. Sim improved steadily, and I was truly sorry that our time together would soon draw to a close.

We had been together for nearly one month, when Mr. Sim returned from work long before the usual time. This meant trouble. Ashen faced and breathless, he burst into the flat. "They are doing the N.I.Z., your hospital. It's dreadful. All those sick folk and the whole staff. It is said they won't leave anyone behind today. Nurse, don't leave this house in uniform. Don't leave at all. You must stay with us. They would arrest you at once. The population is filled with rage. Rumours of a general strike are on everybody's lips."

I had heard enough. Excusing myself I went to the bathroom, the only place I could have true privacy and silent meditation. So, this seemed to be the end. Now my hospital with all its dear people was the target of their wicked planning. I could see them in my mind's eye. All those familiar faces; the terror that must undoubtedly be theirs at this very moment: the elderly, baffled and bewildered; the children, crying and calling for their mothers; others fighting and kicking to be left alone. I'd seen it so often. Methodically, cold-bloodedly, the wards would be emptied. The staff would be compelled to help in this hellish scheme. Then they, too, would find themselves in the army lorries.

Another chapter had just ended in my struggle for survival. Was it worthwhile? The possibilities of escaping ultimate arrest seemed so remote. The chances narrowed continually. Finally my turn would surely come.

However, there was nothing to be done at present. No plans could be made, no ventures undertaken. One had to remain hidden until the raids had died down, or I would be an escape suspect. As long as they didn't approach the houses at the same time we were safe. We were like mice caught in a trap.

When I returned to the dining-room the coffee was made, the atmosphere quiet and relaxed. This time they seemed entirely concerned for *me*. "Nurse, you can stay with us as long as you want. Look upon this place as your home. Come in and out as you like." And he added with a smile, "when it is safe to do so."

I loved that house more than any previous shelter which had come my way. The Sims were such a nice couple, so genuine. They acted so sensibly and with absolute honesty, having the safety of others at heart as much as their own.

From this date, the 13th day of August 1943, I was allowed to use their spare room and make it my home. I tried to show my appreciation by work well done, never calling time my own. I wanted to be of service whenever they needed me, and gladly went 'the second mile'.

Everything went well for some days, and, according to reports from outside, the atmosphere settled once more. Had people become accustomed already to the absence of the large hospital in the centre of the town? The loss would soon be felt. Where would the acutely ill be taken? Jewish people were not allowed in a non-Jewish building. The enemy's rules were cleverly framed. I shuddered while thinking of perforations, acute appendicitis, difficult childbirth. More and more filled my imagination and mingled with broken bones, fiery abscesses and burns. Probably it was better in the long run to die at home than a slow demoralising death out there in the unknown.

A week seemed long enough for self-imposed house arrest. Soon I began to venture out, cautiously at first, but aiming always a little farther from home. One learned to listen for rumours, to search for scraps of genuine news. One looked for authoritative guidance among the chaos of social community life. Amazingly, a clue of leadership was found, and I searched for definite information.

Unofficially, the Board searched for survivors from the 13th of

August raid in order to establish a skeleton staff for those who remained in the large, glass-fronted modern home for the aged in the centre of Amsterdam. They wanted to turn this into an emergency hospital for the time being having both services running side by side.

Could there be a vacancy for me? I would find out. It meant venturing into the lion's den, but then I had a perfectly legitimate excuse for being alive and free: I had been sent on district duty. It had to be now. I longed to go home with some definite news that day.

As I made my way through the glass panelled swing doors, the warmth I experienced radiated a faint sense of well being. It was not possible to see a superintendent, but someone in authority would speak to me 'presently'. 'Presently' materialised after a long, long time, and I was absolutely dumbfounded by the confrontation of an older Sister of the former N.I.Z. who startled me by reproachfully seeking an explanation for the delay in reporting for duty. Did I surprise her even more by reminding her that I was on district duty long before the 13th? I will never know. She ordered me firmly to report for duty as soon as my patient could dispense with my services.

When I mentioned the end of that week her quick reply was that she would like to see me on Friday night so that I could go on duty the next morning. No free time, the only privilege being . . . to be free from arrest.

The next chapter was about to begin, of this I was sure, but, instinctively, I knew it would not last for long. It simply could not. I was so young to share the privileges of the older staff. I had no security stamps on my identity card. In a nutshell, I had nothing: just a faint will to keep going.

The Sims received my news with mixed feelings. They had known that I would have to leave some time, but Friday . . . it had come so suddenly. We had grown close in these weeks, and the mutual friendship and companionship during the recent fearful days made us all sad when we thought of parting once more. Soon this family would join the ranks of the many thousands before them. I would never see them again.

It was about the end of August when I entered the elegant modern building of the J.I. In these days the great amount of glass and the height of the building was eye-catching. Somehow I was proud to be on the staff. 'I would do my best, as always, for the sake of my people, ignoring the hardness of certain superiors.' They too must have been living under constant strain and tension. It was difficult to be reasonable and fair when nerves were torn to shreds.

The junior staff did not enjoy the privacy of a single room. We all lived together in a large dormitory. Our bedside locker was the only privacy we had, but we were very happy and the atmosphere was most harmonious. We talked at night until sleep overcame us. When on night duty we were moved to a ward at the back of the building, on the top floor. There we enjoyed silence, and were free of any disturbance of the day. We didn't go to sleep immediately after coming off duty, but sitting on our beds, nibbling a shared delicacy, we discussed events of the previous night, or simply enjoyed getting to know each other.

A royal treat awaited me in this ward on the morning of my birthday. As I arrived, sleepy-eyed, the girls stood at attention beside their beds and greeted me by singing the lovely Dutch birthday songs. They are so melodious, so hearty, that the singing always touches the hearts of those who hear them, and I was no exception!

The greatest treat was yet in store. The chief cook's daughter, also a nurse, opened a large dish towel and handed us all a freshly made, thick, large pancake. Another nurse had a jam jar full of sugar, and we each received a sprinkling, to crown a treat.

I don't remember enjoying a birthday as much as that one. The celebration was so genuine, so unexpected, so memorable. Days like these meant a great deal amid the constant strain and stress, the fight for survival, and the alertness for spies or betrayal.

A few uneventful days lay ahead, yet towards the end of the week I viewed with suspicion my very colleagues. It requires some explanation for my readers to realise how such a situation could develop.

One of the safest ways to dodge arrest was to find some way to go 'underground'. Underground literally, or 'into hiding' in some way or another. Discussing this, or even contemplating it, needed the utmost secrecy with absolutely trustworthy companions. Finally, financial backing was a necessity, for no one could predict just how long the war would last and, therefore, how long financial backing would be needed. If however, such a plan was discovered by the enemy, immediate imprisonment in a labour camp was a certainty.

Could my reader, therefore, be surprised when I got into a state of terror one morning at the beginning of September when the night porter, just going off duty, called me over to the reception desk. "Dobschiner," he said, "would you like a chance of survival? I've got an address for you. Think about it quickly and see me tomorrow at this time."

He was gone, leaving me shaking like a leaf. Me, go underground? How could I? I had no funds, no financial backing, no connections. Why had he approached me? Just me? I had to keep this to myself. Absolute secrecy was a necessity.

Throughout that day I could not concentrate on the work I loved so much, my people, those who depended on me for care and attention. They and the staff seemed to notice that I was different, that something must have happened; yet I could not tell them.

By late afternoon my imagination had worked itself into a frenzy. I was frightened for the first time regarding the future. It seemed that a trap had been set, and there was no escape. Raids and arrests could be dodged, but when one was attacked along the 'silent road' of so-called security, well, where then was there a way out?

Once off duty I sat in the dormitory, staring into the unknown future, endeavouring to get my position and the facts quite clear in my own mind. Weighing the pros and cons of a chance for survival I realised that, humanly speaking, I had none. I had no one to turn to, no possessions, no money, no connections; a nobody with only the will to live and work for those who needed help.

The will to live? Did I *have* the will to live. Was it worth it? Those I wanted to help; those too, would soon be gone. After all, this and this only was Hitler's final goal—the annihilation of all Jews. Why then fight to live? It would only be for a little while.

My willpower was weakening and once it began to slip the 'couldn't-care-less' attitude was just around the corner. There was only one way open. It was just a chance, however. If I surrendered voluntarily and reported to the labour camp authorities, they might give me a position as nurse in the camp, and by working there I might gain survival. It was a risk, but also a chance I had to take. I couldn't continue on the basis of today's approach by the night porter. I was trapped both ways and could only free myself by deliberately reporting for voluntary arrest.

Yes, that was the answer. One could not live continuously as I had been doing during the past five months—arrest for deportation, escape, seeking work, food, shelter, and then arrest all over again. A continuous cycle of survival and doom. A life on a see-saw, up and down, life or death, changing from moment to moment. The decision had been reached. I would report at The Theatre in the Plantage Middelaan. When? I was not too sure. Some time that week. Probably quite suddenly, when I felt I could not go on any longer.

A fine young nurse sharing my dormitory probably having watched me for quite some time, sought my confidence. Repeatedly she insisted that I should tell her my troubles, but words could not be found for a long, long time. I was under high tension and entirely wrapped up in my own grief. I felt so alone, so lost, so bewildered, so doomed. Yet she talked, and talked, and talked, repeatedly tempting me to speak. Soon I could resist no longer. Her kindness and true sincerity melted my determination to remain silent. Sobbing brokenly I told her of my continual escape during all these months, the fierce reality of the ultimate future for us all, and now the new proposal of the night porter. Why had he chosen me? I had no financial means. I was nothing to him or anyone. I was so frightened. I could not fight for survival much longer. I was tired; oh so tired. I wanted to surrender! I would go to The Theatre tomorrow and then . . . then it would be all over, very soon. I would travel the road all my family had taken. Yes, I would surrender.

Silence reigned for sometime after my confession. Her longing to help was great, but what could she say. We both knew that I had spoken the truth.

Contemplatively, she endeavoured to reason with me: "But, Hansje, the way to The Theatre is a deliberate act of suicide. You know it, and you must fight it. Accept the night porter's offer. There is just a chance that some way out is awaiting you. Some people don't *need* to pay for their keep, but just *work* for their living. Don't dwell too much on how a life of hiding will work out for you. Just take a day at a time."

Wise words, Lena, truly wise words, but my will to fight was failing. I doubted my determination to keep on. The experience of freedom and then being caught all over again was proving too much.

This cat-and-mouse game had lasted too long. I was finished. I couldn't fight any more.

There and then I decided that the next day, the 6th of September, would be the day on which I would commit my 'deliberate act of suicide' as Lena had called it. Just before curfew. I would report at The Theatre and, with a little bit of luck, would surprise my father and be with him on his birthday, the 8th.

While on duty on that last day of freedom, my mind was not on my work, not with my patients. I experienced a strange sensation. I was on duty, yet I was not there. I was away, far away from Amsterdam, among the milling thousands in trains and camps. I was part of despair, part of lost humanity, part of damnation and annihilation, part of equipment for the enemy's game. The cast of their dice would place me forward, forward, forward. Then I would land on a square which would determine my return to . . . almost freedom, but not quite. Another square on the game board meant solitary confinement, until I could redeem myself by certain acts of favour towards my guards.

Oh God, enter this hell and deliver me. I don't want to breathe any more.

'I can't; I won't. Please receive me into Thy safety and peace. . . .'

Lena stood beside me, a syringe in her hand. "I said, for Mrs. Shand." How many times had she told me to give that injection? I hadn't heard her. She looked worriedly at me and replaced the syringe carefully in the kidney dish, resting the needle carefully on a pad of cotton wool.

I was crying inwardly, swallowing hard to avoid an outward display of grief. Lena, sensing that I couldn't keep up much longer, ordered me to leave the ward at once.

"Go to your dormitory, Hansje. Cry hard. Get it out of your system. It won't be long till dinner time, and I'll see you then."

I almost ran through the ward, and along the corridors to the dormitory. My bed was a haven of rest and safety. I threw myself on its cool sheets, pushed my face into the pillow and cried as though these were the last tears I would shed before leaving this world. I sobbed long and fiercely, till, gradually, I felt the releasing of tension. Yes, I would do it: tonight. Calmly I considered my course of action. I would pretend that all was normal, not to arouse suspicion. I would act in a gay and carefree manner for the rest of the day, avoiding my fellow nurses, especially Lena.

'Wash your face, Hansje; get ready for dinner.' The bell would go any moment. 'Get moving. It's a long way to the dining-hall!' The night porter came to my mind. He would be in bed now. There would be no questions asked as I passed the porter's office.

Another glance in the mirror at the end of the room and . . . on stage for the last act. Blithely I skipped along the corridor, down the stairs, and through the front vestibule. No, it could not be . . . the night porter on *day* duty. What could I do? Would he notice me? A big broad smile on his face compelled me to go towards him. Don't worry, I encouraged myself. Tonight I would be free! Free? Well, I meant finished. It would be all over pretty soon.

"Good-day, nurse! Well? Decided?" He waited pleasantly for my reply.

Sighing, I told him that it couldn't be done. I had no means of support, no places I knew, and no need for self-preservation as all my people were gone. "No, sir, no, please leave me alone." That was not the way out for me. He let me go, almost sadly, I thought. Why should a complete stranger worry about . . . about me? I could not understand it.

Dinner was good, but I had always enjoyed what we got to eat. The food was warm and tasty. I said grace and gave thanks sincerely for those meals, meaning every word. What a blessing to have this daily food. During dinner my thoughts were afar off once more. 'Where would I eat tomorrow? Would I eat at all? Was I prepared to give up this daily luxury?' I ate and ate as never before. Lena eyed me suspiciously. I was very excited but tried to hide it. Successfully?

Lena picked up her teacup and sat beside me for this leisurely part of the meal. I smiled brightly. She looked worried. She did not speak and neither did I. We sat together wrapped in our own thoughts. 'Did she surmise what I had decided? Was she keeping close to me for a purpose? Was I acting suspiciously after all? Did she want to stop me going to The Theatre? Did she feel responsible in some way because we were friends, and because she was a little older? I did not want to hurt her, but I had to leave her. I couldn't continue the game. I *could* not.

She pressed her hand on my arm, saying "Be good; see you

later!" I nodded. Yes she would, for a little while more. Poor Lena. I wanted to 'be good', but what was 'good'? Shrugging my shoulders I ceased to philosophise over what lay ahead.

Back on duty. There was a lot of work to be done. New admissions, emergency treatment, comforting of the distressed. I almost forgot my escape plans, my deliberate act of suicide. 'Silly Lena,' I thought, 'calling it that; but she was right, I suppose.' I only hoped I would have time to carry out my purpose. We were extremely busy. I just could not leave the skeleton staff to cope with the amount of work on hand. I would stay until 7.15 p.m. It would still leave me time to get to The Theatre before curfew.

The injections given, the inhalations attended to, the compresses changed, poultices in position, beds made and tidied over and over again: serving the evening tea, feeding the invalids, bedpanning the needy; oh dear, no break! The afternoon had been hectic. Would I ever get away? Now or never. Carefully, I placed the tray with glasses on the centre table, then without looking at either patient or nurse, I left the ward swiftly.

My heart was thumping as I ran up those stairs two at a time. In the dormitory I calmly collected my few private papers and possessions in my small black case. There was my nurse's coat, my veil, my gloves. Without any more thought I hurried down those familiar stairs, through the front vestibule, past the porter's office and outside.

Phew! I had managed it. The porter probably thought I was annoyed with him for trying to save me. He probably would not give it a second thought; or would he? I walked firmly and purposefully towards my goal, The Theatre! My mind was blank, with no thought of the possible consequences entering my head. I saw no one and nothing, I just walked on and on and on.

Twenty minutes must have passed as I turned the corner of the street which would bring me to the door of The Theatre. Suddenly a hand on my shoulder brought me back to reality. Lena! She couldn't speak. She was red, perspiring profusely, panting like a dog after a hunt. While fighting to get her breath and searching for words, she began to cry.

Now it was my turn to be concerned for her. She gave me no chance, but pulled me back round the corner. She was furious. She alone knew my plans, and discovering my absence, she must have run all the way after me. Did she blame herself? Had I upset her so much? I began to worry.

Her very first words I'll never forget. "You selfish, stupid, childish idiot! Get back at once and stop your nonsense!" Looking at her watch she almost pulled me along the street. We had to hurry to be in on time. The curfew was not far off. Oh dear, I had angered her. This outburst was so unlike her, so unladylike, so commanding. She had no right to stop me, yet I could not resist her plea to return.

I went back; ashamed, embarrassed, and as tame as a lamb.

On the stroke of eight we entered the J.I., breathless and exhausted.

"Go to your dormitory and get into bed," she ordered.

I obeyed.

10

THE EARLY MORNING BELL RANG THROUGH THE nurses' quarters. I had been awake for a while thinking over the happenings of the previous night; I realised I was fortunate to be there, to be lying in a cosy warm bed. Had it not been for Lena where would I be now. I would pull myself together and try to be brave once more. In the coming days I would work well and cause my friend no more distress. I was so ashamed. Breakfast tasted wonderful.

Quietly I carried out my morning routine. Everyone behaved in a normal way, and I realised that Lena had not spoken to anyone about last night's incident. This increased my determination to work well.

At lunch time I approached the hall porter myself. He smiled as usual.

"Well, Jan, I'd like to go, tomorrow, if you just tell me what to do. If this is to be the way for me I won't resist any longer."

It surprised me to hear that I had spoken at the eleventh hour. Tomorrow was the deadline. He had to find a girl before the next day as the cook's daughter, who should have gone, was still in bed with influenza. He had chosen me as the substitute to fill the gap. 'To be or not to be that is the question', and it *had* to be. I would go wherever I was led. I had taken the first step; the rest was veiled. Underground, abroad, or a labour camp? Trapped like a rabbit. However, I would at least be going on my own instead of in the packed deportation trains.

"Nurse, you are dreaming. You must listen very carefully in case my duty is changed, and I do not see you again. You will leave immediately after lunch tomorrow, telling no one, not even your best friend, that you won't be back. You will leave the J.I. as if you were going for a walk. Only take the bare essentials and your hand-bag. This is important. You will go to this street and number, which you must memorise before leaving this building. You will walk smartly all the way, do not linger or talk to anyone. On approaching the street corner get ready to sneeze. That is, with your right hand take out a large handkerchief from your right hand coat pocket, then using both hands, thus moving your handbag upwards and over your star, sneeze at the precise moment of turning the corner. From then on keep your star covered till you have reached the memorised number and are safely inside the house. That's all!"

He then told me the street and number. The last was easy to remember. I almost looked forward to the morrow's adventure. After apologising for my mistrust and thanking him sincerely, I made to leave for afternoon duty in Ward B.

Somehow, my work seemed easier, my energy doubled. I coped as in months gone by, I felt bright, almost frivolous. Once more Lena eyed me suspiciously. Was she worrying again? I hoped she was not. Surely the porter would explain to her tomorrow night.

Once in bed, mental repetition of my orders and mental preparation for this step kept me awake till well after midnight. All I could take was my little black case and what I could squeeze into it. I had to look like a nurse on duty, nothing more, nothing less. Oh, I was tired, and I soon fell asleep, my mind well tuned-in for tomorrow's game.

The 8th of September, 1943 was a dry day; at intervals the sun shone, there was a gentle breeze. A perfect day for the great event. Eagerly I attended to the morning chores. Purposefully I dressed some patients, bed-bathing the invalids and elderly. We served their dinner, then settled them for their afternoon nap. Incredible how quickly the hours had passed!

The nurses' dinner. I enjoyed this meal as much as ever. Nothing could spoil my appetite. Worry or strain simply increased the desire for a tender steak or a scrumptious sweet. When we left the dining-hall I made straight for the washroom, tidying myself as fast as I could. All was timed. No one could be kept waiting.

Pretending to ignore the porter, I lifted my coat from a hook in the vestibule and stooped to take my black case from a cupboard in his office. As I stooped, I heard him repeating the address once more. "Good luck, nurse," he wished me quickly. With a wry smile I turned from him. "Thank you, Jan," then I was through the swing door.

Walking steadily towards Amsterdam East, little did I know that this would be my last long walk; for that very afternoon I was to emerge from that house an entirely different person, a new personality.

This walk had a definite aim. It, therefore, was not boring or wearisome. On the contrary, I looked forward to events, whatever they might be. I felt somewhat diffident, however, ringing the door bell of the given address. What would I say? Whom would I face? As soon as the front door was shut behind me, I seemed to be 'under orders'. They needed no reply. "Come right upstairs. Please enter this room and sit down."

I sat for almost fifteen minutes in absolute silence. Is it possible to think in a situation like this? It was impossible for me. There were no noises of any kind from other parts of the flat. I sat and waited in this almost peaceful silence.

The front door slammed. Someone came upstairs, I was sure; but then . . . silence again. Listening attentively, I wondered about this latest arrival but even so I was startled at the sudden robust way in which the door behind me opened.

I rose to my feet which was just as well for I was faced by the tallest man I had ever seen. He smiled almost sheepishly as he tried to make me feel at home. "Sit down, please," he urged. He appeared kindly, but came straight to the point as if time was most precious.

"What is your name?" he enquired. When I told him, he changed it to Francisca. My new name was born!

"We'll make it Frans for short. Do you like that?" It was difficult to smile and say 'yes', but smile I did.

"Well, Frans, you will come with me. All right?" I was taken aback. Raising my eyebrows and frowning, I sought for words to express my doubts about such a life, my fears regarding money, and, generally, the unknown quantity of such a strange life.

He swept my doubts aside. 'Who was he anyhow?' I wondered. Perhaps a secret agent of the enemy? Security did not seem to worry him. Would he take me to H.Q. straight from here? I'd heard of such happenings. Medical guinea pigs or mistresses for the officers' mess! Oh my God, what had I done! Was I in the wrong hands after all?

Oh, yes, his eyes seemed honest enough, or what could be seen of them. They were tired and red-rimmed as if sleep had not been his companion for some time. Was I listening to all he said to me?

My thoughts were mingled with his speech. He was smaller now. His forearms resting on his knees, his hands folded as in prayer, he looked right into my eyes and talked in a most persuasive manner.

"You must come, Frans. You owe it to your family, your parents, all your people. We want to save as many people as we can to live a healthy normal life once the war is over. You can serve your people better if you stay in this country. We will look after you. Don't worry about money; that will come all right. There are so many interested in you and your people. They give donations voluntarily for your keep. You must come; they expect me to bring one girl today. It should have been the cook's daughter: all was fixed for her escape, but because of her illness you were chosen. We have not much time my dear: we get the 3 o'clock train from Central Station."

Still words would not come, and still he talked on and on and on, pulling his chair nearer and nearer.

I sat with head bent, staring into space, not noticing that little scissors were now in his hand.

He reached out to the coat I was wearing, cutting loose the star which labelled me a Jew, an outlaw, one of the condemned.

Was I paralysed? Why did I not stop him? How could he dare to do this? Without the star I could not show myself outside this house.

It was all over in seconds. He coughed, loudly and deliberately. The door of the room opened, and the lady who had shown me in, entered. Wonderingly I saw my star in her hand. Moments later I heard the flushing of her toilet. This was the end. I had no choice. Only one way lay open. I had to go with this stranger.

Mrs. X, whose name I have never learned, entered once more carrying a red flannel dress. Smilingly, she wondered if it would fit me.

The tall stranger left us.

She had taken over.

"I'll take care of your uniform. You will need to leave it here as you will have to go out of this house as unobtrusively as possible. Come, get changed and I will look for a coat." She found one which fitted me fairly well.

Daddy Long-Legs was called in once more. He seemed pleased with the quick and effective transformation.

Then came a short list of instructions.

"You will walk with me as if on a sight-seeing tour of Amsterdam. You speak German? All the better! Speak German only; it will make people turn from us in disgust. A perfect alibi! I will ask you about some buildings we pass. You will enlighten me as my guide, but in German only, please. We will go by tram to the station. Try to look as if you are used to it. Laugh and act normally. I am the stranger; you the German girl showing me around Amsterdam.

Was he torturing me? Or was I really on the way to freedom?

"Good-bye, my dear, and good luck." Did I detect tears in Mrs. X's eyes when we shook hands?

"Good-bye, and thank you very much." I had spoken at last.

The tall stranger now turned to me. "Well, Frans, here we go. Chin up and smile. This is an order!"

We hurried downstairs. Courteously he held the door open and shut it behind us. Quickly we made our way to the nearest tram stop.

No neat queues allowed passengers to file into the trams. When a vehicle arrived, everyone pushed and shoved until you felt like a sardine in a tin. It was even more oppressive today, as the memory of those other trams returned with this pressing crowd. Daddy Longlegs gave me a push and hoisted himself up behind me. He stood there on the platform, clinging to a pole like grim death. When our eyes met he smiled broadly, with sheer boyish fun. "Sie mussen festhalten oder sie fallen in's wasser!" I shouted to him (Hold on tight or you'll fall in the water (overboard)). He roared "Ja, ja, ja; ich werde aufpassen."

It worked. Disgusted looks all around met my eyes. As people went off, my companion moved inside and stayed there till we arrived at the Central Station. It was the quickest journey I had experienced for years.

"Once we are on the train I shall not speak any more, Frans. Don't worry about anything; just rest and relax. All will be well."

I just nodded. I hoped all would be well. If not? Well, it was a gamble. It just had to go well! The train was packed, the noise was terrible. There was adequate time to meditate and reflect, to contemplate and to wonder. Where was I going?

A slight pang of fear arose when the direction seemed unmistakably Westerborg, the central gathering camp, the last stop before final deportation abroad.

He couldn't do that to me! He was so genuine and so honest looking. He couldn't be one of the secret service. Glancing over at him I studied his expression, partly hidden at that moment by a German newspaper. His eyes met mine, and a reassuring nod accompanied by a warmhearted smile sparked across the compartment. I smiled back, then stared out at the landscape once more.

I wondered if we would get any food. It somehow was of minor importance. We were working to a schedule. A task had to be completed, food did not enter his scheme of things. Amazing how soon one forgets one's stomach when safety is at stake.

We had arrived at Westerborg. What now? I looked at my companion, but he ignored me completely. Impassively he stared through the window, as though far away in thought. Once or twice he sighed heavily, then I noticed a frowning forehead. Soon I would learn to understand him and hear of his escapades. At present he was a sheer mystery.

The train still rumbled along. There were frequent and lengthy halts at stations and country junctions. Twice a Wehrmacht train packed with singing soldiers passed us. Darkness fell. The compartment was only half full of sleepy passengers. I dozed once or twice very lightly. Apprehension had not yet left me, there was the continuing underlying watchfulness which was to become my companion and second nature throughout the years that lay ahead.

Everyone nursed their own thoughts. In silence and darkness we travelled along. Lights were forbidden, the blackout was strictly observed. The hours crept on, and with it our train.

It could have been around midnight when I was awakened by the train drawing sharply to a halt. With eyes accustomed to the dark I noted with amazement that we were the only two left in the compartment. No sound anywhere. Further along the train doors opened and slammed shut in the usual way, but my companion made no attempt to leave. Instead, he leaned forward and instructed me concerning the next step towards our goal.

"We will alight presently, but please observe absolute silence. We won't go near the platform. I'll help you down to the railway track. You must walk slowly and silently across the sleepers. Try to avoid the gravel; it's too noisy. I will imitate a bird's sharp night-whistle and you will notice a policeman. He is all right. Don't speak to him. We will follow him, and you will sit on the back of his bicycle once we reach the field road. I will follow at a safe distance. Is everything clear to you? Right! Come on then, Frans, our time has come."

He opened the door, then slowly and silently disappeared below. His hands reached up for me, but I handed him my black case. Having put it down he reached up again, and I accepted the help of his strong arms. Landing quietly on my toes as instructed, I looked around. It was so dark, not a star in the sky. The air was damp, I felt shivery from lack of sleep, excitement and an empty stomach.

Holding his hand, I stepped from sleeper to sleeper. The silence was intense. Long-legs smiled, put his fingers to his mouth and produced a beautiful imitation of a night bird's shriek. Silence! Then we heard a movement. It came from behind the bumpers. Suddenly from nowhere a very big broad-shouldered policeman stood right in front of us. His shiny buttons were the only light in the enveloping darkness. He lifted his hand, we stepped over the rails and followed him. In incredible silence we reached the field road behind the station. I noticed the bikes. It needed to be a strong one to carry this man and my own heavy weight! With a gallant gesture and smile he offered me the luggage rack, so I stepped on, holding gently to the saddle. But he bent down whispering into my ear, "Put your arms around me. It's safer! We have a long, long way to go."

It certainly was a long and bumpy track. For three quarters of an hour we rode along, silently, and at a regular speed. It was a blessing that these roads were flat; hills could have proved a nightmare. Long-legs followed at a distance with my case on his rack. The discomfort eased as I became accustomed to the bumps and bends. I was therefore almost sorry when he lowered his leg and our journey came to an end.

"Here we are," he whispered, pointing to the outline of a large square house standing somewhat off the road. Studying this new landmark in my life, I was so grateful that it had indeed become a sharp reality. I would be 'illegal and underground' from now until . . . the end! Who could think straight in times like these? These two men surely could. Listening to their conversation, there was not the slightest doubt that clarity and purpose governed their minds.

The policeman informed my friend about what was to happen on Thursday night. "It's no use meeting before midnight. I would suggest 12.45 a.m. There still won't be moonlight if the clouds remain heavy. The others will meet us at the back of the Town Hall. We have had an S.O.S. from Limburg. They need 200 ration books, and we must concentrate on identity cards this time as well as ink pads. We only have ten minutes at the very most, but it should be sufficient. The men know their jobs; we'll just be there to supervise and ensure safety. Well, Domie, see you on Thursday then. Get some rest. Goodnight, good night." He slapped my shoulder and I smiled back, thanking him for all his kindness.

One can learn a lot just by listening. They seemed to be involved in a plot of some kind, but definitely anti-German, that was certain. So, my friend's real name was Domie, short for something I supposed, or even a false name, like mine. Not having called him anything at all, I decided I would wait until I was quite sure how to address this extraordinary man.

"Don't dream now, Frans, you'll soon be in bed. Come on, we'll go in by the back door to your new home. I hope you like it. This is my house." I just smiled politely but tensely as we walked up the path to the house. There was not a sound to be heard. The windows were closed and shuttered; storm doors secured the front entrance. Suddenly we stood outside a small, low back door. Silence!

Daddy Long-legs tapped the window in a strange way . . . —, . . . —, . . . —. It must be a code. It resulted in a stirring behind the door. Bolts were pulled back and forwards, a key turned laboriously, twice, then two young men with grinning faces appeared with a "Hi-Domie". They greeted me with "Hello", which I returned. Securely the door was locked behind us. Then 'Domie', as everyone seemed to call him, led me through the dark stone-floored lobby towards the kitchen. Light came through the cracks, someone rushed to open it wide . . . incredible . . . subdued but delighted voices and laughter. "Oh, Domie, it's good to see you." "How are you?" "Hi, Domie." Everyone seemed to be giving him a delighted welcome. The kitchen was full of women. Joined by the two young men and Domie, we made quite a company.

My attention was drawn by a voice from behind all the others: "Hello, Nurse!" Was it possible? The slim young nurse everyone had given up: arrested, we had thought, during a shopping expedition.

So she was safe; as I would be from now on.

They thought me shy. I was only baffled. It meant I was safe now, underground.

Domie, still holding me by the arm, now pushed me forward. "This is Francisca, our new member."

"Welcome, Frans," they called in turn. I smiled a 'Thank you'.

"Here, have a nice cool drink of buttermilk. You'll be ready for that by now." One of the women handed me a large mug.

"Hey, we could do with some more as well," the boys chorused. "We'll all take some more and drink Frans's health!"

"Just one moment, boys, while I introduce Frans to Aunt Jo. She'll be in the study. No buttermilk for me. . . ."

"Oxo," they chorused before Domie could finish his sentence. They all burst into hilarious laughter.

With his boyish grin Domie led me through another door into the hall proper. It was cosy here, warm, dimmed lighting and well carpeted. There were lovely pictures on the walls, and I had a sense of security. He opened the door to the study. "Hello, my darling." Lovingly he embraced his wife. They exchanged questions regarding each other's welfare while I observed the pleasant design of the study. As their conversation grew louder I heard his wife's doubts about bringing 'another one'. Didn't he realise the danger, and that their safety diminished each time he brought 'another one'. "If you only were there, my dear," he replied persuasively, "you would understand why I do it. The situation is growing worse daily, and the cruelty grows with it. We must do what we can, my dear. You must be my partner here while I work over there. We must! It is our duty and privilege." She nodded, and he stroked her head. I was worried, shy and embarrassed.

Domie turned round sharply. "Let's toast our new arrival with buttermilk and Oxo." She chuckled while we walked back to the kitchen. There, Aunt Jo put her hand on my shoulder and with a bright smile, announced: "Well, folks, Frans our new arrival! We hope she'll be very happy with us."

The buttermilk was served and everybody was introduced to me.

There were two boys, nephews of the family, both called Dik. They were known as I and II. Both had been students at a Dutch university who, one morning, had found themselves in a severe predicament. The post brought them call-up papers to work for the enemy abroad. Work for them. Never! Leaving their studies to serve their country was one thing; but to work for the occupying forces—no! Immediately, they left their respective homes and went into hiding, leaving their parents truthfully unable to answer any questions regarding their whereabouts.

They had come to their uncle's residence hoping that no one would trace them so far from home. Dik I wanted to be a veterinary surgeon. He had brought many books with him to keep up with his studies. Dik II's dream was to be an architect, but I was never to see them study the subjects of their aspirations. Their voluntary duties in this unnatural life included many remote from surgery or architecture.

Then there was Lily, the little mouse, a professional photographer from Amsterdam. She was thin, pale and very serious. Her black hair was long and straight, and hung loose around her face. It looked as lustreless as her face. Somehow, I knew she resented newcomers who might put their carefully planned safety measures in jeopardy.

Ellie, the big mouse, seemed more easy-going. She shook hands pleasantly.

The conversation during the introductions made me realise that the people had already been in hiding in this house for more than a year. Incredible!

These, then, were the mice. They occupied part of the attic. Becoming accustomed to thinking of them in this way avoided any slip of the tongue to outsiders who were totally unaware of the secret life in this house.

Ruth, the nurse who had vanished, I had known by sight at the hospital in town. She had been engaged to be married, but now was voluntarily and completely separated from her fiancé.

Everyone had their own burdens, strains and tensions. Strange to say explosions seldom occurred, I was told.

There was, amazingly, much fun and laughter among this curious company. A sense of humour was essential and was happily present.

Domie looked tired and drawn, sitting there on the high stool sipping his Oxo. Both his hands cupped the tumbler; observant or witty remarks would be uttered after every sip or two.

Little mouse was the first to rise. "Excuse me, folks; I'll get on with the work." A smile passed over her expressionless face.

I was interested in that girl. How I would like to get to know her. 'There's time yet, Frans,' I said to myself, 'you've just arrived.'

She was gone. The others took the hint. They too moved off, leaving their tumblers behind.

When I made attempts to clear the remains of our feast, Domie's wife stopped me.

"They'll do till after. Come and we'll have a chat in the study. We'll be in the way while they are getting ready."

Domie followed.

The study was a pleasant room. It invited one to relax by its very furnishings and lighting. Domie did just that, while his wife introduced me to the rudiments of my new life.

"Call me Aunt Jo," she began. "You will soon get used to living with the others. They'll keep you right. Ask them anything you want to know when I am not around. There are a few points you should know tonight, however, before you go to bed. We have certain safety measures which will be shown to you tomorrow. One is of primary importance to all of us. Everybody must act instantly when the buzzer goes for emergency. When you hear it once, just once, don't move! Stay where you are! Be absolutely quiet and wait for a double buzz. That is our 'all clear'. When you hear the buzzer being pressed persistently, it means danger. Follow the others! We have frequent safety drills, and you will be introduced to them in the morning. No more to burden your tired self tonight. Come with me and I will show you where you'll sleep tonight. Tomorrow things will get organised."

I went over to Domie, who was partly dozing. "Goodnight, Domie, and thank you very much for everything; for everything!"

He sat up and carefully replied, "Frans, it is nice to have you with us. I'll see you later."

We climbed the stairs. There was a long corridor ahead of us with doors on either side and a full-size long window at the end. With the shutters tightly closed and the black blinds drawn, we could walk in the brightness of the light which filled this house apparently everywhere. Was it planned psychology to brighten our imprisoned lives?

"Come and we'll see Bas-Jan, my baby boy. He is just eighteen months old, but, oh so sturdy. He might be a farmer by the way he carries on in the garden each day. He won't waken. Come and see him."

He was lovely. A bundle of joy in this strange abnormal world. Would he ever talk about us once his vocabulary increased? His face turned sideways, thumb in his mouth; he seemed in a most uncomfortable position sleeping on his knees, bottom up. Aunt Jo assured me that he loved going over that way. She now lifted him gently, laying him on his side, and covering him with the three little blankets which had previously looked like a ragheap entwined with toys.

"This is our room when Uncle Bas is at home," she enlightened me. "On other occasions we switch around a little for a change, with the exception of the mice. They have their permanent abode upstairs. You'll see it all tomorrow."

She turned off the light and we left quietly, crossing the passage, making for the last door on the left. It led to a small room, the smallest room in the house, I believe. Ruth and I were to sleep there that night till we got organised.

"The toilet is right at the bottom of these stairs. Now get some rest, and I hope you will sleep well."

Alone at last! Looking around I got acquainted with the lay-out of my room. Yes, it was small all right, but I liked it straight away. The bed was broad and spacious. Just as well, as I had never before slept with anyone in a double bed. Tonight I felt like lying down anywhere. There was a narrow table standing awkwardly alongside the same wall with the chairs neatly tucked under it. The other wall was covered by shelves of books, and at the far end there were two doors. When I opened them to satisfy my curiosity I found a small, dark, square boxroom, our 'private bathroom' with a few pails, water jugs and china wash bowls—all articles carefully planned for two. Another smaller door, right opposite the double bed, I imagined, would lead to the boys' room. I curbed my curiosity.

So there I was sitting on a strange bed once more, in a strange house, among strangers, even goyim*, for the first time in so many years. The Third Reich would not allow us to mix with Gentiles but blow the Third Reich! From now on I would be illegal through and through.

I decided I had better prepare for bed as it was after 2 a.m. Quite unbelievable! The house was alive! People were moving about everywhere. The mice went back and forth, up and down, with pails, buckets, jugs and papers. Dik I and II were doing exactly the same. Ruth was on duty in the kitchen. She didn't join the activities of her colleagues. Or did she tactfully leave me to myself for a while?

Would I be safe to venture from the room? What would I say if I met anyone? Perhaps it would be better to wait until things had calmed down a little.

Oh, how tired I was. Yawn upon yawn escaped from me, and I was hungry too. Aunt Jo wanted the cups left till later. That surely meant they would eat once the work was done before retiring for the night. Yes, she had mentioned 'supper' and Domie had mentioned 'see you after'.

How would I prepare for bed? I had nothing, nothing at all. Should I tell Ruth or Aunt Jo? I wanted to brush my teeth, but I had no toilet preparations. Oh, I was so sticky. Now to venture out —where was that toilet? Down below, near the stairs, Aunt Jo had mentioned. Well, I must have a walk, just for some exercise. The carpets felt nice and soft; it was easy to walk quietly, yet I tiptoed gently along. Halfway down I met the big mouse. "Don't worry about the creaking staircase. You'll soon find out which steps to avoid," she laughed.

I could hear the cistern. Yes, that was the toilet. No bother finding it from our room. Over there was the kitchen. There was Domie's voice. I wanted to see him again. Without the slightest hesitation I made for the kitchen.

Yes, Ruth was preparing the food. The bread looked lovely, rather loose in texture and a bit crumbly. She cut loaf after loaf. There was butter and cheese and jam. There was also a row of tins, all shapes and sizes, and I watched her filling each to capacity. "This red one is yours, Frans; you can take it up with you later. This is our flask; we will share it for breakfast. You will get your own

* Gentiles.

122

some day this week." So Ruth was on breakfast duty, and attended to the supper as well.

The tumblers were washed now and surrounded two heaped plates of bread. A large pot of tea was brewing, and those still busy realised that respite was at hand.

Soon we were perched on stools or sitting on chairs. They bombarded Domie with questions regarding the situation in the cities, and for news of friends and relatives. The atmosphere was quiet and serious now, and the discussion concerned the safety of all involved. They urged Domie, persistently, to 'take care' and not to be too daring. He shook his head calmly, reassuring them, but mainly to avoid arguments about this delicate subject.

Aunt Jo joined the company, and I learned about the many varied projects in which these people seemed to be involved.

Little mouse was the first to rise once more. "Goodnight, folks. I am very tired. Goodnight, Frans. I'll see you in the morning. Come and see our place, will you? Goodnight all."

How kind! An extra word for me!

She picked up her tin and flask, and was soon followed by the others.

I helped Ruth to tidy up before we, too, disappeared from the scene.

Domie called me back. "Frans, may you be very happy here. Never feel lonely. We are your friends. Talk freely about anything that may worry you, and ask any questions when things seem strange to you. We are responsible for you and will do everything possible to see you through. You, in turn, will take a responsible part in the safety precautions which are of utmost importance to us all. All right?"

"I promise that, Domie." My answer conveyed utter sincerity.

"You may also call me Uncle Bas if you want. The boys do, and after all you are our youngest."

He knew how I felt and was trying to make me feel at home. Dear Uncle Bas! I left him with a firm handshake, tears in my eyes. I was so tired, so grateful, so speechless. . . . I wanted to go to bed, to close my eyes, to shut out everything I'd seen and heard, to be alone, to pretend to be sleeping and then, peradventure, fall asleep and spend some hours in the land where peace reigned—the land of silence and darkness, in God's loving arms.

Ruth was in our room when I arrived. "Here is a nightgown. I hope it fits you. Anyhow it will keep you warm. It's colder here. We are so far north."

North? I wondered. I would have loved to know where I was, but I knew, instinctively, that this was a question which must not be asked.

"This is your towel. Remember your colour and keep it near your facecloth and toothbrush. We use the same soap and toothpaste, and leave it behind when we move from room to room. Down there are our pails. We keep them covered and use them when we are not allowed downstairs; that is all day until the buzzer sounds for the all-clear at night. It is very important not to use these pots when the signal for 'silence' has gone. Absolute stillness is essential till Tantje gives us the 'all-clear'."

I just nodded. I couldn't take in much more. Who was Tantje anyhow? Who cared? A little cat-wash and I slipped into bed. Ruth watched me as I asked her which side was hers. She did not seem to mind so I chose the side next to the wall, wished her goodnight and closed my eyes.

Darkness, how good. Half past three. When would the day begin in this community? Oh to sleep, to sleep, to dream, to think, to be safe! Safe? Yes, safe! That had been the purpose of this race during the last twenty-four hours.

"Almighty Invisible God of the Universe; God of Abraham, Isaac and Jacob; protect Thy people and save Thine inheritance." After reciting my Hebrew prayers for the night, I gave way to the sleep which gradually overcame me.

11

WHEN I WAKENED THE SUN WAS STREAMING INTO OUR little room. Ruth was up, the shutters folded back allowing each ray of sunshine to penetrate. Sitting on a cushion on the floor, she leaned against the bookcase, cleaning her nails; a magazine on her knee. Her curly black hair, carefully combed, framed a fresh complexion. She wasn't aware I was awake; it gave me a chance for another respite. Closing my eyes once more I drifted into dreams and thoughts, contemplating this new existence.

How long would this war last? Would the Allied Forces win or would Germany conquer Europe and bury us alive? It couldn't be! It would be futile to hide, futile for the resistance to fight their illegal battles, futile to retain a will to live, futile, yes, everything would be futile. The Allied Forces *had* to advance or we would be trapped like . . . like real mice.

Aunt Jo entered, and I heard her whispering voice. "Is she still asleep?" "She was stirring," Ruth replied, "but she has slipped over again. Just let her sleep this morning."

"Cheerio then, but get her up well before dinner comes up, the boys will want to get in soon."

"Right, Aunt Jo, I'll make sure she's up."

That was that. I must try to keep up this pretence just a little longer. It was quiet and comfortable here and I felt so relaxed. Better not open my eyes again, it would be fatal. Time passed, how long I could not say, then Ruth moved nearer the bed. She sat down and I breathed as naturally as I could. Was she looking at me? Oh dear, I'd better stretch and groan a little. . . .

"Sh, sh, you're all right, Frans, wake up, sh, quietly though," she whispered. "You'll soon need to get up, the dinner will be here at any time, then the boys and the mice will want to join us."

I sat up straight!

"See this window; always crawl past it, never walk upright near any windows, especially when the sun shines."

I understood. Stepping from the bed I crawled along the floor to our washroom; Ruth was still beside me. "Take your hot water bottle; you must use the water in it to wash your face. There are only the two jugs, you see, and this little glass jug is for drinking only." Hesitantly, she added, "Look, Frans, you've got to use this pot during the day, then empty it into the pail. Rinse the pot with your washwater and put the lid on the pail, it gets emptied at night. Let me know if you *have* to go down stairs, I'll show you the drill."

That was that, I understood. I would learn. When I opened the doors of the hidden washroom once more, Ruth had made the bed. The table now stood in front of it with chairs at either end. There was a tablecloth, but a lonely blue and white piece of corded binding puzzled me, lying there all by itself. I wouldn't ask. Everything had a meaning, I would know in good time.

A quiet tap at the door. "All right, Frans? Shall I let them in?"

"Yes," I replied.

It was 12.30 p.m. The boys entered rubbing their hands. They chatted with Ruth. I had nothing to say. Then the mice tiptoed in, and joined in the chatter. I had nothing to say once more. I just watched and listened. Would they really accept me? I would do my best and adhere strictly to safety regulations. Lily, the little mouse, announced conscientiously, "There will be a safety drill later this afternoon, it will let you know the ropes, Frans." I nodded a "Thank you."

Three sharp buzzes. Frightened, I looked to Ruth for guidance. Dik II jumped to his feet and disappeared. No one seemed perturbed. Ellie sighed, "Ah, dinner!" Moments later Dik arrived back with a wooden two-tiered tray. He carried it in front of him, and it seemed heavy. What a gorgeous smell. There were serving dishes with vegetables and potatoes and a large plate with pieces of meat. There were knives, forks, spoons and corded pieces of string, all different colours.

We sat round the table. My place was on the bed beside Ruth. The plates were quietly handed round, cutlery picked up separately and laid in position, the serving dishes, serving spoons, salt and pepper placed on the table. The pudding and fruit was shifted to the top shelf of the tray. What now? We all sat ready. I just watched and waited. The boys folded their hands and bowed their heads, then all said "eet smakelijk" the Dutch for 'bon appétit', and Ellie began serving the meal. Quietly I recited the Hebrew thanksgiving for this superb food. Potatoes had already reached my plate, and now vegetables and a piece of meat. Well, this was it. Mother had said I should eat, keep myself healthy and not worry about Kosher* food anymore. Oh dear, how could I eat it? Dear Lord, I want to be faithful to the customs and traditions of my people. Must I eat this meat?

Lily wanted to know if I had no appetite. Of course, I had an appetite, but this meat. . . . "Don't you like meat?" she asked.

"Oh yes, I do," I assured her, "but not today if you don't mind."

"Sure we don't," they answered in chorus. Lily lifted the meat on to her plate and cut it in five little pieces. With surprise I noticed how eagerly the others swallowed their extra treat.

Now I, too, enjoyed my meal, a meal without any more snags. The gravy was delicious. I mixed it with my potatoes. I ate and listened to their newsy and strange conversation. It was so different from the normal chatter of daily life in the world of soldiers, arrests, raids and curfews.

They talked about weather forecasts; forces of wind which would allow them to grind wheat, mill their flour, bake their bread for several days ahead. Often it seemed no milling was possible. It was too noisy, too dangerous, since those who passed the house might hear. Then, as the bread was rationed, they needed to buy it from shops all over the district. No suspicion had to be aroused that this household needed more bread than its quota.

They talked about the British Overseas News Service. I marvelled! What did they know about those?

They talked about printing papers. Whose duty was it for this afternoon? They wanted to bring me 'up', I suppose, to the domain of our mice.

They talked about messages needed, lists to be made as Nopje was coming later tonight. We were interrupted, "hi, Tantje," they chorused. The cheeriest looking young girl I had seen for a long time, entered our room. Her smile spread right across her face, and she broke into hearty laughter at the welcome she received.

* Meat killed and cleaned according to Jewish ordinances, then pronounced: 'clean'.

They complimented her on the superb dinner adding praise for other small tasks she seemed to have performed on her day off. "Meet Frans, our latest addition," they said together.

"Yes, I've heard all about you, Frans," she beamed, "I hope you will be very happy here."

"How do you do, Tantje," I smiled. I withdrew and sat on the bed once more. Oh dear, I wish they wouldn't talk to me. What could I say? I felt so out of it all. They were so used to each other, and I didn't want to spoil their company. How would my arrival affect them all? I was determined to see that nothing hurt them, that everything should go on just the same, if they would only leave me alone. I would learn to be kind and polite and quiet and cause no one any worry or offence.

Ruth showed me the blue and white piece of corded string. "That is yours," she informed me. "Remember your colours. You use it to tie your cutlery together just as we have done." Chuckling, she added, "You must lick them clean, very clean, also scrape your plate, we use them again at teatime, they don't get washed until night, you see. We do all the family's dishes together, it saves water, unnecessary noise and time."

I tied my cutlery together as instructed. Tantje lifted the double tray and left with a quiet "Cheerio for now."

"Well now," Ellie took the lead, "see you all at 4.30 p.m. All right? I've got things to do. Cheerio all." Lily followed.

"Come through, Frans," Dik II beckoned me, "and see our room, it will give you a glimpse of the road."

Excusing myself from Ruth I followed the boys through the small narrow door. I had been right the previous night. That small door led to the boys' room.

Oh, it was beautiful! It was a real room with carpets, dressing-table, two wardrobes and the most beautiful lits-jumeaux I had ever seen. Two single beds, joined as one with a common headboard, winged by two lockers. It was a bright room graced by colour drapery.

"It's really the spare room," they informed me. "Yours belongs to Tantje, but she shares a room with Nopje downstairs just now. We all encroach on each other's territory," he casually remarked.

I nodded. There was the road. They held me back from approaching the window. I had already forgotten. There was no traffic, except a bicycle approaching. We must be right in the country. Straight across from our house was a small church, and along towards the left I noticed some activity. It was a shop, the boys confirmed this. Along came a car, and we drew back a little. They smiled, "Well done, you're beginning to learn."

"Thank you for showing me your room, I will see you later, I had better get back." Once more I withdrew into the privacy of my room. *My* room? Our room!

Ruth wasn't there. The place was tidy again, and I sat down on a chair. What now? Surely I could not sit here doing nothing, day in day out? Yes, there were plenty of books, I would read many of them, but not today. I felt sleepy again, but I had better do nothing meanwhile. Soon it would be 4.30 p.m., then I could climb the ladder to higher spheres. So I sat on and travelled once more the paths of memory thinking of all that had happened to bring me here. Strange, very strange!

Domie walked in, quietly. Everyone behaved quietly. I rose to my feet, but he beckoned me to remain seated. He stayed for almost half-an-hour. I did enjoy his pleasant company. He talked so naturally, so confidently, dispersing any worry which previously may have clouded my mind. He asked questions about my home, my parents, my family, my background. I told him and he listened, genuinely interested. He assured me that the war couldn't last much longer and that things would be normal very soon.

He explained that he would need to leave home again that evening, but would be back at midnight on Saturday. There was more work awaiting in Amsterdam.

Putting two and two together, I reckoned he would leave after his raid on the town hall, taking his catch to Amsterdam in order to supply the Resistance with ration books and identity cards. What a man!

"Good-bye, Frans, I won't see you till the weekend, be good! I trust you will settle down soon."

"Cheerio, Domie, thank you, thank you very much." He was gone. I wanted to cry. Why couldn't I? It would make me feel so much better. Oh, Domie, why did you have to go? Why didn't this world have more people like him? So unpretending, so honest, so straightforward and so pure. So mature and yet so boyish and adventurous. Why did he do all this? What was he, who was he? What was his job? Wait . . . no it could not be? Perhaps he was employed here? No, he wasn't the kind of person to be a cleric. But there was that church and they called him 'Domie'. What did it mean? It could, it must be, yes it must be short for Dominee. That is the Dutch word for Reverend, the minister, the minister of that church perhaps? That meant he must be a Christian man. Oh dear. I had heard about Nuns who grabbed Jewish children, saving them from the hands of the enemy. Then they were hidden in these Convents and later baptised. Oh my God, save me from such a future. Don't let me be captured by Goyims. I want to remain faithful to Thee. Rather die with my people, than live like a Goy.

Had my worries foundation at all? Only moments ago I had admired Domie for his purity, his honesty. No, he couldn't be one of these people. He was neither nun nor priest. He was some kind of ordinary man, no, an extraordinary man. I would trust him even if he was a Dominee. After all, he would respect my faith. I had nothing to fear. Our God, after all, was the only true and living God, the God who created heaven and earth and all that dwelled therein. He couldn't and wouldn't be beaten by any false gods. He who had succeeded throughout the centuries would succeed now. My faith was strengthened, I was His by birth.

Ruth appeared once more. "Ready, Frans, the mice are waiting to receive thee!" It sounded so funny. We tiptoed along the hall and were faced by a rather frightening hole containing a ladder. "You first," I suggested to Ruth. She gladly agreed and ascended without the slightest fear of tripping. I followed. Three smiling faces beckoned me. How on earth did they get up and down the ladder with their pails, buckets, jugs and junk? Incredible! All right, I would do it. Carefully, step by step I reached the summit. What I saw made me marvel! One had to choose one's words carefully. It was a sheer impossibility to show my true feelings.

Poor mice, what a life to lead, shut off from God's pure countryside in such an attic. Yet it was better than to exist until extermination in one of these death camps.

They waited for a verdict, but all I could manufacture was, "Thanks for your welcome, sorry for being so clumsy." The attic was dirty, dusty and filled with every kind of useless article. I looked around and followed them carefully through this maze, until they showed me their home proper.

"Well, this is terrific, you are miracle workers. Have you done all this yourself?"

Separated by rough curtaining their sleeping quarters lay before me. Plain iron bedsteads and odd feminine articles. That was all. Ellie explained, "You see, nothing but the table must remain when the danger signal goes. We must wipe out any traces of life up here within seconds, then disappear. The curtains come down and we mess up beds and other articles with newspapers and sacks. It must look as untidy as any attic does. There is some cleaning up I can assure you, when the 'all-clear' goes."

I understood. A little anyhow.

"It's the same down under with you and the boys. Ruth will show you the ropes, won't you, Ruth? Rule number one for us all is 'don't spread yourselves out! Don't make yourselves at home! Be ready and able to quit in seconds'." How easy it is to misjudge a situation. On purpose they kept this attic as uninhabitable as possible. No raid should betray a sign of habitation. I wondered, was it possible?

Happily none of them suspected the way my thoughts lay, they were ready to show 'the ropes'.

"There's not much among these beds to show you," Ellie continued, "but look among the beams." I saw nothing, but pretended I did. "See there, that's where the boys pick up Radio London. We receive true news of the progress at the front lines and the war in general. We receive secret messages, useful to *our* organisation only. We all help to print the news we receive and some of the schoolchildren, tested and absolutely 'safe', take a few among their school books into town, then hand them to their appointed professor or teacher when giving their notebooks for correction. No one speaks a word, Frans, they just act, and thereby become part of this great resistance movement undermining the enemy. No classmate knows of the other, no one knows who-is-doing-what. They are absolutely trustworthy. Even their parents don't know, Domie chooses his children from the Bible Class. Isn't it superb?"

I could only shake my head, I was speechless. "What a people, tremendous, even the children!" I muttered.

"Yes, even the youngsters," Ellie continued. "You haven't met Sientje yet. She is wonderful. She works here daily, helping Aunt Jo and Tantje, and looking after the baby. She knows all about the secret life in this house, yet her parents know nothing, neither does her boy friend. She leads a normal happy life of any teenager, yet inwardly she is carrying our burdens."

I continued shaking my head in sheer astonishment. What could I say? Lily took over. "This is the mill. Here we mill our grain when it is a good stormy day. The motor makes a horrible noise, but when it is stormy . . . oh boy . . . we do all we have in store, it sees us through for a few weeks at a time. Dik I is our baker, you should see him at work, he's wonderful. Did you taste this morning's bread?"

When I told her I had slept until dinner time, consequently missing his home baking, she chuckled with delight.

"Go and get it, we'll share it for our afternoon break. I have some jaffa juice and you supply the eats." It sounded like a party. I would risk the dangerous descent to get that bread.

"Stay here just now," the mice advised. "Wait until the boys come up, they might be willing to show you their secret transmitter."

Eventually the boys arrived but they didn't join the female party. They began to oil 'their apparatus', whatever that entailed, and they swung around and behind the beams as supple as monkeys. They fetched and fixed, they carried and shifted. What and where did all this activity lead to, I wondered? Was it necessary? How did they fill their days and still look busy?

"You must join our keep fit class," Ruth suggested. "You need it and it's fun."

When I asked what form it took and when it was held, they assured me that it was open most of the day, and straightway the five monkeys, as I termed them secretly, lined up holding on to the vertical beam, and began swinging their legs alternately in wonderful formation.

"This takes the place of a daily walk," they explained.

"But let's calm down," the big mouse advised, "we are overwhelming our baby with all that we're doing. Ruth, please get Frans's breakfast. I'll pour the jaffa juice, and we'll settle down to a chat and let Frans tell us more about life in the outside world."

Ruth went and came back, yet I had heard nothing. The silence with which all activities were performed was a sheer revelation.

We sat in the curtained-mouse-hole on beds, table and floor. We felt cosy, united in a common bond of illegality and separation from

132

normal life. That the mice had lived here for over a year, and the boys nearly as long, was a thought which did not escape my imagination. How was it possible? This was only my first day, yet already it seemed like years. Their questions were endless. What Domie couldn't tell them, I had to fill in. I told them about this past year. The dodging of arrest which affected all the people in the towns. The raids, the rough and cold attitude of the soldiers. The hospital's final chapter. They asked about my own people, my home, my belongings.

It was a heart-to-heart afternoon, probably the first and last.

Altogether it had been an unusual day. Domie had joined us, urging us never to lose heart, to keep going, to persevere even when spirits were low. No one else could inspire us as he could. Peace and calm radiated from his slender, boyish personality. His sense of humour could dispel anxiety and fear. Courage and determination became our crutches; we wanted to walk well with these for his sake.

He was leaving us that night to attempt yet another rescue mission, then our life would be hum-drum again, according to the long term inmates.

"Pssstt." Dik II rushed to the ladder. It was Tantje. "Early tea tonight, folks, it's catechisatie,* the kids will be here at 6.30 p.m." Some club I imagined. One by one we descended. I did not like that ladder and was glad to see the daylight in our room.

What should I do now? I sat down, rose to my feet, picked up a book, sat down again, pretended to be fully immersed in its subject and thereby persuaded Ruth that I had settled at last.

Three sharp buzzes; I looked up enquiringly.

"Tea!", she said, "the boys will get it."

I nodded. They arrived with double tray, teapot and mugs. The top shelf was laden with homemade bread, butter and jam, a large piece of cheese and a pot of syrup.

I wasn't hungry, but smiled because they did. I pretended to be eager to taste the food, by rubbing my hands in anticipation as they did. I ate, but slowly, to avoid their questions. If only I could be invisible. They seemed so content and happy together. Why had Domie brought me here? Did not my presence upset their unity and routine? The girls were tuned-in to each other, the boys were

* Confirmation class.

pals and their cavaliers. I was so immature, so inexperienced. I must find a way of service. I could do a lot if they'd let me, if I did not deprive them of a job. That was the problem: too many people, too few jobs, to fill too many working hours.

The boys discussed Aunt Jo's latest suggestion. It was that we should rise earlier each morning, lead more normal lives, have regular hours to boost our morale and attend to set duties; then retire at night at a more reasonable time.

We resisted such rules and regulations strongly. Could she, with all her love and goodwill, realise how we felt, confined to certain rooms during the day. How glorious it was to be able to move freely around the house after midnight and to linger as long as possible in that state of semi-freedom? We only wanted to retire when our bodies and eyes were truly tired and then . . . then just to sleep on until we wakened to yet another day which required our undivided attention in care, silence and patience.

It was true, we had to consider one another. It was necessary for Aunt Jo to retire early, she always had a strenuous day ahead—the responsibility for her little boy, her home, the safety of us all, and a club which she ran. She was such an active person, she needed her rest.

We, on the other hand, were geared to an entirely different existence. We needed more sleep by day, shortening its hours, and more activity by night. We would do our best to be as quiet as possible for those who rose early.

I listened to their discussions and learned of their problems. This seemed to be the most dangerous part of the day, the time when the silence buzzer would call us unexpectedly to immobility as callers or visitors came to the house. None must become suspicious by strange noises upstairs. A normal family atmosphere had to be preserved by all the visible members of the household.

We began to settle down for the evening. The mice retreated to their attic to do 'odds and ends'. The boys chose a book and I joined them. Ruth took up her sewing basket. The hours dragged on.

The door bell rang often and loud. There were many voices, young ones, mingling with Domie's, Aunt Jo's laughter and that of the visitors. Little Bas-Janneke could be heard as well, he must have been out all day with Sientje. She was like a nannie to him.

He adored her and her people, I was told; and it was just as well, for this house was a strange home in which to bring up a little one. What would happen once he could talk properly? Would he tell anyone about us? Could he betray us? He could say 'mice' but that wouldn't mean a thing to anyone. In the country most people were plagued by mice.

They had promised I would see the little fellow that day, but I would have to be patient till he came, perhaps before he went to sleep. I wanted to see him. Life didn't seem so serious when a child was around. Silence had truly engulfed us. We listened, yet didn't belong to the life around.

What had happened in the town today? They must have missed me at the hospital. Suspected arrest, that would be the rumour. Yet, we were safe. Safe as long as no one found us. If only my parents could know this. Where were they now? Poor, poor people; in tremendous hardship, cold, hungry, almost certainly without proper shelter, privacy or clothing. Were they still together? I doubted it? Oh, my dear, dear people. Why? why? why? Deep down in the most secret part of my heart I hoped they would no longer be in this world of woe. It was unbearable to think of them at hard labour on road building or in gravel pits. Nonsense! How could thousands upon thousands do such work. They were not needed, they were just surplus bodies, unwanted life . . . oh Lord God, annihilation, that was the purpose of this terrible treatment. No, they couldn't be alive. This was September, and I had had no news since April. Five months, five months of life in a whirlpool, and now . . . now it was at a standstill, sudden, abrupt and silent. I had time to reflect. It had all been real. We still had to cope, but in some respects only. Others were ruling our lives, for good. Over there others ruled their life . . . into destruction. Dear Mother, dear Father, why oh why had you to experience so much agony, heartbreak and loss in your life? Would I ever understand? If you will suffer, do you worry about me? May your senses be dulled to worry and wonder, may you just exist until the Almighty releases you and you relax in His protecting arms . . . for ever . . . until we meet again.

Oh no, I must restrain myself, I mustn't cry. I would go to the wash-and-toilet cupboard, close its doors and cry there, no one would see me. Everybody was so quiet, Ruth was reading now.

Carefully I rose from the bed. She looked up, signalled to me to sit down, pressing her finger tightly against her lips.

No, no I could not; Lord help me, Father, Mother . . . pleadingly I looked at Ruth, then pressed my apron against my flushed face and cried bitterly but silently as never before. She left me alone; I felt grateful. I wasn't ashamed anymore. I just felt so alone, so hopeless, so unable to help, so finished. Oh my God, take me too, why not me?

I felt relieved and relaxed once I had calmed down, but also humiliated, and shy, for surely Ruth would tell the others. Quietly I lay down on top of the bed and closed my eyes, pretending to sleep once more, and there I would stay until the all-clear gave us renewed freedom for the evening.

Ruth read on and I finally dropped over.

When I wakened it was dark, the shutters were closed, lights were on and the door was wide open. I could see the boys going downstairs. Ruth was also there with a bundle of washing in her arms. Domie walked in. He was dressed in the clothes I knew so well. Cheerio all, be good, Frans. We will meet again at the week-end. I must go now or I'll miss my train.

"Bye, Domie," Ruth hesitantly called, "be careful!"

"Good-bye, Domie," I added, "be careful!"

We listened quietly as he ran down the stairs, waving once more. Aunt Jo's voice, "Bye bye, God bless you. Take care!" They shut the door. He was engulfed by a dark moonless night once more on his way to seek and to save those who otherwise would be lost . . . forever.

Deep in thought I stared down those stairs where moments before my saviour had gone, gone to save others.

Ruth, interrupting my train of thought, enquired if I'd slept well and if I wanted to come down with the others and help with the chores. Yes, I wanted to, very much. It was easy to copy the others and to use one's own common sense.

My duty from now on was the care of our washroom, cupboard and toilet articles in general. It was great to feel busy once more.

There was just enough water in the jug to rinse the pot. Carefully I poured it through the divided lid into the collecting pail. The emptying of this pail, its cleaning and disinfecting, was always the first duty of the night. Once this was out of the way one could feel more normal and human.

Secondly, the wash bowl. I took it down, washed and cleaned it thoroughly. Then a second pail, the collecting pail of the day's washing water. Carefully I walked down the stairs, as it was heavy and I mustn't spill it. Aunt Jo insisted that such a volume of water was beneficial for the already overloaded pipes of this one toilet. So down it went! Both pails back at their destination, clean and shiny for another day's use, I concentrated on the filling of all containers; the large jugs for washing and rinsing purposes and two smaller glass decanters for drinking water.

Ruth was still busy with the washing, so I continued with duties which I knew were ours. The others were running around with breakfast tins and flasks. I copied all I saw. Collecting our tins and flasks I put them on the draining board in the kitchen. The flasks were rinsed and filled with water, the tins were washed out.

Thinking that the boys had finished with their mops and dusters, I requested their use, but they pointed to other brushes, mops and dusters, there being enough for all of us. With a choice of 'tools' I climbed the stairs once more. Actually one searched for excuses to use this Jacob's ladder, a healthy and wholesome activity after hours of forced immobility.

Time passed quickly after dark. Soon it was midnight. All work done we gathered around the table in the roomy kitchen. Lily had been busy preparing our meal. Tea was made, the bread buttered, now we could lounge and relax. Aunt Jo came in to bid us goodnight. The chatter began; small talk, serious talk, gossip and news reviews, and, most important, duties to be allocated for the night.

Dinner and tea dishes had to be washed, potatoes and vegetables cleaned, breakfast prepared, flasks filled. There were delightful hours ahead of us yet!

I listened and learned. The beans would be pulled soon, and they would need cleaning and bottling for the winter months ahead. It was a big job, but Aunt Jo had a cutting machine. After cleaning and stringing them first, they were put into a small hole, a rotary handle turned and turned and out came the stringless beans, cut evenly in a huge pile. We would all take part in this operation until all the beans were securely bottled and stacked in the store. When I saw the preparation for the maintenance of our mortal

137

bodies, I marvelled. There were stacks of bottles of all descriptions. Carrots, peas, cauliflowers, cabbages, beans, cherries, gooseberries, strawberries, blackcurrants: all gathered from this rich and fruitful land and garden. The mice had done most of the work long before the boys had come to join the working party. Several times a week a bottle was opened and savoured, hence the stock had to be maintained, replenished by those foods which were in season. They talked and talked, informed and questioned me, and when 3 a.m. brought our conference to a close I was delighted to lead the way to lighter spheres.

And it was the evening and the morning of my first day.

12

DURING THE SECOND NIGHT, SLEEP WOULD NOT COME. There was so much to digest. I'd seen and heard more than any book could tell. I could imagine how flat and uninteresting life must be to them, now that the pig was gone. They had only just finished the bottling. "It should last us throughout the winter," they had said. 'Uh! Pig. How revolting!' However, it might be delicious, I would wait and see. We had never touched pig, it was against our religious customs and tradition. I thought, 'It is funny how the different races eat foods appealing to them alone, chocolate-coated beetles, eels, oysters, pigs and hundreds of other things of whose existence I wasn't even aware.'

The butcher had come and silenced their beloved animal for good. No one had known about her. She had been with them ever since she was a piglet given to them by a local farmer who knew of their plight. Deep under the Church Hall they had dug a large hole or pigsty; there Rosie grew up for better or worse. She was fed, cleaned and loved day by day, or rather night by night. The hidden family and hidden Rosie became friends, now her voice was silent and she lay buried and broken in tightly sealed bottles.

Poor Rosie, she'd been sacrificed for many, now I was to see the underground pigsty, our gateway to escape if the danger buzzer sounded. In this disused hole there were benches; also large aluminium milk containers protecting important papers, photos and manuscripts against the perishing damp which attacked any goods left in the open.

The tunnel lay straight ahead. I couldn't see it till tomorrow but they had described it and told me of its origin. Once Rosie had been put 'to sleep' the gang had started their major project, the digging of the tunnel. Pail by pail they removed the sand, building scaffold inch by inch, shoring up walls and ceiling as the passage progressed. Dik, as amateur architect, had sponsored the project, now the finished article might have to prove our salvation.

139

Tomorrow . . . tomorrow . . . this was enough for today. I couldn't think further, oh for some sleep.

At ten I was wide awake, but as Ruth was still asleep, I didn't dare move. Another day of care and silence. As soon as my bed companion stirred I would fetch the flask for our morning cup. Oh, I had forgotten, this wasn't traditional 'morning tea' in bed, we called it breakfast and sat at the table!

Aunt Jo brought us some mending. Bas-Jan's jackets, Domie's socks, silk stockings with big holes and ladders belonging to Tantje, Aunt Jo and Nopje.

Nopje, I looked forward to meeting her! They'd said such nice things about her, she was also engaged to be married. She had been born in the Dutch East Indies and had a brother who, I gathered, worked with Domie. I understood she was very artistic and very pretty.

Sientje had gone home after bringing Bas-Janneke. We didn't see very much of her, yet she knew all about us and was safe and trustworthy.

Sometime today the buzzer might go; for danger this time! One had to be prepared to act immediately. All traces of life had to be removed and we had to disappear below the platform in the Church Hall, lower ourselves down a small hole into the disused pigsty and along the tunnel. The time taken had to be improved on each time, decreasing from practice to practice.

There certainly wasn't much conversation, not even during the 'safe periods'. Every now and then a brief sentence passed between us. The boys came to fetch a book or ask a question, but on the whole the morning hours would be quiet and we never saw the mice. Although they made us welcome they certainly didn't encourage us to visit their quarters. They had learned to live alone and appreciated their privacy.

At midday everyone gathered once more in our room to await the three buzzes which would bring the double tray and my second dinner in this secret abode—a very strange life.

After our meal the hours dragged on as before. Dik I suddenly stood behind me as I stared through the curtains at the small stretch of road which could be seen from this side of the house. One certainly never heard any of the others approaching if you weren't facing their way. We all wore soft slippers or gym shoes. "Did I give you a fright?" he smiled. "Why don't you come into our room? You could then study the road from a different angle. There isn't much to see, but you'll soon get to know the villagers and learn to recognise any strangers. One of us always has the road under observation. If any intruder should come up our drive, we can sound the buzzer, even from here, you see," he pointed at a switch.

"Can I come with you now, then you can show me your light switch, just in case I touch it accidentally."

"Don't you dare!" he warned me, waving his finger right in front of my nose.

I liked him. He didn't seem to be under the same strain or tension; at least he didn't show it.

We slipped through the connecting door. Ruth stayed behind. The boys' room was so very airy, so colourful and tasteful I couldn't help remarking on this once more. The bedspread was from Suriname and the woodcarvings on the wall from Java.

The shutters inside the windows had a venetian blind effect. They were shut at present. This allowed us to observe the road but did not let anyone see movements inside the room. It was bright and sunny: we needed many such days. Feeling more at ease with the boys, I ventured to ask some questions. Dik told me that we were far North, actually one hour's cycling distance from the German border. He encouraged me not to be frightened if I saw soldiers on the road, as they sometimes passed this way on routine patrol or on leave. When I asked him if his Uncle Bas had any connection with the Church across the road, he smiled.

"He happens to be the *Minister* of this parish."

Oh, so he was a minister! Now I'd plenty to think about while watching the road—these people, the church, a minister! A *Christian* minister. He hadn't looked like one when he had kidnapped me. He had behaved oddly, more like a climber, hiker or tramp. Yet . . . his personality was fine, sincere, precise and purposeful. A strange human being. A minister! that meant he would be at home on Sundays.

Ah well, live and let live, my Saturday would be over by then. I would keep the Sabbath quietly by myself. The other Jewish girls were certainly not orthodox. None had mentioned worship or prayer. Only the boys were not ashamed to pray in their usual way at the table.

I had always said my prayers. It came natural, like breathing out and breathing in. I couldn't remember when I'd learned them or how small I was when taught. The worship of the Almighty Creator, the customs and traditions of our fathers, were interwoven into our homelife.

Although no prayer book was saved from our belongings, I knew enough to keep me going. On Saturday I would deliberately let them realise that I wished to be left alone during the morning hours, even if it meant praying in our washroom behind closed doors in the dark. It really did not matter as long as my heart had the right attitude. Then on Sunday I would respect *their* day of rest, and would do any job to allow *them* more freedom.

The fields looked brown and healthy. The mustard seed in full bloom gave the country a colourful panorama. Children on bicycles passed by frequently, mothers with little ones in chairs on the rear wheel, others with chairs at front and back. Bicycles seemed to be the only form of transport. One could even see elderly men with soft hats riding them. These, I imagined, were farmers, while workers carried tools across their shoulders. I could only see one shop at the corner, but Dik told me there were several in the village.

When would I meet Bas-Janneke? Perhaps at the week-end when Sientje was off? That was a possibility.

The door opened. There were the mice, followed by Ruth and a stranger. Everyone seemed to have wakened up, the atmosphere had improved perceptibly, there were smiles on all their faces. The newcomer crossed her arms over her chest, bowing deeply before us as one doing homage, and mumbling some strange greeting. The others bowed jokingly in return. She came over to me, "Welcome here, Frans," she said giving me a firm handshake, and I knew she meant it.

I liked her too. She had a lovely complexion with a smooth skin, and her cheeks looked like two rosy apples decorated by two dimples whenever she smiled. Her chestnut brown hair was combed right back in a tight bun, but little strands, here and there, naughtily escaped and hung over her ears.

We all settled on or around the large lits-jumeaux.

She opened her bag: to me it seemed like a party . . . out came toothbrushes, peppermints, newspapers, magazines, thread and

elastic, a comb, a pair of braces, pencils, a torch, shoe laces and . . .
a box of chocolates!

"That's for you all to share around. *My* treat, actually from
Dedde too. We had some spare coupons so we put them together
and . . . hey presto . . . chocolates for the community."

She was thumped on the shoulder by one and all, then Ellie
opened the box and we shared it round. What a treat! We bombarded our visitor with questions, longing for news from the outside world. There were sad stories to listen to, but she also had us
in fits of laughter, pianissimo. Crescendos were forbidden at all
times and under all circumstances. Having saved up her days off
she would be with us over the week-end and all the next week. A
fine prospect I thought, she was like Domie in some ways, yet I
couldn't put my finger on a particular aspect. I suppose being a
secretary, working close with a person day in day out, sharing secrets
such as foiling the enemy would bring an affinity of behaviour and
action.

When she had left us, we all knew the day wouldn't be boring
any longer. Each one had something new, something to give their
attention to, something to think about. Soon after Nopje had gone
I almost jumped out of my skin; the emergency buzzer sounded,
and my heart beat rapidly. Ruth grabbed me by the arm and we
slipped to our room. I just watched her as she hid pyjamas and
personal belongings behind a panel in the wall then she checked
our washroom and pulled me with her down the stairs.

Avoiding the kitchen door, she opened a smaller one and signed
for me to follow. I just noticed a crop of hair disappearing. The
boys! Ruth crawled on her hands and knees, quietly but quickly.
I followed her example. There wasn't much headroom, I couldn't
crawl as fast, and as my rear hit each horizontal beam of the platform overhead, I had to flatten my body even more. Relieved, I
reached the hole and followed Ruth down below where she waited
to close the hatch behind me. Then we joined the others in the
pigsty. We looked at each other and smiled. Lily, however, pointed
at her watch. "Too long," she said, "still too long. Four minutes is
far too long."

"Cheer up," Dik II consoled her, "next time will be better!"
There we sat and waited until the 'All Clear' allowed us to haul
ourselves through the hole, then back along below the platform

143

ceiling and out into the hall proper. We slapped and brushed each other's clothes before going to our respective domains.

Aunt Jo and Tantje helped with the brushing, assuring us that we had 'done well' and 'not bad at all', yet Lily, shaking her head, objected and insisted that it was 'too long'.

We spent the rest of the afternoon and evening enjoying Nopje's gifts of papers and magazines.

Soon our evening routine would begin and with it freedom to walk around the house, so much appreciated by us.

We knew how to do all our chores quietly and smoothly, avoiding disturbing all 'normal' movements of the household.

There were extra jobs tonight since Domie would be home tomorrow for the week-end, and we wanted to do as much as possible so that Saturday night could be a family night.

The days and nights passed with monotonous regularity. One learned to sit still; to listen for the unexpected. I began to distinguish buzzer from buzzer. I looked forward to visits from Nopje. Although she never had orders from me, I having had no money at all for more than a year, she did include me in her treats to the little community. She always had a surprise, however small, for 'the baby of the gang' as she liked to call me.

Somehow it seemed that we were imprisoned here, imprisoned for our own good certainly, but for how long? No one could tell, no one dared to estimate. When the boys listened to the B.B.C. they returned with either glad or glum faces. I never asked for details. Their expressions spoke as clearly as words as far as I was concerned.

Time dragged along, slowly, uneventfully and silently. Inwardly however, my active temperament could not adjust to this inactivity, this silence, and implicit obedience which I owed to all for their generous hospitality and tolerance of yet 'another one'.

My nervous system was taxed, taxed beyond all endurance. Tension not known before, increased daily within me. Our nights were short but peaceful, yet my mind worked overtime and drove any sleep from me. Dawn broke far too soon to another day of silence and monotony. Loneliness, fear and a modicum of self-pity produced a strange effect on my weary mind.

One unforgettable night I did not join the others in the nightly

144

chores. I was obstinate and told Ruth in no uncertain language **that** I *wouldn't* come down! She first endeavoured to persuade **me**; pacifying, comforting and encouraging what was left to inspire. Soon she gave up. I didn't seem to hear what she had to say. After she had left I cried and cried, sobbing into a heavy bath towel. I was hot and got hotter still as time passed. My throat was sore and I felt feverish all over.

Aunt Jo came up and tried to reason but it was of no avail. The more she talked the more I sobbed. I could only mutter "I'm so sore, so sore, so sore."

Yes I was sore all over, but mainly my head. I had never felt like this before; it frightened me and a vicious circle formed.

Aunt Jo ordered me to get up and led me through the hall **into** her own bedroom. Bas-Jan was asleep, deep and sound as usual. 'You will stay here tonight," she announced. "It's more peaceful for you and the others as well."

Peaceful or not my pains grew worse and the tension increased. Oh to die, to be free of all this. Oh my head, my poor head. A red hot saw seemed to be splitting my head in two, slowly **but** thoroughly going deeper and deeper. I wouldn't live through it, I couldn't bear it. I whispered for a doctor. Often and persistently I called for a doctor.

Aunt Jo tried to explain that no doctor knew of our existence and that she could not possibly involve another person in our secret and thereby expose him to danger, while, at the same time, enlarge the circle of the trusted.

I couldn't understand the implications; I was sick, I needed a doctor and I would get a doctor, I *had* to! Aunt Jo tried to reason with me again, then she became tough and firm. I still ignored all her words and cried and sobbed for a doctor. Oh what pain, Oh what a life! Not conscious of the time that had elapsed I was at last confronted by a stranger who called himself a doctor.

"Doctor, oh Doctor," I cried, "please help me! I'm so sore, so very sore. My head, oh my head."

He held my hand, felt my pulse, examined my hot body, peered into my eyes, ears and nose, hit my knees, arms and ankles with a little hammerlike object, then gave me a long and deep injection in the leg. A relaxing sleep mastered my painful body, and I was **at** peace.

The following night the doctor visited me again, and I was calm and free from pain. Aunt Jo left us together and he explained what had happened to me. He gave me some tablets and instructions to stay in bed over the week-end. "Think it all over, my dear," he suggested. "Face facts and the situation as it stands. Accept reality but have hope in the future. You are in very good hands, in the *best* of hands. Good luck and good-bye!" He shook hands and left.

I had experienced my first migraine! It would be my companion in the years to come. I would have to learn to live with it whenever it came upon me, then pray for its departure . . . some day!

Quickly I rose and tidied the bed, switched off the light and went to my room. Domie would soon be home, I didn't want him to know. Doubting the discretion of the others in this matter, I went to bed, and dozed fitfully.

After what must have been hours, my door opened. It was Domie. Domie with two mugs of tea on a tray. I sat up straight, tears welling up in my eyes, as I apologised sincerely for what had happened in his absence. He didn't want to hear anything about it, just emphasised repeatedly that he was sorry I had been in such distress. Only then did I realise that he was the only person who wanted to listen and would understand. I was and always would be to the others 'the extra one', 'the added security risk', 'the new-comer'. I could not blame them but, at the same time, I could not alter the position. I had come to stay. Selected by Domie.

Tomorrow was Sunday, he wished me a good day.

Funnily enough, I could not imagine him in a long black gown like a minister. Yet he was one. He would have to preach sermons and guide his congregation. He would have to be at many a grave-side and comfort many a mourner. I supposed he would be good at that. He didn't need to *say* anything, he simply *was* comfort *himself*, his *very being* inspired courage, courage to go on.

Next morning the boys were dressed smartly. Jokingly I asked if they were going out. To my surprise, they nodded. In little Dik's eye was always a sparkle. He would tell me what was going to happen.

Evidently the Sunday morning routine followed a rigid pattern. Once the service had started, with the organ playing and the people singing their praises, the boys would tiptoe downstairs, press a clothes-hanger between the connecting-door and settle beside the toilet, to worship the God of their Salvation.

"You can come too," he added, "Ellie sometimes comes." Politely I declined, but eagerly assured him that I would love to see Domie all dressed up.

He burst out laughing. "I'll tell him," he assured me, "I'm sure he'll come."

I'd done it! Now I would see my kidnapping tramp in holy robes. Perhaps I wouldn't even like it. Perhaps he would be different. I shouldn't have asked to see him all dressed up. I admired him just as well in rough clothes.

Dik was gone. I would just have to accept the result of my curiosity.

The door opened, "Oh my word, Domie," slipped out of my mouth. He was his usual self and enquired sheepishly if he were respectable enough to go. With my very best wishes I sent him on his way. I was left alone to reflect on Domie's new image.

He was a minister, a *real* one too. I could not get over it. He looked beautiful and majestic. Those clothes made him look even taller. His narrow face and thin hair seemed unequal to command all that there was of him; yet his eyes and his very personality spoke of a greatness with which he walked hand in hand, a phenomenon difficult to define yet powerful in experience.

I could hear the first hymn, men, women and children's voices mingling. The boys would be sitting beside the toilet mouthing the words without a single sound. We had been under the platform on which Domie was standing now. The services were usually in the Church but between mid-September and mid-April the Church could not be heated sufficiently to draw the villagers from their home fires, hence this special arrangement. The boys liked it, as it enabled them 'to go to Church'.

The hour passed quickly, the boys had to disappear before the worship ceased. We all sat together on the bed and watched those smartly dressed farmers and their families leaving the drive by bicycle or on foot.

Dinner was later on Sundays, but when the familiar two tier tray arrived, it was worth waiting for. There was a three course dinner, fruit, soup, cabbage, meat and an extra piece of fat to mix with the potatoes.

One had to be very tactful and polite to decline such delicacies as pork with its fat. Tantje had begun to know me, she now always sent some extra gravy or a little butter to moisten *my* potatoes.

There truly was a different atmosphere within the house on a Sunday. Would it be like that each week?

The afternoon was spent lazily; reading, musing, sleeping, we were free as usual till the hour of darkness. Free, but compelled to be extra silent. Visitors, callers, even children loved to come and go freely on Sundays. This had to continue or suspicion might be aroused. A few young boys and girls knew all about the illegal community, although they had never met us. They were looked upon as secret helpers. Once told where to go and what to do they acted without question and with precision.

After tea we continued in quietness and idleness. Sunday was the longest day of the week; it was most trying mentally as well as physically.

We never saw Domie after tea. He spent some time with his wife and son as well as time alone in meditation before the evening service. Then, when the last Amen rang through the hall, Domie would walk calmly and reverently from his pulpit, through the connecting door and disappear into his study. Aunt Jo awaited him, helped him to change and be out of the house in his old clothes, and on to his bicycle in record time even before the organ had quietened and the first parishioners had left the building.

With gathering speed he cycled towards the station three quarters of an hour away and just managed to catch the last train to one of the large cities, to seek and to save the lost, lost among thousands of others being herded into trains, lorries, camps and gas ovens.

He would mingle with the crowd, pass his messages to resistance workers who moved about just as freely as he did, and receive reports regarding the special desperate few.

Who really were the desperate few? Were they not all those hundreds of thousands? Yet only a few had a chance, some here others there.

We were among the few and we had to be patient, to endure the *isolation*, instead of the *desperation* among the doomed milling crowds. We all had to face up to whatever lay before us.

The evening was well on. Not long now and the all-clear signal would allow us once more to stretch our legs, exercise our bodies and do some work in the house which so hospitably was our continual shelter.

A new week lay ahead. Yet all were alike, did we really look for variety? Monotony surely was better than the variety which we had known so well in the days gone by. Yet there was variety even amongst the most sleepy monotony.

I remember one morning the danger signal buzzed in all our rooms. Fortunately it was around ten thirty in the morning. We had risen, tidied the beds and eaten our breakfast.

My tongue was frozen to the roof of my mouth and I was shaking at the knees. Everyone was responsible for their own belongings so I checked that none of my night attire was lying around; then, racing down the stairs, I followed the others and being the last, Tantje shut the connecting door behind me. Crawling on my hands and knees I soon reached the hatch which gave access to our underground passage. Ruth had just lowered herself and reached out for me.

Each one nursed his or her own thoughts and only communicated by looking into each other's tensed faces.

A full half hour, to us an eternity, then the all-clear sounded throughout the house and in our secret passage. Voices and steps came nearer, but still we did not make a move. In all our minds was one thought, one thought only: had he or they whoever they were, discovered the buzzer and forced Aunt Jo to divulge the correct signal to get us out without resistance?

The steps were right above us now, it could not be Army boots. Then Tantje's voice: "Are you still there?" followed by her usual chuckle.

Dik I made the move. He sped to the hatch door and pushed, while Tantje pulled and laid it gently open. Dik helped each of us out and followed last, covering our opening until the next time.

Our voices mingled excitedly. Tantje was bombarded with questions.

"Get upstairs now," she urged, "I'll be up in five minutes with some hot coffee and then you'll get the whole story."

Tense, almost paralysed with fear, we slowly made our way up to the boys' room. The sun seemed brighter since our time in darkness and silence underneath the platform.

We settled down on the large bed. Aunt Jo joined us, smiling as usual but strangely white around her nose and forehead.

"Well that's that over!" she said calmly. Tantje arrived with the coffee, her broad grin showing her large white teeth. How casually and coolly they accepted their responsibility!

Between them they told us what had happened.

Two German soldiers had marched up the drive after their car had suddenly screeched to a halt. The noise had alerted Aunt Jo and as she saw them jumping from the vehicle, she had instinctively given the alarm signal for us to disappear. Evidently, the soldiers had rung politely at the front door and when Aunt Jo calmly enquired what she could do for them they had asked if they could come in! They were shown into the study and asked if they wanted some coffee, but this they had declined.

Shyly and slowly they began their story. A nice young Dutch girl at the border had been friendly with them for some time now. They had seen her regularly during their off duty periods and last week both of them had become sure that this girl should be the bride of the younger German soldier. Could Domie marry them in a religious ceremony in the Church or quietly in his vestry with witnesses? The soldier had friends in his battalion whom he could bring to the Manse.

The whole incident had shocked us considerably, although none remarked on the effects. We could not settle to our daily routine, instead we lazed about till dinner time, emotionally recovering.

13

MUCH OF OUR EXTRA WORK DURING THE AUTUMN consisted of cleaning, preparing and bottling vegetables and fruit for winter consumption.

The afternoons remained as tedious as ever. Occasionally I would help with the assembly and stapling of Illegal-News for distribution among the trusted, but mainly we were left to ourselves.

Mending, knitting and reading were the three main occupations we were able to pursue. I had nothing of my own to mend and the household mending was pounced on by all four females. I was chief soler of socks and stockings, amazing everyone with my special knowledge in that field, and delighted that my apprenticeship had not been in vain.

Knitting was not my forte, I left it to the mice who produced some beautiful and useful articles of clothing for little Bas-Janneke.

The boys had started to plan for St. Nicholas. This is one of the most observed national celebrations of our country and we, too, were planning to enjoy it. With their nimble fingers and inventive brains the boys created models and composed humorous poems to explain their creations which were then presented to us.

Domie, a key figure in the resistance work, was often required to help in rescuing allied intelligence men and arranging the smuggling of them out of the country. Several had landed by parachute in some fields near the Manse, others came just for a night, and then disguised as Dutch farmers, would leave the following evening.

We never tired of teasing Domie about this side-line.

Dik made up a long poem about his parachute side-line sung to the tune of a Dutch National Song. It was to be given to him on St. Nicholas night, together with a parachute made from a handkerchief and a soldier cut from a clothes peg. We all would have copies of this song and serenade him as he entered the room.

There were presents, mostly handmade, for everyone in the

151

house and they were placed in a large clothes hamper in the months previous to December 5th.

We had extra sweets that night and each one received a large solid chocolate letter, the first letter of their name. There was hot coffee and no one went to bed before dawn broke over the countryside. It was a true midnight feast with all the trimmings a government could afford to give their occupied nations.

Soon the people of Holland would prepare themselves for Christmas. This is a religious festival, slightly commercialised as everywhere else, but not as widely spread as the national St. Nicholas celebrations.

Christmas connected with Church and Worship, would be more serene and yet joyful, they assured me. Well, no doubt we would sense some of its atmosphere even here in our quarters.

Since going into hiding and therefore unaware of the true dates of my own Jewish festivals, I had come to terms with my conscience and Creator to observe the festivals simultaneously with the Christian festivals. While they prepared for Christmas I prepared my heart and imagination for Channuka, the feast of freedom from bondage after a struggle with the enemy long ago, when Judas the Maccabean became the national hero. A miracle occurred amongst the ruins of the Temple: the everlasting light above the Ark also smashed, was now extinguished. Oil had to be found, so that it at least could burn to the Glory of God and in thanksgiving for victory granted. Yet only one drop would drip from the once brimful container. One drop! Sadly it was poured into the cold dark lamp . . . just to let it flicker to the glory of the Living God who never would forsake His children. They might be ungrateful, forgetful of His loving kindness again and again and disobedient to His commandments but He would remain faithful! Just let it flicker for a moment, from the grateful heart of him who had found it. But lo . . . a miracle . . . the one drop burned and burned so brightly for eight days and nights, long enough for a new container to arrive from a nearby town.

Eight long days! Nevermore would the children of Israel forget that their God was alive and showed Himself to them in signs and wonders in every situation.

Could He not do that nowadays, I wondered, could He not intervene and bring our sufferings to a close? Why did He permit all this mass annihilation, this separation of children from parents, husband from wives, families broken, many driven to mental breakdowns, desperation and suicide?

Could He and would He prove himself once more, and stop this cruel oppression? Had we, as a nation, really transgressed so deeply? Would He forgive?

Last year we had celebrated Channuka at home. I was in bed with scarlet fever. My parents received my gifts with the words 'God with us'. Where were they today? 'Oh God, be with them as Thou has promised of old', I prayed.

Yes, I would celebrate Channuka in my heart, I was determined. Aunt Jo's Christmas lights would be my Channuka lights. No one would see the worship of my heart to the God of my fathers. If only I had my Hebrew Prayer Book, my Old Testament Scriptures. But who was able to take such risky items on a flight into hiding?

From my earliest age I had been taught to recite prayers of petition or thanksgiving in Hebrew. Prayers and blessings for dozens of occasions. Songs and Hymns for festivities and Holy Days. There was plenty stored in the cupboard of my memory and heart that would carry me through these years. The stories of the early days of my people gave me encouragement during many a dark hour.

There was the story of Moses; his birth, the tragedy of his hiding during early childhood; how much like some of our children today he was. There was his faithfulness to the God of his fathers while dwelling in a Gentile home; I, too, would be faithful and walk in his footsteps.

Then one remembered the account of Jacob and Esau, the fighting twins. How sad to have battles and separations in family life! This, too, was like many a home today and it taught me again how Almighty God had patience with his erring children and would guide them, bringing good out of evil.

I thought of poor Joseph. His jealous brothers deceived their father and sold the lad to strangers, who took him to a far country. He must have been terribly frightened down in that deep pit all alone, before he was brought up and given to these men of a different nationality and custom. How cruel can one's own flesh and blood be . . . and yet, see how kind and helpful Joseph turned out to be when these selfsame brothers were near to starvation. That's how I imagined God would be some day. He would forgive and accept His wayward family. Joseph was like Moses, a man who remained faithful to the God of his fathers, although far removed from all religious influence.

If he could do it, so could I, hidden away in strange premises, separated from all childhood customs and observances; I too would be like Joseph, yes I would! After all, God is so high and mighty and understanding He would see my heart's devotion and surround me with the same love which he had shown to my forefathers.

Aunt Jo had written an outline for the Christmas service. She asked if our printing machine could make a hundred copies or more and if we all would get busy stapling the sheets. We did this that same afternoon. They looked very pretty. Young Dik had sketched some twigs, stars and flowers here and there on the front page. One looked almost like a *Magen David. I asked to shade those twigs with green ink and give a touch of colour to each service sheet. They were as delighted with the suggestion as I was with this extra piece of work.

They were Christian hymns that appeared on the pages. Some had the word 'Israel' in their verse, which greatly surprised me and made me wonder just where the connection could be. Others had a spirit of worship and thankfulness right through them which was most impressive. It was strange to see Almighty God as the focus of their worship, their prayer, all in straightforward Dutch. It was appealing and certainly crystal clear in this direct approach.

The second page of the programme had a story; their Christmas story. Glancing over the line I noticed that the Jews came into it as well and once more I was certain that these Christians must know more about us than we gave them credit for. Very strange indeed. Before the week-end all literature was stencilled, assembled, stapled and colourfully shaded. A splendid piece of work Aunt Jo had called it and we all agreed wholeheartedly.

Yet Christmas came and went, but we, the secret occupants of that house, knew little of what it meant to those who were free. Ours was a royal share of the Christmas fare, but that was all.

1944 made its entry quietly. We welcomed it with heavy hearts. What would the future hold for us in these coming months? We approached them as always on a day to day basis.

It seemed as if these early weeks in January were like a very slow

* Star of David.

motion film. No encouraging news from the front lines. No ray of hope for our people. No break in the constant arrests which continued around the clock in all parts of the country. 'Patience and courage' was our motto for 1944.

The silence between us increased. What could we tell each other? Even during our midnight freedom the work was done swiftly and quietly. Always one of us had a sense of depression that cast a general feeling of pessimism over everything. The boys usually could inject some ray of hope when thunderclouds hovered over the women folks.

The big mouse would reflect on days gone by, while little mouse frequently was 'utterly sick' of life in general. Ruth craved for her beloved fiancé with whom all contact had been severed and I just felt alone, belonging nowhere and to no one. We made our own plans for each day and thought our own thoughts.

When spring came our blood stirred and the longing for freedom was more difficult to restrain. We were permitted to sniff the cool dark night air while standing at the open back door. The finest privilege of all came to us when spells of sunshine enveloped the house. The long hall upstairs had the benefit of a full length window at the far end. Aunt Jo would open it wide once two of us were flat and still on the carpet. There we would sunbathe gratefully, accepting every ultra violet ray which came our way. We had set times, which had to be strictly observed. During changeable cloudy days, five minutes for two was reasonable, while on bright sunny days we could relax and sleep for half an hour at a time. We practised deep breathing exercises, and imagined we were at the seaside. But when the bedroom door opened and a quiet pssst came our way we knew to roll over on our stomach and crawl quietly into the room, making space for the next two who craved for the sunshine. Weather permitting we went through the same routine during the afternoon. These were the happiest days.

1944 did not bless us with the good weather everyone had hoped for. It depressed our spirits and made us wonder if the war would ever end.

Among the hundreds of books lining the walls of almost every room, I found a beautiful coloured illustrated children's Bible.

Was it childish to delve into history, a history which fed an inward faith in the invisible Creator of the universe? These stories

155

were so familiar, interwoven in my very being from an early age. Yet they were far more full of meaning at the age of eighteen and in these surroundings than during primary schooldays. I knew myself to be part of the people with whom God had dealt from century to century. Throughout my reading it became clear to my conscience that it was essential for man's peace and security to follow God's plan of living. One should seek from the Greatest of the Universe, wisdom, guidance and advice for one's daily life. To please and obey Him should be one's chief aim and to be His servant the greatest privilege which any human being could receive.

The conviction had grown within me that the final work in history would be with and from that selfsame Almighty and Invisible God; the God of Abraham, Isaac and Jacob.

He would continue to influence and surround individual lives, continue to choose his Moses, Joshua, Joseph and Rahab. He would chasten his Nebuchadnezzar, Pharaoh and Haman. He would deal with people in authority like Solomon, Saul and David. He would speak through his present day Jeremiah, Isaiah and Malachi.

A great awe for the God of our fathers stirred in my soul, worship had a new form and meaning as day succeeded day. I realised that I could worship without words or prayerbook. My inner self knew it had been accepted by this Eternal being, resulting in almost child-like contentment and happiness amidst sordid captivity and inhibitions.

The continual reading in clear Dutch resulted in clear faith and a longing for a new revelation of His Being in our own time.

Certain passages of the Prophets' exhortations and their condemnations were totally unfamiliar to me. They were my 'Latest News' and more important to my daily diet than the B.B.C. broadcast of front line progress. What outspoken characters these, often lonely, men of God were! They cared not for personal danger as long as God's will was proclaimed. A general theme was common to all; God would one day send the Messiah. He would deliver Israel and call nations to see true light in God, discovering His eternal purposes for mankind as a whole.

What a plan! A mighty plan indeed! How wonderful it would be to witness such interventions in history. Would it work? Often the book made it clear that a plan like that would not be accepted by mankind in general, but that a 'Remnant 'would believe and be saved—the old story all over again. It was the same in Noah's days. Only a handful believed, only a handful was saved. Men would defend and build firmly on their own intelligence, disregarding the higher invisible power and then like the Tower of Babel collapse. History repeated itself even in the pages of my children's Bible. Almost unconsciously I entered a part of history previously unknown to me, yet strangely familiar. It still dealt with the people of Israel but new characters had entered the scene, names I had never been taught, events which had never been mentioned at home or in school lessons. Scenes which took place in Synagogue and Temple, according to this Bible, registered a blank when searching my memory. Yet all the stories were so obviously Jewish and revealed the God of our father so lovingly.

Why had I previously been so totally unaware of all these personalities? Why were these stories and important events so obviously connected with all I knew from childhood and why did these Christians have a Bible on their bookshelves which dealt with my people?

'Oh my God, I wish you could answer all my questions with the voice of a human being. You are in hiding as much as we are,' I used to think.

One person outshone all others in these stories—a new prophet born in Israel. Some called him 'Lord', others 'Master', some 'Messiah'. He was also laughed at and even rejected like all Prophets before Him. Men of God had to face hardship sooner or later. I liked this one, this stranger to me. He was more realistic, not so 'square' as the older ones who had lived before His time. He seemed to be 'with it' in many ways. In other respects He was as steadfast as a rock, even speaking out to those in authority when another would have flinched and tried to be tactful in order not to offend. He was honest, thorough and fearless even in the face of the fiercest opposition.

He was born in strange circumstances. Strange indeed and yet, why should anything be strange or miraculous if God is behind a situation, for then a strange incident becomes the most natural happening on earth. Is it not miraculous or strange that flesh and bones called 'humans' can feel, can see, can hear, can communicate with words, can sympathise, can radiate trust in each other, can act, hurt or heal? He Who IS life, can surely create life in the way

157

He wishes. Nothing is a miracle when God is behind a situation. Nothing!

This baby boy was worshipped by Wise Men from the East, even His own mother and father were baffled by all the commotion. When it was His turn to become *Bar-Mitzwah He was found among the elders of the temple discussing subjects which were far beyond His years, instead of going home with His parents for the festive reception which every Bar-Mitzwah boy was privileged to enjoy.

He helped in his father's workshop and yet His heart was strangely entwined God-ward. He learned and taught in the Synagogue where He also worshipped Saturday by Saturday. He was interested in the under-privileged, the sick, the poor, the elderly. He was cautious among the rich, respecting their difficulty in finding a way for personal contact with their God. He hated and furiously condemned religious exhibitionism and outward piousness.

I learned to respect Him for His deep insight into human nature; for His dealings with men and women of varied characteristics.

He was unusual. He called God 'His Father'. So did I, of course, but He acted on that relationship and was as close to Him in effect as I was to my father when we were still together.

His relationship and worship were less traditional than I had known it. His outlook and behaviour to God was more up-to-date. Although a Jew like myself, He practised His faith in an unorthodox manner and yet it impressed those around Him more than the traditional way of the fathers.

Some wanted to learn from Him and follow Him. First He dissuaded them, then began to call some to come with Him. Almost like a command. First two, then four and so on. They just left everything in their home and even their daily work to obey His compelling command. Inwardly my spirit was deeply moved. He preached new and strange things regarding the approach to Almighty God. He drew attention to the fact that HE was the Way, the Truth and the Life and that no one could come to the Father but by Him.

That was tough meat to digest. 'I did not feel He should have

* The Jewish equivalent of entering manhood, maturity; being confirmed during a ceremonial synagogue service.

158

made such high and mighty statements as that. It somehow lifted Him above all previous prophets. But then, if He *was* that promised Messiah, then He had every right to speak like that! If so, we should accept and worship Him as such. No, He couldn't be. If He were, why was the world in such a mess now. But if He was *not* the Messiah, who on earth was He? He definitely was Somebody special and Someone secret too, because no one had ever told me about Him,' so I ruminated.

Whoever He was, I liked and admired him greatly, especially the way He stood up for righteousness, purity and every straightforward thought and word. It hurt me that He was constantly misunderstood by so many and even thrown out of Synagogues and called unkind names. If I had been alive then, I would have stuck up for Him, I'm sure. Definitely I would have gone with Him on His travels! He had the right idea about God and life in general. He could have taught me a great deal.

As the weeks and months passed by, His life became part of mine. The readings about Him and incidents concerning Him became more important to me than anything else in my own environment. I found I could tolerate my isolation without frustration, always longing for the next opportunity to learn more about Him for He had become my hero.

One Sunday morning in February I carefully enquired of the boys what drill was necessary for the Sunday morning visit to the space between toilet and Church Hall. Not at all astonished they advised me to bring a blanket and hotwater bottle, and to follow them when they gave me the signal. That morning I listened to my first sermon. Uncle Bas spoke loud and clear. His voice inspired me with more awe and reverence for him than ever before. Filled with sincerity and authority, it reached my inmost being. He read from John chapter 13 and elaborated on the service aspect of Christ's ministry and the lesson it should be to any who were contemplating throwing their lot in with His. 'You call me Master and Lord? You say well, for so I am, if I then have washed your feet, you also ought to wash one another's feet! In short, I have given you an example, that you should do likewise. The servant is not greater than his Lord. Happy are you if you understand this, know these things and do them.'

"No," Uncle Bas said, "it does not lie in the washing of feet only. Service to your fellowmen must cover *every* aspect of life; carry each other's burdens and *so* fulfil the law of Christ.

"If you had lived in His day and bicycles had existed, all of you here would have been pleasantly surprised because after worship you might have seen Jesus Christ in the shed behind the Church Hall, finishing the blowing up of your tyres!"

I enjoyed the company of my Bible and my new found prophet and hero, Jesus. At times, unwillingly, I realised that the Christians also knew someone called Jesus, but I rejected the possibility that it could be the same one as my Jesus. Grudgingly protecting Him from heathen claims I crowned Him with Jewish glory.

Why did my people not talk about Him and learn from Him. It would have done them so much good. I had to find out more about this once the war was over.

The events of His life progressed in a most extraordinary way. Was it a story, a play or reality? He got himself into awkward places and situations, actually refusing the easy way out and saying that He had come into the world for a purpose and that purpose was to die finally like a criminal. He came to overcome death with life.

I hoped He would manage somehow, and secretly wished Him success in His venture.

When I read of how horribly He was treated, how cruelly He was betrayed and tortured, I saw in my mind's eye hundreds who also were illtreated and attacked during riots and daily arrests in the streets of Amsterdam. But why was He singled out? Others had nothing to fear. It was in the main, His very own people, fellow Jews who instigated all the trouble. Why, oh, why? I was torn between the two opinions of worship and attitude towards God. I had become a spectator weighing up both claims.

My people brought Him to a Roman Court in order that Pontius Pilate would sentence Him to death. How could they do such a thing? I was furious! This Roman Governor told the crowd on several occasions that there was no reason to crucify Him. Why did they not give up and cease to torment and persecute Him?

He was tremendously humble and even concerned for the eternal destiny of his enemies. He prayed for them. He even healed one who was attacked by one of His followers.

When they took Him up a hillside to nail him to a wooden cross, all my deepest feelings were roused in sympathy for the meek sufferer and in disgust and bewilderment with my own people. How could they do such a thing! It was their fault that heavy nails were hammered through these hands which only had done kind deeds and blessed so many. How could He endure such pain; His body hanging there in mid air, His feet pierced as well, and His poor arms almost pulled out of their sockets by the weight of His body.

No death in the whole Bible was described so fully. This faultless being; this godly prophet. His own people had wanted it, *My* people. Why? Surely all these followers could have stood by Him! In the end all had left Him to go the last bit of the road alone!

I was certain now that it was all meant to show with unfailing certainty that His was the final victory. He would endure all the pain and humiliation and then . . . then when everyone expected Him to die with the other two criminals, God would deliver Him and He would climb down from the cross, and be crowned Messiah of Israel and the world. But still He suffered, how He suffered! His mother stood and watched it all. How could she have done it? I would have stayed at home weeping in frustration at my helplessness and loneliness. But she had stood by, to watch with Him, to comfort Him by her presence, to let Him feel that He wasn't alone. Incredibly, too, He was concerned for her. He had said to one of His friends, "Son, see your mother." He wanted him to take care of her and for her to have someone to take care of. How considerate of Him to arrange comfort and friendship for those He had to leave. He told His executioners that He was thirsty. They gave Him no water, but vinegar to drink. He was no coward; I had realised that long ago. He even prayed for those who hated Him. When one of the occupants of the other crosses asked Him very sincerely if He would remember him when He reached the Kingdom He was talking about, Jesus told him that today he would be with Him in paradise! What a magnificent statement! Did these people standing around still not realise that this Jesus was no ordinary human being?

I did! And although I had grown fond of that new Person, and admired Him, at the same time the situation frightened me a little. It seemed that Jesus, Who lived centuries ago, had, in some unexplainable way, taken an interest in me with a loving touch. Although we couldn't see each other or communicate as human to human, deep in my heart I was assured of His victory over the cross. While still reading of His agonies, in myself I wished for Him to show the power that was His, and free Himself from that cross. I knew He would do it, and as I read on I waited eagerly for the moment when this would be described.

The agonies continued, the drama unfolded itself in such a horrible manner, almost breathtaking was its tension. Near to agony was my own desire to see His victory reach its climax, then unbelievably but true, a short cry touched my thumping heart, "It is finished," and he gave up the ghost. Oh my Almighty God, why? All that now penetrated my broken spirit was the description of the thunderstorm and the fear of those who stood around. Thunderstorm . . . there was one in my very soul and body. It made me feel unwell and drew me into a deeper solitude than any resistance movement. To encounter a sense of personal loss would never compare with the intimate personal loss of that day. I had lost hope, a friend, a victory, a miracle. I had lost One I loved dearly, although I had never met Him, except within the pages of this book. He was of my own kith and kin, one of my people, my history, my hope. One beloved of God and of many ordinary Jewish people of those days as well as non-Jews, yes, even non-Jews felt attracted to Him.

Somehow that Personality, that Prophet could be the one admired by the people I lived with. But why? Why should they be so drawn to a Jewish prophet, when I, as an orthodox, educated Jewish person, had never even read about Him before.

It was a puzzle! I was too baffled by all I had read, by my deep disappointment and by the unexplained behaviour and defeat on the cross. Now all was lost to me. Secretly I treasured a dead, unreal hope, clinging desperately to its memory, mourning Him, who had for days been my shining example of love.

According to the custom of my people I mourned for Him seven days. I abstained from all but the necessary food. I banned all reading from my daily routine. My thoughts were wholly centred on my loss and a deep sense of depression settled upon me. I was weepy, edgy, moody and unhappy.

None of the others knew of my personal loss, my great grief, hence I was watched with deep concern. This irritated me considerably. After seven days, according to the law, I gradually returned to normal work. Although still full of a tragedy which had impressed me more than I dared to admit to myself, I endeavoured to appear careless and lighthearted. This new behaviour must have disturbed our little community even more. We were so linked up with each other that the most frustrating atmosphere developed when one or other of us stopped talking for a day or two. It did happen and we learned to live with it, but it created a divided group spirit. "What's the matter?" was a frequent question. If the person wanted to talk all would be well pretty soon. If, on the other hand, a constraining silence lay on a burdened heart or mind, if he or she just couldn't speak about it the situation would be more serious and drag on for days.

At that time I created such an atmosphere. How could I even have tried to explain to anyone all that had impressed itself on my mind over the past few weeks? The situation had to be worked out slowly and thoughtfully. I was determined to find out why the family which gave us such generous hospitality harboured these books and others like them. Of course, Domie was a clergyman, a Christian clergyman, but what had this to do with *our* Scriptures being in *his* home. And then the story about this unknown Jewish prophet called Jesus. What a mystery it all was! I'd even found a black book which clearly contained all our Pentateuch, the Psalms, our major and minor Prophecies, and yet there was something different about it. There was not a Hebrew word to be found anywhere, Hebrew letters yes, but just a few, for example, in the 119th Psalm. There were, too, many books I'd never heard of.

This section, at the back of our Bible, was separated from the rest by a blank page, followed by an introductory notice which read 'The New Testament of our Lord and Saviour Jesus Christ'.

Jesus Christ! There it was again! The same name as I had found in the children's Bible. Here was the same story in Biblical, old-fashioned language.

It must be a special religion, I thought, a leaning towards the Jewish faith, hence their kindness in taking us in. I forced myself to shut my mind to all those thoughts of the last few weeks, deliberately trying to reject all these writings which were so very confusing. The days passed by occupied in the usual way. Slowly I came to a halt in my discoveries, outwardly indifferent and almost the same inwardly. If only my feminine curiosity would bring me the true peace I longed for. There was an underlying unsatisfied urge to find out more from either that black book or the children's Bible.

True, I had suffered disappointment, but why not act as an adult and read the rest of the story which I would find in the remaining pages of the book. It would do no one any harm if I studied the customs and religions of other people, especially those of the people who must have been motivated by this religion to such an extent as to endanger their own lives and those of their family by saving and sheltering us.

I wanted to do this, I was drawn to read and search; yet I was too lazy or too tired to make a beginning.

During waking hours and during the hours of darkness, when sewing, sunbathing, eating or washing-up, my thoughts dwelt on the unfinished subject. My craving had to be satisfied. I would read once more the chapter of my personal loss and then continue with the story of what had happened after His death.

Again I looked at the coloured picture with the three crosses, I studied His face and those who stood near. The whole event was alive once more as it had been some ten days ago. 'Now I know that You couldn't come down from that cross' my thoughts silently told Him, 'It was crude and cruel to do such a thing to You, because You were good, kind and somehow different from Your predecessors. Had I been with You throughout your travels, I would have stood by You. I wouldn't have let anyone touch You, Lord. If they would have listened to me, I would have drunk your bitter cup for you. You didn't deserve it, Lord.' Lord? Why did I call him Lord? Never! It was strange; but it didn't matter, my ears didn't hear what my heart reasoned. My mouth would surely refrain from such audible statements.

Back I went to history and its unfolding. With a deep sigh I settled for chapter 20, part of this unfamiliar book called 'St. John'. It was now the first day of the week and Mary went back to the sepulchre with spices. She was determined to anoint the body of Him who had been so understanding to her, and so considerately kind at all times. They would preserve His dear body as long as possible foiling the attacking elements which sought to reduce all matter to dust and ashes.

Deep in thought and with sorrowful countenance she walked

steadily to the place where He had been left on Friday. Then she saw the stone had been rolled away from the opening.

What could have happened? Excitedly she ran ahead. When her eyes had grown accustomed to the twilight in the tomb she shuddered with fear and sudden shock: the place was empty! What next? Numb and weary, Mary stumbled into the bright morning light. What could she do? Who could have been so crude, so disrespectful, to assault the body of Him who only came to bless, to do good and point men to the only hope in life and death. Yes, it was true, He had made enemies in His lifetime. His purity had uncovered all wickedness, all hypocrisy. No one could hide their true motives under a cover of godliness. He saw through it all. His eyes would pierce one's very contemplation of evil doing, would make one halt with sheer shame.

Were His enemies no longer frightened, now that he lay still and cold? Did they want to destroy any bodily memory? Why had God Almighty never interfered? He surely lived close to Him and was obedient to His will. Had He not earlier, during His service to God and man, been confirmed with the words: "This is my beloved Son in Whom I am well pleased, hear ye Him." How then had God allowed this atrocity, to scandalise the image of the dead?

Having fought back her tears for so long. Mary now gave way to her grief. She felt as I had done during these past ten days, and again I joined in her sorrow.

Incredibly, the story took a remarkable turn, someone had come near to Mary and had spoken these words, 'Woman, why do you weep so bitterly, whom are you looking for?' Not interested in the identity of the kind gardener, she replied, probably without looking at him, 'They have taken away my Lord and I don't know where they have laid Him!' Almost unaware of the brief pause in conversation, she was startled when the same voice called her name, reassuringly, lovingly: 'Mary'. When her eyes met those of Him who had uttered her name, she knew with indisputable certainty. 'Master!' Surprised and delighted she fell at His feet, longing to kiss His blessed hand once again.

Gently He evaded her. 'Don't touch me yet,' He said, 'but go into Galilee and tell my people what you have seen and heard, I will meet them there.'

'Master!' Dropping her spices and balm. Mary hurriedly left, exuberant and radiant with joy.

Joy! Didn't I know how she felt! I could have jumped with the thrill I experienced, but I had to be so quiet. I knew it, I knew it, I'd known it all along! Death would not be able to triumph over Him. He was a true prophet of the Most High, and favoured by God above all who had gone before Him.

Lifting my heart to God I prayed that He would raise up some-one like this Jesus today, one who could perform miracles and deliver us from all this persecution and discrimination. It had been a story with a truly happy ending. I read on, delighted with the miraculous change in events.

The incidents took place in a clear and precise manner, easy to understand, yet puzzling in reality.

Why had I never been told about this part of our history? It clearly was a historic event, yet it never had been mentioned during my junior or senior education.

I had to find out and I would!

During the next forty days this living Prophet showed Himself to many, still teaching, still pointing people to God and talking about His future; about His invisible reign through the Spirit once He had left the earth. He told those standing around too, that He would 'return in like manner'.

That was that!

From now onwards one read how He worked through all those lives which allowed Him to use them, as a tool. This was pictured in a very realistic way.

Then my favourite portion began. It taught me more than almost anything I had learned previously. It spoke of an orthodox Jew, a Rabbi. He, too, was confronted, like myself, with the new Prophet and His claim of Messiah. He had never met Him, but had heard all about Him and believed that it was a hoax, someone blasphemously claiming to be sent from God. He would fight for the faith of his fathers: the preservation of the truth: the one Eternal God. There was born one who was to fight a holy war, one whose aim was to destroy those who called themselves Christians. Permission to do this was granted to him and letters of introduction to Synagogues in other parts of the country were safely tucked away in his leather pouch.

166

As he journeyed along thinking about the ridiculous situation to which his people had succumbed, he heard his name being called. Repeatedly he looked at his fellow travellers, who in turn wondered about their leader's behaviour. Who then was calling his name? Hesitantly he ventured to talk to apparently no one. 'Who art Thou, Lord?' The answer was the severest blow the young Rabbi had encountered during his professional career. 'I am that Jesus, whom you are persecuting.'

He could not see anyone. All of a sudden his eyes were blinded. His fellow companions didn't quite know how to console or calm him. He wanted to be alone to think. He had been humiliated and defeated by the very Prophet he sought to destroy.

When he arrived at his destination, he was a different man. The new believers there were frightened of him, knowing his reputation. They feared a strange trick when he wanted to join them. Those who had been awaiting him were also at a loss, for instead of denouncing this apostle Jesus, he uplifted Him in all his conversation and humbly acknowledged His living personality, telling everyone about his extraordinary experience on the Damascus Road.

Yes, it was a moving and realistic story and according to these writings this Jesus was alive, living again through the lives of those who allowed Him to use them.

A beautiful account, but not of much use for me or my people who were hunted from generation to generation. Why did Almighty God allow all this hardship, suffering and death? Where was the answer?

14

I HAD READ A LOT IN THE PAST FEW WEEKS. IT HAD KEPT me quiet and probably widened my outlook. The daily monotony took over once more. We heard horrible reports from the cities. Arrests and atrocities continued and we were tired of waiting for the end.

Domie hardly came home now. He was suspected of illegal activity. Rumours had to be taken seriously; one could not afford to take a risk. Sometimes he came after dark for a brief spell with his wife, to bring us news or to help us with any trouble that had to be faced. Long before sunrise he would be gone, once more on his way through the high cornfields opposite the manse, his trusted territory. If the enemy was near, the corn would protect and afford a means of escape.

His visits became fewer and fewer. The strain, tension and worry increased each day. The manse was under suspicion. Quick action was called for.

One night in April 1944, when we were assembled in the kitchen we heard that familiar knock at our back door. It was Domie. We sensed at once that something important was afoot and we called Aunt Jo.

Domie told us that orders had been circulated for his arrest. The manse might be searched. We all had to leave. Accommodation for each one of us had been arranged, and our exodus would begin at midnight tomorrow. What we had feared so long had come to pass.

Each one dwelt on their own position. Each one craved for survival. Yet no one could do anything. We had to wait and see what was planned for us. Our lives were in their hands. Quietly we went through the evening routine, only more thoroughly than usual. All possible clues had to be destroyed. We packed a few personal toilet articles and went to bed.

The next day was unusually burdensome. It was the last time we were ever all together.

'Oh for a Jesus Christ today', I thought. If ever I needed assurance regarding the living God, it was that day. That night we were to be taken to an unknown destination. I needed Him to give me courage; I coveted deeply His assurance of protection.

The two boys were very composed. They went about their daily tasks quietly. After an early evening meal Aunt Jo asked us to get dressed and bring to the dining-room all we intended to take with us. All that I had fitted comfortably into my little black case. Clothing was unimportant. My body could take care of that. I wore several pairs of stockings and socks, a few sets of underwear, dress, skirt, pullover, jacket and coat. Walking was rather a cumbersome job, but all these things had to be taken care of and would be necessary if I reached my new home.

Aunt Jo had settled herself at the piano. She played her own Church songs. They sounded bright and sensible. The boys sang tonight and so did she. We girls listened and some of us followed the words in the little song book. Personally, I wouldn't have minded singing some of them, if only that name 'Jesus Christ' hadn't appeared on practically every page. I couldn't bring myself to pronounce it. A solution was easily found. I *did* sing! Once I got the tune I began to sing, but all honour ascribed to Jesus, I, in turn, passed on to Moses! Whenever they assured their Lord and Master of implicit child-like trust in times of danger, I assured Moses of the strength I gained from his fine example and service to God and man. 'What a friend we have in Jesus' became 'What a friend we have in Moses'.

This singing session was the nearest I had known to normal life for more than a year. It passed the time through the hours of dusk till we all had to leave and it lifted the strain from our heavily taxed shoulders.

They came for me first. I shook hands with everyone, thanked Aunt Jo and Tantje for all they had done, and waddled, heavily clothed, out of the room. Aunt Jo saw me to the back door and asked if there was anything else I needed. I had hoped she would ask me. There was no other way to tell her. Rather shyly I asked if she would allow me to take the little black book from upstairs with all the Bible Stories, and if she could spare it, one of the song books we had used that night. Not at all surprised she consented and asked me to wait a moment while she fetched them. It was the first time I had openly mentioned the strange book.

The police officer had arrived; it was time to leave. Could it be imagination or was Aunt Jo's kiss warmer this time? While passing through the dark garden I picked a pansy and slipped it carefully into my book. I treasure it to this very day, pressed among the pages of my little black book.

As when I arrived, so now, I travelled on the back of a bicycle. The journey was almost as long, and just as uncomfortable, although I was more padded than on the previous occasion! Our journey ended before a row of grey stone labourer's cottages. The police officer rang the bell of one of the houses. The door was opened, but no one could be seen or heard. No words were exchanged, but an arm stretched out and pulled me inside. Once the door was shut and bolted, a voice whispered, "Sorry, no light, my dear, no one must know you've come, you see."

It was a relief to know that the ordeal had passed so quickly and without incident. The lady was kind and informed me that they had one other illegal person in their home. I would have to share the bed inside the wall cupboard. The doors were opened at night but closed during the day. As at the manse we were only allowed to move at night, but more care had to be observed in this new abode. A ladder from the hall through a skylight led to the attic. We climbed this ladder early each morning before the sitting-room curtains could be opened and the blackout removed. The hatch was then closed and we had to endure silence till the hatch opened for the delivery of meals or for an occasional chat if no visitors were expected.

A pail with lid provided for our personal needs up there. Did my new landlady wonder why a broad smile spread over my face? I gloried in the promotion to a 'Pail-and-lid mouse'. Now I had the status of the Manse Mice. 'Where are they?' I wondered. As I began to drift dreamily along this line of thought I must have missed some of the instructions. However, I was soon brought back to reality as she prepared to introduce me to my bedmate and fellow 'Diver', as we illegals were conveniently called.

She led me to the little sitting-room at the front of the house, opened the door and there . . . standing beside the table in this small room was Sister Moony—a department Sister of our Amsterdam hospital, dreaded by most juniors!

Sister Moony! No, I needed no introduction. We knew each other too well and this meeting took me entirely by surprise. Smiling faintly she shook my hand. I, in turn, felt it my duty to reciprocate by producing a faint smile as well.

Once this formal, unnecessary introduction was over, I waited automatically till she offered me a seat. A duty atmosphere was in existence!

My new landlady, who introduced herself as Tantje's sister, brought each of us a mug of hot chocolate and some biscuits. Then it was time to prepare for bed. Sister Moony led the way. At night we were permitted to use the kitchen for washing. I followed wherever she led me . . . ultimately to bed.

Bed was the cupboard behind the doors which I had seen previously. The mattress was held firmly between the wall and an outer horizontal plank. The bed was immaculate and I was invited to get in first. Sister Moony pushed a chair near to the doors and I began my journey-on to the chair—over the plank, kneel on the creaking bed—rub the soles of my feet against each other to lose the last speck of dust before partly disappearing under the blankets on my side of the bed.

Sister Moony—in bed with me! The nurses' home in the hospital would have been split wide open with hilarious laughter but I felt no such temptation. On the contrary, as soon as my head touched the pillow, I crossed my ankles and folded my arms. Sister made herself comfortable and insisted I move over another two inches. Now my left side rested against the wall. Pulling the blanket over that shoulder I began to contemplate this new situation, but my mind soon went blank, and I slept the sleep of exhaustion.

Next morning Sister Moony wakened me with tea and bread which I consumed as soon as I managed to sit upright. Still feeling sleepy, I was in no mood for conversation. This suited the boss who began instructions to her junior. I must rise as soon as I had finished my tea, make the bed, close the doors, wash in the kitchen and follow her to the attic.

Doing as I had been instructed, I soon reached a tiny room among the thick beams. This quick ascent was greeted with a smile of approval. The ladder was removed, the latch closed and we settled down to quietness till the hour of release, at Sunset.

Downstairs the husband began to pull up all blinds, open the windows and doors, answer the milkman and baker. No one suspected that up in the attic two human being were awaiting a favourable end to the war. I was sad and unhappy in my new surroundings. It was exasperating to have Moony around me all day, and probably she felt the same about me. It is difficult to learn the lesson of forbearance and patience!

We saw our landlady only three times each day—halfway through the morning, when she opened the hatch and handed us potatoes and vegetables to clean, lunchtime, and in the afternoon, if the house was free, to hand up a cup of tea.

The rest of the day I was under Moony's authority. Every morning after we had settled down for the day there was a short lecture on the benefit of healthy bodies in time of physical restraint. These bodies had to be exercised to keep them supple, fit and healthy. She would show me what to do. Then I began to realise why we didn't get fully dressed downstairs: 'gymnastics' was her ever important theme.

It must have been funny both of us marching round behind one another in stocking soles and underskirts! Moony's hair hung down her back and swung to and fro with every jerky movement. Whether I felt like it or not, I had to follow Moony around that attic, morning after morning.

During the long hours of each day I often tried to make conversation, but soon realised that there, too, I was an intruder. She was interested in conversation only when she could tell me 'what to do'! We developed our own mode of life.

No news of the war reached us. We depended on what the enemy broadcasts stated or explained. We only existed. I became dull and very passive. The manse life had been more active, especially in the evenings. The mice and the boys would discuss matters of interest and I could listen and learn, while Nopje and Tantje popped in and out with news, humour, or just a cup of tea. This was like solitary confinement, as my companion was not interested in my presence, indeed resented this intrusion into her haven of safety and quiet. She didn't want cheering-up, conversation or discussion. We lived, ate and slept together, yet we were miles apart.

I turned again to the God of my fathers and began to read my little black book. I made no effort to hide my interest and her presence did not worry me. The attic became my cloister. I learned more during my brief stay there than I did anywhere else in the years that lay ahead.

The Psalms, the Kings and Prophets and once more the New Testament thrilled me. It seemed strange that all the stories of the Children's Bible were in this little book as well as our old scriptures. They fitted in and I delighted to read them. In the fifth Book of Moses, chapter eighteen and verse fifteen, Moses talked of a new prophet to rise from amidst the nation. He should be heard and obeyed. To me this was none other than this outstanding Person, this Jesus Christ, born into our nation, one of our kith and kin, brought up in the law and prophets. He spoke with authority and full knowledge of our history, our backsliding, our means of return and restoration.

The room we occupied in this grey stone house attic was small, but attractively furnished and decorated. While the mice in the manse had only the bare essentials we enjoyed a splash of colour in furnishings and decoration. Instead of the actual countryside, we could look at pictures representing the finest scenery of a free country. When continual sitting became tedious and a strain, a divan along one wall allowed us to stretch out. Mrs. Goody cared for us with true concern and love. Our meals were wholesome and nourishing: nothing was lacking except our freedom.

And so we lived, or rather existed together, by day and by night. Sister didn't allow her junior to forget her place nor her professional standards. I was a prisoner in a double sense. I had to do as I was told by her, who was my superior in years, rank and sentence. I complied with the wisest course under those circumstances!

Days and weeks dragged by. Horrified, I discovered that all gladness had drained from me. Would I ever know how to laugh again? Laughter hadn't been in evidence for many months. It was dangerous from the noise point of view, and indeed what cause for laughter could be found in such monotonous conditions? To think that I had ceased to be glad, I who had to be constantly checked by teacher and parents alike for my happy-go lucky way of living; I had forgotten how to laugh! This realisation frequently brought tears to my eyes. It made me even sadder and lonelier than before. 'Whom have I in heaven beside Thee and who is there in earth whom I would desire above Thee', was the deep cry of my heart.

More and more my thoughts turned to the God of the impossible.

He was explained and portrayed so clearly by this prophet Jesus Christ, that I almost felt that I knew Him—that I could depend on Him—that I could take Him at His word and live according to His advice. It only worried me when this Jesus Christ made definite claims regarding His purpose on earth or His authority; or proclaimed His apparent divinity and the part He played in our approach to the Almighty Creator of the Universe. Some of His own words would come to me:

'No man cometh unto the Father, but by Me.'

'I am the Way, the Truth, and the Life.'

'Come unto Me . . . and I will give you rest.'

'All power is given to Me in heaven and in earth.'

'I am come that they might have life.'

Unconsciously, He had stolen His way into my life, and I could no more think of God the Father without visualising Jesus Christ. Slowly but surely, God became a reality in my thoughts. I learned to consider Him; weighing my actions and aims as they would affect Him and His cause.

Wistfully I wondered if He would use me in the same way that He had called and used others throughout history, so clearly described in the Old Testament Scriptures. I would love to be in His school, learn from Him and be a blessing to others, whatever the cost.

As day succeeded day He must have drawn me closer and closer to His heart, for my Scriptures were a constant oasis in this perplexing and frustrating desert of underground existence.

When I read of how God called His people to Himself, I marvelled at His patience and shuddered when I saw the hardness of their idol worship—ignoring the God of their Fathers, depending on their own strength, rather than turning to the source of all wisdom. So steeped were they in tradition and monotonous religious observances, oblivious of the fresh wind of personal contact with the Almighty, who wanted to act as their Father.

Meanwhile I feasted on the vast variety of revelation which presented itself to my eagerly questioning heart and mind. The fact that this Jesus Christ was so intensely Jewish and yet so opposed by the leaders of that day, was a continual puzzle. After all, we knew that God had promised us a Messiah, the one who would open up a straight way for sinful man to His Fatherheart. A true Lamb

174

of God which would take away the sins of the world, a new and permanent substitute for the Temple sacrifices which no longer could be held.

What reason did we have to disbelieve this Jesus, when He claimed that He was that promised Messiah who would die for our sins and rise again to be the first of those to conquer death?

Public opinion? Public opinion voted against Him and won! The masses listened to second-hand reports, put about by those who wanted supreme control of Temple affairs and taxes, those who wanted nothing new. They wished to retain the monotony of stale tradition without a breath of life.

It had all happened so long, long ago. If I had been there at the time, would I have joined Him, followed Him, served Him? Of course I would, I reasoned with myself. He was worthy of the devotion of every human heart, and therefore of mine. Such a pity that it had no bearing on life today, yet I liked this additional prophet, this Sinless Servant of all and yet apparently their Master.

This new discovery commanded my undivided attention. The New Testament became to me a more and more up-to-date account with a similarity to events which were taking place in our own age. I could imagine Domie, Aunt Jo, Tantje, Nopje and Sietje as disciples of Jesus Christ.

The thing which never ceased to baffle my questioning mind, was the strange phenomenon that all the people I knew who followed Him were not Jewish at all, and had no apparent connection with Judaism, its religion or tradition—they were Gentiles of all nations, yet they prayed to the God of Abram, Isaac and Jacob. They sang the psalms of David and read the prophecies and were interested in Israel as a country. If they left this Prophet and His name out of their prayers and songs, they could be Jews of a high and sincere status, and could be instructed in our rituals and dietary laws and strengthen our ranks beneficially.

As it was, the whole scene appeared upside down. The Gentiles used *our* Holy Writ, learned from *our* prophets, worshipped Almighty God and His messengers, and yet . . . they were not Hebrews.

If these war days taught me anything worthwhile, it was the true Biblical history of my people, their aspirations and hopes, their longing for God's revelation in a Messiah of His choice.

175

A plaque above the door in our little attic attracted me. The message was true, as if the dead thing knew me through and through, 'Man looketh on the outward appearance, but the Lord looketh on the heart' (I Samuel 16.7). So true! Neither Sister Moony, nor anyone else knew my heart, my searchings, my contemplations; they all saw the outward appearance, only God knew my heart!

He knew that I would be His servant if I could. He knew that day by day over the past few months, my love and devotion for Him had increased. He knew that I believed that this Jesus was our Messiah and that I was bewildered that my people did not recognise Him as such and give Him their individual allegiance. God wanted to use the Jewish people to be a blessing to the world, wherever we might be situated. Instead, we lived like introverts, denying our revelation and rejecting the redeeming gift of God.

No one had seen God at anytime; this Jesus claimed that He came from God and explained His greatness, majesty and nature by living among us. But He died; then rose again. Death could not hold Him, the Bible claimed. He opened up a new life, showing us immortality and the opportunity of eternal life through faith in His sacrificial death for us. He came to die for us so that through His death and resurrection we might be cleansed, forgiven.

A vital truth surged through my very being—death and . . . life! He's alive! He worked and pleaded still with humanity, it was *He* who had been busy with me all these months. His vast almighty and penetrating Holy Spirit had pierced my iron curtain of reasoning.

'Rabboni, Master, *my* Master and my God!' A supreme sense of absolute safety and belonging filled my excited and happy being. Within seconds meaning, purpose and security presented itself to my reason. There was hope for this world, hope through this unknown Saviour, this Jesus Christ.

To the amazement of Sister Moony, I left my potatoes half peeled, laid down my knife, rose from my stool and without an explanation left the little room. Outside among the attic beams and in a little corner of the roof, I slowly knelt down, clasped my hands in absolute surrender and closed my eyes to all around.

'Rabboni Joshua Hamoschiach, Master Jesus Christ!' It was all I could whisper. Deep thankfulness and love to Almighty God for His inexplicable revelation and gift flooded my entire being.

God cared! He cared after all! He was interested in His people!

If it is possible to be humbly-proud, I surely was that. I belonged! Belonged for time and eternity to the God of my Fathers, the God of Abram, Isaac and Jacob, because of the mediating death and resurrection of the sinless Lamb of God, Joshua Hamoschiach. No more did I fear my enemies. If I was arrested I knew it would be God's will that I should enter a situation to bring His comfort to others. Was I ready for such a task? I was no Paul, or Peter. I'd only known my Master for minutes. Again Biblical truths flooded my mind. 'Have not I made the mouth? I shall be with you; I shall go before you. I shall give you to speak in that hour, what you should say. Only be strong and of a good courage. Heal the sick, cleanse the lepers, proclaim the good and acceptable year of the Lord.'

Privilege went hand in hand with responsibility. I wasn't to be allowed to rest in my joy and happiness. He had chosen me as a channel. All He required was my willingness to be used by Him for whatever He required.

That day I was truly emptied, an empty channel. If only I didn't choke it by selfish interests or foolish fears. 'Pray without ceasing! Watch and pray that ye enter not into temptation!' There they were once more, the words from the Scriptures. My heart was lifted up almost continually. He remained close and dear and was always interested in all my doings. He listened to my regrets and His advice was always correct.

By the end of that day, Easter Monday 1944, Sister Moony, having watched me curiously, asked why I seemed so pleased with myself. Not having spoken with her, I was surprised that she knew. I was conscious of suppressing a smile at times but didn't realise that my inward happiness had spilled over and made her wonder.

What could I say? "Almighty God is really terrifically wonderful," I beamed. At this she frowned, peered into my face, then shrugged her shoulders, sighed and went on with her book.

Inwardly I repeated 'terrific and wonderful'. Yes, He was all that and much more, but we, His creations, were so far away from His will and His purpose for our individual lives. Futhermore, my people . . . their unnecessary suffering . . . the fear among young and old . . . the premature murderous death of all those millions

. . . war . . . hatred. *God* was terrific and wonderful, but why not *we* His children? Were we His only in name now? Had we, as a people, gone our own way, become introverts instead of listeners and His obedient followers?

Oh! All the world was in a muddle; all the world was full of turmoil; all the world! The world consists of people. People young and old. This means I reasoned, that change of attitude, a change of heart by individuals would make a better world. *Individuals make or mar the world!*

Here I was, I could not do otherwise, I'd love to follow the way of God mapped out by the Lord Jesus Christ. It spelt love, truth, purity, freedom, joy, salvation and perfect assurance of a living eternity in Christ's presence.

'Don't fear what men do unto you, they can only kill the body but not the soul. Fear rather Him who can destroy both body and soul in hell.'

That was strong language, but He had said so, and His words are spirit and truth.

During the next few weeks I simply devoured all I could of both the Old and New Testaments. A new world lay before me, a life that was endless and a future that was secure however much men interfered. My mind and heart more active than ever before, I knew myself secure, cared for and of value to the Majestic Creator of this universe. I suddenly knew myself rich, with riches no one could take away.

This gift of 'security' came at just the right time. Mrs. Goody gently broke the news to me that I could not stay with them till the end of the war. It was too dangerous in such a small house to cope with two illegal persons. She was not too sure of her grocer, baker, butcher, etc. Ordering food for two and buying what was necessary for four people could easily arouse suspicions.

During the next few days events moved rapidly. We had visits from the courageous nursemaid of the manse and from Tantje. They brought news and equipment for false identification cards, finger prints and passport photographs. The items were equally divided between them and safely tucked inside their brassieres.

My name, date of birth and address were false, while a real fingerprint and photograph ensured a semblance of reality. All further preparations were completed without my knowledge. I would be collected, handed over, deposited, re-collected, changing hands several times and deposited again. This process would continue during the long journey South and although no one was aware of it at the time, it actually continued to the very end of the war. I would never know how long I would stay at one house or in one village. Most people would introduce themselves by an illegal name or none at all.

While Uncle Bas was our key figure in the North, Uncle Henk was his counter part in the South. A sensitive spider's web of trustworthy people and homes were at his command. He endeavoured to find hideouts suiting the needs and temperament of those seeking refuge. It did not always work out satisfactorily, but his efforts were tireless.

Soon I, too, would enter this conveyor belt of human ingenuity, but as transporting could only be done on dark and cloudy nights, I had to wait for one more week. It gave me time to prepare myself mentally for the most daring ordeal yet.

But first I had to go for a night and a day to the manse. This bit of information gave me great pleasure. It would be wonderful to see my old haunts again, to finger the books which were so dear, and to speak with Aunt Jo about my Saviour and Master, the Christ who had revealed the God of my Fathers to my searching heart.

Sister Moony's good-bye was as cool as had been her general attitude over the past few weeks. She wouldn't miss me, of that I was certain. Glad to be alone in her domain once more, my departure was a matter of delight to us both.

15

IT WAS PITCH-BLACK WHEN I LEFT QUIETLY BY THE
front door, walking smartly away with a gentleman who passed
our door at the appointed time and signal.

Two bicycles waited at the far end of the next street. When I was
handed one I realised what was expected of me. Silently we cycled
along the dark country road until we reached the manse. Once
more I entered by that familiar backdoor remembering a similar
entry some nine months before.

Aunt Jo awaited me with a delightful supper. This time it
seemed as if I were a Queen. I almost felt sorry for poor Sister
Moony in that lonely attic. Yet she had seemed happy and un-
disturbed. She had no enthusiastic Francisca to ruffle her smooth
waters now.

My kingdom was very quiet, almost unnaturally so without all
the familiar faces and temperaments. A night and a day was all I
would spend in this house which I would enter no more. I slept
little that night, yet I rested unafraid of all that was before me:
One more day, a day of mental preparation for what was to be the
biggest ordeal yet.

As dawn approached I dropped off to sleep. It was nearly midday
when I woke up refreshed and rested, ready to listen to all the
important instructions for the coming night.

Aunt Jo was as calm as usual and so was I. It now seemed a
thrilling adventure to beat arrest and death continually and in so
many different ways. After dinner we moved into Domie's study
and Aunt Jo began to talk. Her instructions were short, to the
point and unemotional. Only at the end she added smilingly,
"Remember, it is written: 'Lo I am with you always, even unto
the end of the world'."

My nod of the head assured her that I understood. Of course I
knew that I depended on God's presence with me right through
danger into the safety of yet another home.

There was little more conversation during the evening hours. What could we say? Everyone's life was so disjointed, broken and lonely. Aunt Jo had to face the rest of the war on her own. Uncle Bas couldn't come home anymore. Arrest and perhaps the death penalty was all he could expect if he were caught. Yet on an occasional dark night, a tall lean figure would emerge from the cornfield and tap the familiar rhythm of the secret code on the shutters of the window. He would spend a brief moment with his loving wife, his partner and help through these difficult years. He couldn't see or touch his son for the boy was now at an age when sheer enthusiasm would tell everyone that 'Daddy had been home'.

Our thoughtful silence was interrupted by the hymns which Aunt Jo played and replayed, as if to impress their message on my heart. Tantje had joined us. Language was unnecessary. The atmosphere was filled with the presence of Him Who was our security and Friend. An occasional humming of the tunes being played was the only other sound.

'Uncle Bas, that shepherd of the sheep, that true pastor of the needy, would have prayed with us', I thought. 'I'm sure Aunt Jo and Tantje would be able to do that too', I reasoned; just to commit me into the care of the Almighty. 'I'd love that', I thought, the way my father had placed his hands on my head that dark night when he was arrested. I could almost feel, at that moment, both his hands on my head and hear a mumbling of words. Yes, I would ask for prayer.

"Tantje, could I see you for a minute? Alone?" Surprised, she looked at me and nodded with her usual big grin.

Beckoning me to follow her, she left the room. "Well?" she enquired in the hall.

"Would you pray for me, Tantje, pray with me now, before I go away?"

A scarlet flush transformed her face within seconds. I then realised that no one had ever asked her to do that before.

We went into another room. She didn't light the lamp as the black-out had not yet been attended to. Expectantly I sat on the nearest chair, my hands folded in surrender and my eyes closed.

After a short silence, Tantje spoke, slowly and simply. She addressed our invisible Master reverently. Confidently she asked Him to take good care of us all during the coming night, to let all plans work out smoothly and to restrain the enemy, foiling any Satanic raids and arrests. "Let all be still this night to let these people escape freely." After the 'Amen' we joined the others. Aunt Jo told us that the time had come. Everything was timed precisely; we had to keep strictly to schedule.

This was the real 'good-bye'. We all realised it and made it short.

The weather had changed in our favour. It was stormy, dark and dry when Nopje and I left this dear, dear house. The lashing rain during the day had penetrated the hard clay road and the railway line. The ground was soggy and our wellingtons were sucked repeatedly into slithery bogs. Walking was hard work but we had to keep going. Our object was the 'Urlaub-train', only for Wehrmacht, which crossed over the border at 1.15 a.m.

Having left at 11.30 p.m. we found ourselves well into the wilds by midnight. It was pitch black and who could blame us for shaking with cold and terror when we saw two small lights coming our way? The order 'On your tummies, don't move' was obeyed instantly. When the patrol had passed and their lights well away, we continued our trip. Soon we reached the railway line. Nopje placed her stick with a white sock attached, firmly in the ground. It had to guide her on the return trip. From that point, continuing in a straight line, she would reach the safety of the manse once more.

We struggled along the right side of the rails towards the station. This would be the longest lap, nearly one hour, and the clay was so soft and slippery all the way. Near the end two more people came in our direction. One carried a light and we took shelter for a moment. Then Nopje followed them and I noticed that one was very tall. Domie! The other, an officer, walked ahead and we all followed at the given sign. We walked smartly and purposefully so as not to arouse suspicion. At last the firm concrete of the platform was under our feet. We took off our wellingtons and changed back into clean shoes.

Everything depended on the next five minutes. No fear must enter our hearts, yet mine was thumping and puffing in rhythm with that engine.

Nopje pressed my hand lovingly and firmly, then I walked on with Domie. He opened the door of the nearest carriage. We were in the 'belly of the whale'. It was the Urlaub-train all right, packed with Wehrmacht returning from leave and now going back to the front line, back to duty.

I marvelled at the calm way in which Domie sought to settle me for this long and dangerous trip. In speech and mannerisms he fitted in well with the soldiers in uniform and civilian clothes. Roughly sliding open compartment door after compartment door he shouted: "Nirgends Platz? Schrecklich." No seats anywhere? It was necessary to shout in German, for it didn't arouse suspicion. I kept close behind him, wondering where he would land me eventually. Then my fate was decided. He pushed me forward and exclaimed: *"Na Endlich! Aufwiedersehn und gute Reise!"

"Until Utrecht," he added more quietly and looked deep into my eyes. That meant everything to me. Then he gave me his pastoral blessing and committed me into the care of the Shepherd of our souls. The compartment door slammed shut and in the dim light I moved slowly towards the only vacant seat. Who ever could imagine me here? Who ever had ceased to believe in miracles?

My seven soldier companions blinked a sleepy eye at me, I excused myself in proper German and everyone went back to sleep as if doped by a power from on high. Strangely enough I, too, was ready for sleep and settled myself comfortably among them and drifted off into dreamland.

As this was the only stop on the other side of the border, the train rattled on towards Utrecht. When it eventually jerked to a halt, everyone wakened almost at the same time grinning at one another.

Calmly and slowly I rose, stretched and rubbed my eyes once more then left with a kind **"Aufwiedersehn, alles Gūte!"

That was that! I felt refreshed when I slipped on to the platform already busy with milling crowds. Ordinary people, men and women going to work. It was exciting to mingle with people and to be one among many. While enjoying the glories of my present state, someone came straight towards me, using the deceptive German. I was greeted like an old friend. "Gute Reise gehabt?"*

This was the password, and joining in the game, I walked alongside him towards the next link in the chain. It was another train on

---

* "At last! Well, good-bye, and a safe journey!"
** "Cheerio, all the best!"
* "Did you have a good journey?"

another platform and my companion placed me in a special compartment. Two people smiled at me. They seemed to be father and son, and I smiled back. Contact had been established and we continued an apparent unattached relationship.

This part of the journey was almost normal. It was wonderful to be 'free' and look, move and act like an ordinary person. As it was still early morning and I had no one to talk to, I settled into a happy and relaxed spell of daydreaming.

Hungry as I was, I realised that eating was quite out of the question. Slipping another sugar lump into my mouth I felt fully satisfied and continued my daydreaming with closed eyes.

This was to be a long day, a long journey. It was most fortunate that a healthy sleep overtook me most of the time. I was hungry no longer. The body becomes acclimatised to situations like this. The silence between my fellow travellers was hardly noticed; everyone seemed busy with their own private thoughts and no one felt it necessary to break it.

Towards evening we entered the most southern part of Holland. I'd never been here before. Even the countryside looked different to that at home. Everywhere there were hills and valleys, quaint villages and far more churches. It looked like the evening rush hour. The passing stations were packed and the roads were amazingly busy too. Our train did not stop at every station, but the compartment began to empty itself slowly. At last the two men and I were alone. The older man was around forty years of age and the younger one, introduced to me as his son Dirk, was about eighteen years of age. After a friendly welcome they gave me a sandwich box containing slices of bread and cheese still juicy and fresh. The boy had a small fruitshop in his pocket and the orange he produced was a slice of new life for me! Not much was said until they realised I was now ready for the next step.

Heerlen! We left the train and mingled with the rush hour crowd. Everything was timed perfectly. They took me to a lonely farm outside the city boundary where a delightful meal awaited us. I was allowed to wash and change my clothes. Once properly laundered they would do some other young girl. My new outfit suited me remarkably well. I began to feel the thrill of adventure.

Oom Henk and my hostess withdrew to discuss the arrangements for the next twenty-four hours. Dirk and I discussed superficial matters including the ever pressing remarks about the weather.

When our Seniors returned, we learned that their decision was to make use of the last dark night and deport me at once after midnight. Here I was called Francisca officially, as my false identity card confirmed this now. I was now two-in-one. Soon I learned to be one. My new name became part of me, my age, occupation and address practically a reality. I lived and moved as Francisca Dobber.

Our way ran through cornfields. It was dark, but not cold and far more peaceful and less frightening than the previous night's journey down South. Gentle breezes waved the corn gracefully and made it sizzle like a panful of nourishing chips.

Why all this care and love and detailed attention to see me through? Why were so many endangering their own and their families' lives? For me?

I learned from my guides that while I was being conducted to safety terrible things had happened to my fellow undergrounders. The mice had been caught, after being placed in selected families by people like Oom Henk, Dirk and Domie. Some traitors had smelled out the illegals and betrayed them for material gain. The mole, best friend of the mice, had guided and guarded their travels but he, too, had been caught.

He was strong and fit and had a chance of surviving, but the mice, especially the little one, couldn't stand up to it. Suddenly arrested, she was dragged to a prison in Amsterdam, then to a camp in Westerbork and from there. . . .

The worst was confirmed by a letter which reached Aunt Jo some time later:

'Friday afternoon, while standing on the station at W. I saw a long train passing which had come from the central camp at Westerbork. From one of the cattle trucks, three women, standing behind an open latch covered by barbed wire called something to me. I could not get very near because the whole station was full with the enemy police force which kept people from getting closer. I knew these poor people wanted desperately to tell me something, then I made-out your name and address. They wanted to greet you once more. I hereby pass this message on to you.

Yours sincerely, Captain K.'

Would world opinion not soon melt the enemy into final surrender? How long could we and all like us hold on? How many thousands more had to be sacrificed by bombing, starvation and murder, torture, gas chambers and notorious terror before the final end was in sight?

Preservation? One *had* to go on. No more surrender could be tolerated from us since we had been saved so long and at so great a cost.

We arrived at a quiet little street and oom Henk tapped his secret code message on the window. A door opened and we entered the dark house. Once fully sealed off, the lights went on in a small room. It was difficult to see at first, having been out in the dark for nearly two hours.

We exchanged greetings in a whisper while I expressed my usual words of thanks for 'having me'. A cup of tea was poured out and after eating some food oom Henk and Dirk took their leave.

I did not like to see them go. They were the last link with my dear people up North. Oom Henk assured me, however, that he would be back in a few days' time.

Quietly my new housemother guided me to a room with a double bed. Her teenage daughter was sleeping and I had just to slip in beside her. She knew I was expected and would meet me in the morning if I was awake before she left for work.

Hesitantly I tiptoed around in the unfamiliar bedroom. Hesitantly too, I endeavoured to avoid the unavoidable; sleeping in the same bed with an absolute stranger. Sister Moony was bad enough, but now this! All the time my conscience hammered inside me with thumps of indignation. Was I daring to question or reject those who endangered their own lives, sacrificing their comforts in order to save me? Furthermore what about those many thousands who knew nothing of this luxury offered to me? The thought of them shook me into acceptance.

Having carefully attended to personal necessities, I stepped just as carefully into the 'pre-heated' bed. Sheer exhaustion took over and soon I knew no more.

The sun was high in the sky when I opened my eyes. The space beside me was cold indicating that my bed-mate must have left long ago. Daydreaming had become a pleasant occupation.

The room was barely furnished, only necessities and a few cheap ornaments on a very battered chest of drawers. The bed had, well, not quite clean sheets, and this made me push the top sheet from my chin, but . . . I was safe!

No one in the camps had warmth and shelter like I had. How ghastly for the mice and the mole! Secretly I wished for them what I had wished for my own relations, that soon their sufferings would be ended.

The door opened slowly and quietly. A cheery and healthy looking face popped round the door. "Are you awake?" my hostess enquired. "Here, put these slippers on if they fit, I've made a fresh pot of coffee for us both."

I did like that lady! Such a motherly, hearty and wholesome soul. My ideal dream of a farmer's wife. But was she? Was this a farm? Who was she anyhow and where was I? Did it matter? Of course it didn't. One didn't ask and didn't want to know. She called me Francisca and I called her Moeke. Every one was just Mum and Dad.

The day dragged along slowly, I helped with simple and quiet jobs. If you had two hands and a willing heart you seemed to be acceptable anywhere. This home was no exception. Every now and then a rewarding smile made me understand that my Moeke was pleased with her charge.

At last it was time for the evening meal. I met the teenage daughter properly. A nice bright girl who just happened to nurse a little nervous twitch in her eye. Rather attractive, I thought.

As we chatted during the evening hour, I sensed she harboured a kind of sorrow for me. Here we were together, discussing subjects of equal interest to us both and yet living lives which were miles apart. The one had freedom, the other enforced captivity. One a life of planning, the other just a patient waiting. Hers a life of sacrificial sharing, mine, of necessity, that of a helpless recipient. Her nature indicated her mother's true and genuine friendliness. There was just one factor which made me shudder with horror and fear . . . her hair was alive! And I had lain so near her the previous night and would have to do so in the nights to come. And, oh, I hated these little beggars! No, I must not show my fear to my new found friend. She must have grown accustomed to her inhabitants and caressed them now and then with a dainty gesture of her fingernails.

That night I invented an excuse, and laid a towel on *my* part of the pillow then casually wrapped it round my head. Jokingly, I told her that I felt it draughty at night. She thought it funny but did not seek to stop me doing what I wanted. Our conversation at this stage was soon overpowered by healthy sleep.

At the crack of dawn we rubbed our eyes. "Did I keep you awake?" I enquired. Probably she wasn't used to sharing a bed either. She assured me that it was just 'one of those nights' and that it had nothing to do with me. This I doubted, but appreciated her tact.

Tomorrow would be the third day and oom Henk would come to check if I had settled down and if Moeke wanted to keep me. This was a transitional period and the family were carefully considering the keeping of a permanent refugee. Would it be me? I hoped sincerely it wouldn't. I didn't mind the place, the people, the atmosphere, but I hated the creepy-crawlies so near me at night. Could I mention them to oom Henk? One just couldn't hurt Moeke, yet she ought to know for others would feel like me in days to come if nothing was done to exterminate them. A difficult situation, probably funny in normal times.

That night I lay awake for a long, long time, almost listening for conversation among the animal life. They must have declared a state-of-emergency, the decision being 'either she goes or we go'. They knew, but their owner didn't; she slept the sleep of the righteous!

Carefully I combed my hair next morning. Very carefully indeed! As never before I studied mirror and comb. My brushing was almost furious, while standing as if bowed before a throne. Anything to descend would thus reach the floor in ease, avoiding my shoulders or the chance to fall down my neck . . . och, och . . . it sent many a shiver down my spine.

Somehow the enemy must have sensed my attitude. It seemed as if they found me entirely unworthy of invasion and permanent occupation. None had been eager to sample my island. I was still alone!

A delighted Francisca welcomed oom Henk that afternoon. He thought I looked so much brighter and really rested. He enquired how I'd settled and if I wanted to stay. In reply I elaborated Moeke's kindness and warmheartedness, the good food and the happy atmosphere in the house. I assured him of my gratefulness for all his

188

careful planning and sacrificial spending of time and money. More and more he wondered, screwing up his face into a searching attitude.

Once my stream of compliments was fully exhausted, he calmly enquired, "And what's on your mind, my dear?" You could not fool a man of his insight. Hesitantly I informed him that my bed-mate had . . . lice!

There was deadly silence for what seemed a long, long time. He nodded understandingly and mumbled, "I see, I see." I too mumbled "Sorry, sorry." I just didn't know *what* more to say. How silly to be fussy about lice, when millions faced cruelty and death! Yes, I *WAS* sorry, sorry that I minded those innocent little creatures.

Oom Henk looked serious yet his eyes and attitude did not seem to be influenced by my army of little creatures. Something was wrong somewhere! One had learned to sense an atmosphere. The enemy must be on our trail. Point blank I asked him where things had gone wrong.

"Fransje," he said with a deep sigh, "we have just beaten them! Word has come through that they have invaded the manse, searching for illegals. Thank God you had left. That one night back there evidently started new rumours. Only Aunt Jo, Tantje and the baby were in. As it was 10 o'clock when they arrived the wee fellow was sound asleep."

It was terrifying to hear of these soldiers in our manse, running through our orchard and the questioning about a 'Hole in the privet'. It was a convenient escape-route into the fields beyond, but that was none of *their* business. They had questioned Aunt Jo non stop, I was told. She had played on their human emotions by telling them that she was expecting a baby. Their rough reply was that it did not matter in the slightest even if she were expecting three babies. Then they used the unborn baby as a weapon to break her resistance and betray those for whom she had already suffered so long.

No, she had not given us away, even although in sheer irony, the inspector in charge assured her in a 'fatherly' manner that it was absolutely stupid to place the safety of herself and her whole family in jeopardy for mere Jews. . . . When that attitude had no influence on her steadfastness, he became furious and told his men

189

to get her into the lorry to continue investigation after a night in a cell at H.Q. They never gave the slightest indication where to take the little boy, so Tantje had rolled him in a blanket and deposited him with one of his 'uncle farmers'.

Before they drove Aunt Jo to the cells, they'd even searched the church across the road, after wakening the church officer at midnight with a demand for 'the key'! We were thankful they had evidently been unsuccessful, even there; who would expect to find a wireless set and receiver at the very top of a church tower.

Oom Henk had given me plenty to think about; I just marvelled how all this news could be passed on to us without post or telephone. The organisation did an extraordinary job.

We talked long and in detail about the sudden breakdown in security measures up North. We realised that meticulous care must be taken in every contemplated move here in the South.

Oom Henk agreed that for security reasons, my unhappiness in this home might prove an irritant. He would re-settle me that very night, explaining somehow to Moeke that I was unsuitable for this particular home. Reasons were never referred to.

It was not quite a moonless night when oom Henk and I set out once more on our flight. This time it was of short duration. We landed in a home at the other side of the cornfield. A staunch religious house, apparent to anyone entering. There were fonts for holy water at certain corners. Large and small crucifixes adorned the walls of the hall and bedrooms and my new Moeke wore a golden cross and chain around her neck. She was young and quite pretty. When she introduced her two children to me I stiffened with fear. The girl was just six and the boy had turned four. They realised my sudden fear and worry, and assured me that the children were 'all right', they would not speak, they understood that we had to be hidden, had to be protected by . . . them! They liked the idea and had promised not to speak about us. Us! I remonstrated? They smiled and whisked me up those stairs. Who next, I thought? They wouldn't do that to me? I was not to remain in suspense much longer: I recognised my fellow room-mate and smilingly I walked forward reaching for her outstretched hand—the assistant head of our kitchen staff in Amsterdam. We were pleased to see each other.

In this suburban home I lived a fairly normal life. Naturally Mami and I were barred from all downstairs activities, but upstairs

190

had its compensations. We had a glorious view from our window. The path among the cornfields was in direct view. We often saw Oom Henk long before he appeared at our door. He came more often to this address, using it as a sort of H.Q. for the families in this area. He was one of many visitors frequenting this home, and was not, therefore, noticed as an odd man out.

The district struck me as a devoted religious community. Mami confirmed this and told me about the many religious festivals she had watched. Many processions had passed her window and priests were seen in their flowing robes visiting the homes. Choirboys in angelic dress carried containers, swinging them from side to side, or forwards and backwards and every now and then she heard a bell.

I told her of the religious observances in my home up North and we compared notes. Both of us agreed that these people were devout Christians, yet they were different from the boys and Uncle Bas, Tantje, Nopje and all the Christians up North.

Mami and I enjoyed many a serious chat. She thought me silly, however, when I assured her that the Christians read our Bible and held our prophets in reverence. I told her about my discovery of Jesus Christ, the Jewish prophet, who claimed divinity and humanity in one.

She warned me not to meddle in such matters as the learned Jewish elders had known about this since the days of its origin. I ought to steer clear, she advised me, of false teachings and learn humbly everything about my own religion. It baffled me. "But this *is* our religion," I insisted, "the trouble is that our people *don't know* it, they *have* to be told, Mami, they *have* to."

I just couldn't understand why she asked me to calm down. She thought it was better to leave well alone. When I urged her to consider Christ's claims and search for the truth for herself, she politely asked me to keep off such subjects as it could not alter the present world turmoil. She hit me with the statement that if this Jesus Christ was *really* still alive and if God *did* care, we would still be at home with our families instead of being imprisoned here.

"But the people did not *want* him," I argued. He *is* alive, but won't *force* himself into people's lives. He wants to be *invited* to live within a human being. Then, and only then will he rule that life and others through it. It is because the majority of people from all nations do *not want* Him to rule over them that this present turmoil exists.

She shrugged her shoulders then asked me point blank, "Do you believe that He is still alive?" I assured her that I knew that for sure, as He now lived within my life, at the controls of my deepest level of reason and purpose and action.

"Well, Fransie," she sighed, "you are no longer a Jew. Such a faith makes you a Christian; you may as well leave your hiding place and mix among the Goyim" (a name describing all non Jews).

Now it was my turn to be shocked. It was almost too funny for words. "You really go too far, Mami, one doesn't stop being Jewish when the faith of one's forefathers has at long last materialised, and one feels that reality deep within one's being."

She thought differently and we spent the rest of that afternoon in deep thought. She was the first Jewish person with whom I had discussed this new found faith, but I could not fathom why this faith was 'non-Jewish' and made her almost shudder. It was more of a puzzle to me why non-Jewish people glorified in *our* past.

Truly the world was upside down in more ways than one!

16

THAT SAME WEEK I BEGGED MY FOSTER PARENTS TO ASK
their minister to pay me a visit. Mami had become very stand-offish
and I just had to find out a few things from their minister. It explained in my New Testament that Communion with Christ was
essential and that we could represent that communion with Him in
the elements of bread and wine which He once had shared with
His disciples. This thought appealed to me; I was, therefore, determined to request such a communion and its blessing from their
priest. A week or two elapsed before I noticed him in our street. I
then knew that that would be the day. It had at least given me some
time to prepare my heart and thought-life for this supreme moment.

Poor Priest, did I startle him as well? First Mami, and now him.
He was shocked at my request and replied by asking me several
'vital' questions. Was I a member of the Roman Catholic Church?
Ridiculous, of course I wasn't. Which was my Church, he wanted
to know. None, of course. He looked perplexed. I explained that I
knew nothing about Churches and its people and that I only wanted
'The Communion' because it was the wish of Jesus Christ that we
should do this 'very often in His memory'. Surely, such a wish
could be granted. *His* wish. I could get it only through a Church. It
did not matter to me *where* it came from. The clergy knew *how*
to administer it, so . . . let them grant it and give it!

Only months later did I realise that this 'Communion' was
nothing more than the normal breaking of bread and drinking of
wine which was observed regularly in most Jewish homes. Jesus
Christ had observed that habit Himself, but then one night He
gave it a unique meaning, an everlasting importance to the human
heart and soul, which made that act a deep bond between Himself
and the partaker, an eternal tie.

That day, however, a human being denied me this intimate
ceremony, as if any human being had a right to do so!

It just couldn't be correct. Jesus said '*Whosoever* will may come',

193

and, 'Come unto me *all ye* that are heavy laden . . .'. No exceptions were made by Him. He had not once asked a human being if he or she was a member of The Roman Catholic Church. I knew instantly that I was on the wrong road whatever anyone might wish to say. No explanation was good enough. After this incident I took objection to all the images around me. They were images of disciples, apostles, Christ's earthly mother and a dead Christ on the Cross. Did it not state clearly in The Ten Commandments that we must not make ourselves graven images of anything which is in heaven or on earth or under the earth. No, this was not the road to pursue. Uncle Bas' religion had been so different, so pure and clean, so friendly and full of understanding and love. I would find out some day, I thought.

My foster parents were charming anyhow. I did not mention my conversation with the priest and its effect on me. Let them think I had just looked for pastoral comfort. The clergy were among the few to be trusted with the illegal members in a home. They had had no fear in sending him up to our room.

Mami had kept to herself during our conversation. She *must* have listened in, I thought, but she would not discuss our meeting. We got on well together, in spite of our different beliefs, and many a common interest would be heatedly discussed. We laughed a lot and were happy in our comparative freedom. This pleasant situation came to an abrupt halt one lovely sunny afternoon.

Obviously we did not wear the coarse and practical underwear which was customary in this farming community. It was my silk pair of pants which betrayed us and the little six-year-old who saved us. Excitedly she had run into the kitchen "Mummy the neighbours are wondering about the pink pants on the line. They are Fransie's, Mum. Who hung them out?"

It was enough; a hasty kiss for our little saviour then oom Henk was summoned. Yes, it was only suspicion, we all realised that, but one just couldn't chance the beginning of such a rumour. For our host's and our own sake we had to leave that very night.

How many more upheavals, how many more homes and beds? Dozens. Can I remember them all? Most of them, but not all. One night here, one night there, instinct told me not to settle anywhere, to keep my belongings together. I learned of necessity to be very tidy.

We spent that first night in a transit home, oom Henk's own

house. To me it was like the manse up North. In and out. None of his teenage sons worried about who came—when; and left—when. Hence no upheaval was experienced when I entered their home suddenly that night. There was the ever ready emergency bed in the cupboard of the sitting-room wall, and I slept, convincing myself of the airtight security of this H.Q.

Next night on safari once more. Once more? Would I have dared to face the next few months if I'd been told that the life of a frog was to be mine? Here, there, everywhere. In and out of homes or byres, fields or offices. Thumping heart, panting breath at times not daring to breathe, listening and sharpening the sense of hearing for the sound of danger.

Needless to say it was a shock to me when one night no one came to collect me from the house I'd occupied the previous night. Could it be true that I was to stay in this pleasant little prefab home of a real mining family? A miner who rose at 4 a.m.—an exciting experience.

Here it would *really* be tricky to hide. A miner's prefab-cottage. Houses and houses on this side and the opposite side of our street. It was simple: stay in the back bedroom all day and move to the children's room late at night once they were asleep. Here, too, I was told 'not to worry' if the girls should see me. They were perfectly 'safe'. Fancy, another lot of four- and six-year-old chatterboxes! This was a real spell of 'hiding', no exercises all day and none at night. Just silence, complete silence and no company. Jo was busy with the usual household chores and Wiel was either down the mine or sound asleep in the room where I kept my constant vigil. It may seem an impossible situation, but aren't we all creatures of habit . . . one can get used to anything!

My summer in this happy Roman Catholic home carries only glad memories. This was a truly devoted family, almost childlike in their faith and their religious observances. We were one in our faith in Christ and our desire to please and serve Him to the best of our ability, looking constantly for His help, strength and wisdom, where our own showed its limitation and insufficiency.

We all had hoped to celebrate the end of this war together. United in our prefab we had many a daring plan for celebrations in street and the local community centre. One can, therefore, imagine our horror and shock, when, without the slightest warning, the now seldom seen oom Henk rang our doorbell. The instruction without explanation was short and to the point as usual. Constantly he looked at the still bright sky. "It seems it doesn't want to get dark tonight," he smiled. "You've got to get out of here right away, Frans," he said seriously, "someone has been talking."

Sadly we parted company that night, we who had lived so happily as one family. How I would love to see all those faithful people once more. A pilgrimage of thankfulness, recapturing the moments of long, long ago. What has become of them all? The older ones? Will they still be in this world of tears and laughter, or have they been promoted to the place where love and security exists, the universe where the true Master of our lives reigns for ever? What has become of those little ones? Would their memory stretch that far back? Do they remember the war, those strange people in their house? Most of them will be married or scattered far across the face of the earth, searching perhaps to lessen a burden or soften a sorrow as they had seen their parents do many years before.

There were some more frog-like jumps before me night by night, till eventually, another foster-home opened its doors. Here I was once more promoted to the attic. Not to avoid the child, for it was only a young baby, but Mary was worried about her own father. Both she and her husband had sought for months to find a way to alleviate the lives of the persecuted. The problem was how to fool her father who obviously sympathised with the occupying forces. He could not be fooled, the secret had simply to remain closely guarded. They would accept a persecuted child or woman, and she would live among the low beams in their attic. A person who had no hope of life would not mind deprivation, they reasoned, and it was always an extra penny for the housekeeping in these difficult days. The organisation would pay for the upkeep and apart from that . . . it was always an adventure into the bargain, although a dangerous one.

There I spent most of my time in true solitary confinement, more mental than physical. My thoughts had always been my own, but here, here it was different; one could not utter these thoughts, mould them, discuss them and get fresh ideas.

Never before did I have such close fellowship with Him, the invisible Christ, whose existence people deny. Our acquaintance became strong, our friendship secure, my dependability in Him absolutely unshakeable, a certainty which I have proved in every smallest detail till this very day.

Some of His attitudes have puzzled me. I still don't understand the depth of all His suffering for those who care to associate with Him. The free entry into a living union with Him, if an individual trusts in that divine blood, shed for him or her. I have proved this union with Christ and have also experienced that His promises are dependable and pregnant with fulfilment. With Him one can live through the toughest problems, the most dangerous situation, the loneliest experience. He promised to be with us always, and He is with us in every difficulty. One just cannot doubt Him, when He has proved Himself dependable in every aspect of life.

With warm love He surrounded me in that bare attic. He gave me courage when the air raid sirens sounded their fearful piercing tone. When others ran to the shelters, He stayed with me. His Holy Spirit, able to be everywhere at the same time, covered me with security. I knew myself loved, even when no human being considered my need. His cross became my symbol of ultimate victory. I wanted to possess one, just to hold it, to touch it, to finger its outline. To have one for visual encouragement when days looked black and sadness overwhelmed my inner being, when homesickness and longing for my people created a sense of destroying self-pity. It was the cross which pointed at all times to the Victory after suffering and death.

The potato knife was strong and sharp. With it I shaped carefully two pieces of wood of the same width, which I found among the beams. Not able to join them with nails, having to avoid hammer blows, I pressed in some tacks in the centre and soon had fashioned a cross of my own. Pleased with my joinery effort I set to to paint it with shoe polish, and then rubbed it to a lovely shine. From then onwards, furniture polish enhanced its beauty! If you could see it today, no roughness in the wood would remind you of its origin.

The cross accompanied me on many a journey, one just around the corner, just after its completion. For some days a general feeling of malaise had invaded my body. The food which reached me at regular intervals through the hatch in the floor would only be touched, I just could not eat. I wanted to drink all the time, anything to soothe my thirst. I developed a cough, a nasty almost choking cough. It worried my landlady as much as myself. Would anyone hear me? This must never happen. It could cost us our safety and consequently our lives. Suddenly it happened . . . the cough was preceded by a whoop! I knew enough about infectious diseases to recognise whooping cough! It shocked me to the core. How could I, a teenager, a nurse, have caught this childish infection in this solitary confinement? I just couldn't stop myself coughing. Was this to be the end? Mary was not too pleased about the whole affair. Could anyone blame her? But who else would want me? The Lord would need to help, need to show me a way out of this extraordinary predicament.

Whooping cough without a whoop? Could *this* be the answer? It obviously was not! The cough became worse and so did the whoop, only I began to feel a little more like myself between those attacks. Certainly I felt worn out, but I could lie on my mattress in the corner whenever I felt inclined to do so. Here I could think, cry with self-pity and be angry at myself for giving in. Yes, my mattress and its covers provided the perfect solution, but then I had another idea. I had heard about injections for whooping cough. Could we ask a doctor to come and give me some injections? Mary wouldn't hear of it. She was scared stiff. No outsider was to know about my presence in her house. It couldn't be done. Having discussed it with her husband she confronted me with their decision: the whoop *HAD* to go first thing on Monday. I had to go out, pretending to be a visitor, turning and waving back at the garden gate. I had to turn right and make my way in a straight line towards the city. There I had to look along the nameplates of houses and choose a doctor myself. I had to promise my hosts not to divulge their name and address; the responsibility had to be mine. They would give me money to pay the bill, then they charged it up to oom Henk and the organisation.

I got the message. I understood. If I chose the right kind of doctor, all would be well. Should I, however, choose a wrong address, then this could be the finale.

It was most upsetting, especially when the Allies were so close. Surely, I thought, the war could not last much longer. The Americans were outside Maastricht. A few weeks more and they could be here. The atmosphere outside was one of tension and expectation and penetrated into our house by way of my hosts.

'Perhaps,' I thought, 'the outside atmosphere could provide a cover?' I had to reach a decision immediately. Day and night I was plagued by the cough and its accompanying sickness.

Next morning was the day of days. At a quarter to ten, with a thumping heart and a happy bright face, I set out from my prison into the freedom of an entirely strange town. Waving gaily at the garden gate as instructed, I then closed it casually and left like a normal visitor.

Turn to the right, I had been told. I walked firmly on and on until I felt safe. Suddenly I realised that it was fun and a sense of enjoyment flooded my entire being. Yes, I would find a doctor, but not as near as this, let the walk take me that little bit further 'into freedom'.

Soon I reached the 'Harley Street' of the town. By simply counting 'one, two, three,' the bell of the third house was decided upon. Bravely, I asked to see the doctor; the receptionist showed me into the waiting-room. How would he react? Oh, the horrible cough again and again. I wished he would hurry up. Would he object to the infection in his surgery? The bell . . . oh, he was a handsome youngish man in his early forties and dressed in a immaculate white coat, so common to our continental medical men.

"Good afternoon, Miss . . . ?" He enquired.

"Miss Dobber," I hurriedly volunteered.

Politely he ushered me to a seat opposite his desk and straightway invited me to tell him what was wrong. No words were needed to oblige him on this subject, as a spasm of whoops and coughs supplied the answer.

Smilingly he raised his eyebrows, and equally smilingly I started my story once my breath had returned to normal. It did not take long to realise that my new stranger was perfectly safe. It was with a sense of great relief that I left house No. 3! A fully dated card with the course of injections to come was in my pocket.

Grateful thanks from heart and soul rose heavenward. Almost sadly I trotted homewards, cheered only by the thought of the injections to come and its accompanying outings.

That night I felt brighter and better, physically as well as emotionally. There was plenty to think about. My mind dwelt on the walk, the people who had passed me, the noisy playground, the snatches of overheard conversation at traffic points, the general feeling of expectancy which could be sensed on many a face.

Could it really be true? Were the Americans outside Maastricht? Were the Allies advancing, or was it a wistful rumour? It just *had* to be true. Our people worried about the starvation in the cities, and if the situation became worse, we, too, would have to endure this hardship. Who then would be willing to help such a one as me?

Next morning I compiled a list of injection dates on the back of my calendar, then intertwined them with happy Sabbath days and the coming resurrection day: Sunday. It would bring me into August. My nineteenth birthday. One learned to plan and enjoy occasions in the most miserable surroundings. Certainly I would celebrate my birthday, I had *so* much to be happy about and happy I would be, at least on my selected days at the back of my calendar!

As life became drearier in my attic, my Lord became closer, and as life became more dangerous because of Mr. Metzger, Mary's father, the news of advancing troops inspired courage.

We *had* to make it! We simply *had* to! Nothing must happen now! If Mary would keep me, just a little longer. My cough improved daily with the injections and undoubtedly the doses of fresh air during my outings aided the convalescing process. I promised repeatedly I would keep very still when her father entered the house. His voice could be recognised, quite unmistakably. But Mary raised mountains of obstacles, one especially—"and what if he wants to do some work in our attic, some modernising, the fixing of a water tank, etc?"

It was not difficult to sense just how scared she was, almost sorry now to have meddled in illegal affairs. I just *could* not leave her. Oom Henk had not been to visit me for many weeks. He didn't know about the whooping cough, my outings and the certain knowledge that Mr. Metzger was a 'sympathiser with the occupation force'. How could oom Henk find another place for me at this stage? The atmosphere just vibrated with liberation and expectation. Who would want to bother with illegality at a time like this?

Personally my mind was made up, I would be brave, see it through to the end, whatever that end might be! I pleaded with the invisible Almighty for sanity and reason to return to Hitler and his followers all over the Continent. I believed firmly that it was still not too late for him to renounce his own foolish decisions before more damage was done. If he would only publicly confess his failures, and surrender. I prayed and pleaded for him and devotees like Mr. Metzger . . . but it had not to be. They, too, were determined to see it through to the end, even if that end was total destruction.

The bombing raids increased as the troops approached the direct line to our town. Shell explosions were sharp and destructive. Frequently I held both hands over my ears to help deaden the crash which followed the eerie approaching impact. Every time I gave sincere thanks when my hosts returned from the shelter and I had survived another direct hit on my attic.

The last injection was due the day before my birthday, hence my inward celebration was observed that day with an overflow to the next. Never before had I felt an excitement comparable to that day. You could have believed we were free already. Dutch ladies boldly wore blue skirts, white blouses with red embroidered roses, or plain red bow ties. No one could accuse them of wearing the national colours. The explanation would be that 'all our other clothes have worn out and no new coupons have been available for a long, long time'.

One was almost sorry for the Germans in our town. They hurried about almost sheepishly, embarrassed by their very uniform. To me they were just men, husbands and fathers, far away from home and loved ones, who had followed the herd and were fighting for their country and Fuhrer. And now for them, as well as for us, the end was in sight. Would they be permitted to serve their time as prisoners of war, or would conscription to the fighting area be inevitable? Did they think about their future at that late stage? A life, or death by blasting.

That day, the 29th August, 1944, I stretched my outing to its capacity, not even thinking about how worried Mary might be. I walked and walked along quiet country roads and through busy shopping areas. The windows were decorated with flowers and pictures, displaying only a little of the goods still available for sale. It all looked very attractive, but rations allowed one just the smallest share.

True it was summer, but to me it was more like spring, spring in the air, spring in the hearts of men and women, spring which even affected the little children. The advance was steady, the retreat of German troops on the other hand very noticeable.

* * *

Up North it was a different story. There was despair and broken hearts among those to whom I owed everything, even my very life.

The month of August spelt serious trouble for the manse. Once more the Germans had arrived to search the place. This time it was for illegal food, such as corn and wheat which was kept in sacks upstairs. They 'arrested' them and labelled each one for collection. Eventually it would undoubtedly find its way to a German officer's stomach. Why they had brought rifles we would never know, but Aunt Jo insisted they should take them out of her house when one young man left his accidentally at the back door.

A few more weeks of peace had followed, very peaceful weeks indeed. Frighteningly peaceful! Then one day Nopje cycled up the front drive towards the house, the little fellow got his usual kiss at the gate, but Nopje's mind was elsewhere, Aunt Jo told me later. She had stared at the manse, when Aunt Jo asked the fearful question, THE question which mattered above all: Nopje nodded in affirmation. Yes, Domie, had been arrested!

A young local policeman, after winning Domie's trust, had gathered as much secret information as possible, then betrayed him to the Gestapo. When the arrest was made, he allowed himself to be captured as well. Domie never knew therefore, who along the line had been unfaithful and led him, and many others, into the bottomless pit. His payment? Some cash and the promise of promotion.

Nopje carried a little note which had come from Haarlem. It contained these words: 'You may have heard by now that your husband has been arrested in Haarlem. He is being held in the main prison and is very brave under the circumstances, as he knows from where to draw strength. He wants you to know that he loves you dearly and that you too must be brave. Something is going to happen very soon. Be courageous!'

Later, more specific news became known. Domie had been arrested in the company of two German officers who had deserted and also a Jewish person. During cross-examination they had done all in their power to make him mention names of the rescued. They had tortured him as a means to 'soften him up'. His nose had been broken and his eardrum as well. It was a miracle that his eyes were not damaged as they set on him with rubber-loaded sticks.

Naturally the illegal movement did all they could to free Domie, although it was like surmounting a stone wall. Yet a plan was laid to 'lift' him from that prison on a Saturday. Everything was well prepared, and there was no reason to contemplate failure. Then on the Friday he was suddenly transferred to the infamous Gestapo prison in Amsterdam. From there, no escape was possible.

So that was what the writer had meant in that little note 'something is going to happen very soon'. It had not to be. He now seemed to be imprisoned in iron shackles. Poor, dear Domie.

Oh! that bright, hopeful month of August down South with us was a black night for my people up North.

On that fateful day, when this bad news had been brought by Nopje, Aunt Jo made arrangements to leave the manse. She too, would be on the 'wanted' list. Safety was of utter importance for her and the boy, and besides, she was heavy with child.

Mary, the mother of Jesus, set off on a donkey to flee from her oppressors and find shelter elsewhere for herself and the infant Jesus. That night, Aunt Jo set off on her bicycle into the unknown. It was 9 p.m., the little fellow settled in his basket fixed to the steering wheel, while a small case was attached to the back carrier: this contained all her earthly possessions.

Wearily and alone she cycled carefully many, many miles, not knowing how to answer the constant questioning of her small son.

No, she didn't know herself when they would return home. Nor did she know when he would go to bed. She was weary, oh, so weary. When darkness fell she requested hospitality at the nearest manse. Thereafter it was a case of one manse this night, another one the next, avoiding too long a stay at any one welcoming home. Finally she reached Winschoten where she gave birth to her second son, Erik.

It was to be another six to eight weeks before it would be safe to go back to her own empty residence. The Youth Organisations had been marvellous. Under Tantje's expert direction, they had cleaned the whole building, making it liveable once more, and preparing it for the sad homecoming of their minister's wife and children.

As I stood at the edge of the pavement, crushed by other well-wishers, waving and cheering the slowly approaching American tanks, tears dripped unashamedly down my cheeks. Here I witnessed the liberation, freedom was mine, the nightmare was over, over for ever but . . . no Uncle Bas to whom I could express my gratitude. No one close, no one who belonged to me and no one to whom I belonged, except Him, the Creator of the Universe, Who had revealed Himself to me in the person of Jesus Christ and Who had, in the form of His Holy Spirit sustained me throughout this time of fear and danger.

We were free, but Holland itself was still tight in the grip of the enemy. This last winter was the worst one for the people of Holland and the North. It was the infamous hunger-winter of 1944/45. People exchanged their gold and silver for potatoes and bread. The black market did a thriving trade. Some became rich overnight while others faced poverty and hunger for the first time in their lives.

That winter goes down in our history as the bleakest for centuries. Yet here in Limburg people began to live. Their lives and mine experienced a new lease. We were free, happy and eager to breathe to the full. This physical and mental expansion showed itself everywhere in different ways.

Mary plainly told me that they could not possibly keep me any longer. They had not heard from the Organisation, which, translated, meant 'no cash was forthcoming'. I took the hint and informed her that I would leave at the week-end. When she wondered where I had found a home so soon, I simply said that 'the home' had been waiting for me. This, of course, was a pure act of faith and trust in Him Who had so far planned the road for me.

On Wednesday I roamed the streets again. I possessed no money, not a cent, so all my joy was found in the gladness of my heart, and gratitude to the countless dozens of people who had knowingly, or unknowingly, contributed to the preservation of my life. I thrived on thinking, planning and the determination to use the health and strength left to me to be a blessing to all with whom I came in contact, just as others had blessed and loved to the best of their ability.

Jesus said, 'I have given you an example so that you may do as I have done . . . once you have realised these things, you will find your happiness in doing them' (John 13. 15, 17, *Phillip's translation*).

I had many examples, countless examples. I had seen Christ at work in people of different age groups, professions and social standing. They had but one thing in common: the selfless devotion to the Christ, Who had become my Master and Lord as well. My thought was, 'Would I be able to serve Him in such selfless fashion in the service of my fellowmen?' 'Would I be able to suffer misunderstanding, sneers, cold shoulders, unkindness and continual hardness of heart as He had done?' 'A servant is not greater than his Master', Jesus had warned.

Would I be able? I did not dare to answer, even to myself, such a searching question. 'There is no greater love than this—that a man lays down his life for his friends' (John 15.13 *Phillip's translation*). That was what Domie, my Uncle Bas, had done for me. I would never be worthy of such a sacrifice. With Christ's inward help, I would try to live a life of love, giving and sharing all I had and all I was. Yes, the greatest lesson for me had been the truth that the most valuable gift to others is the gift of oneself. No goods of any description can compare with the value of the sharing of one's love, one's time, one's devotion and sincerity. This is the gift which costs such a lot; not in money, but in time, and love. This is the gift, the most needed gift for which humanity really craves. A human being wants to know that he or she matters, matters enough to be worthy of sacrifice. Christ showed the way and Domie followed. He, too, gave himself, shared himself. I had mused so deeply that I had not noticed that I had returned to the street and house where Mary lived. Hesitatingly, I stood there for a while, when a tap on my shoulder made me turn. There was Mrs. Heemskerk, our neighbour across the street. "Coming for a chat in the garden?" she persuasively asked. Of course I would. Anything normal was always welcome. It was only a small pocket-handkerchief of a front garden, but to me it was Eden!

With another motherly pat on my shoulder she assured me that a cup of tea was in the pot. She left and returned presently with the tea and an extra chair. Within minutes we were involved in the most complicated conversation as if we had known each other for years, yet this was our first meeting. She had seen me come and go from Mary's house, drawing her own conclusions; she knew I was an illegal. She enquired what I would do now.

It was in the reply to Moeke Heemskerk, that my ideas crystallised. I heard my own voice telling of my predicament, my hopes, my determination and plans for work. It was a mighty jungle. I saw a Ben Nevis before me, bringing the chatter to an abrupt halt.

There was a long silence, and even when I felt constrained to talk no words would come. At last Moeke asked in a quiet and warmhearted voice, "Would you not like to come and stay with us just for a little while, Fransje? Just to experience the feel of a normal home? I have three girls, one is your age, you would love it, Frans. Do as you like, but learn to live normally again."

Was I getting too sensitive? Tears welled up into my eyes. I could not answer her at all. Here was my open door, all ready before the week-end. How would Mary feel about her neighbour. . . . Then my material poverty brought me to my senses. I told Moeke that I had no money for my keep, that nothing had been heard from the Organisation for a long time. Of course, I would look for work at once and give her all I could. She stopped my flow of words assuring me that I would just be one of the family, sharing all they were able to afford. My next objection was the consent of her husband and children. They knew nothing of her decision, and might well object. This statement evoked her hearty laughter. She dismissed all my fears in one sentence. "I don't need to ask them, *all* of us would love to have you in our midst. I am the Mother, I *know* my family." It almost sounded to me like the voice of Him who said, 'I am the good shepherd, I *know* My sheep'. Surely the Heemskerks were some of His sheep, I had no doubt about it. I felt the invisible trade mark.

Thoroughly happy I left that front garden going straight to my attic in Mary's house. Going down on my knees where no one could see me, I gave humble thanks to Him who had continually watched over me.

After dinner I lay on my mattress quietly and thoughtfully, a pencil and paper clutched in my hands. Much had to be planned and essentials attended to. The foremost longing of my heart could not be satisfied. How could I begin to search for my parents, brothers and other relations? Holland was still at war and heavily oppressed. No mail could reach the destination of our Red Cross H.Q. All the same I would make statements and have all details ready and in perfect order for the legitimate enquiry, whenever that would be.

On Saturday I would move to the Hermskerks, and spend an official Sunday in a Christian home and take my first walk to a church, their church. I could hardly wait. If only Uncle Bas could know . . . how would he be spending his Sundays? As any other day? Not knowing when the call would come for yet another cross-examination; not knowing when another transfer would take place; not knowing how long he had to live or if he might be released suddenly. I prayed: 'Oh, Uncle Bas, may God Almighty be in these walls, be inside you, to strengthen you and soften all the hard blows by the example of His own endurance when under persecution.'

One Sunday in Cell A 119 he expressed through the medium of a stump of a pencil and a piece of toilet paper his deepest feelings:

> I knew that Thou dost always watch the humble
> and those who wait for Thee,
> Therefore I had this certainty,
> I'd never be alone;
> My broken heart be healed by Thee in time.
>
> But I didn't know that Thou wouldst come
> bowing deeply, entering this low door,
> Witnessing a golden light astreaming through the window
> transfiguring our shamble here with scented melody.
>
> That rising reverently these walls would face Thee,
> pronouncing a three-fold "Holy Your Majesty"
> All the bare structure with folded hands would praise Thee
> because of old and now, Thy ways are merciful.
>
> And I? For bread and water I do give Thee praise
> partake communion with all Thy Church which strays,
> In here, Thy Name's uplifted by angels and poor me. . .
> while all creation Thy works can't fail to see.
>
> How possibly could I lose so soon
> this unity with Thee my Lord,
> Conversing here with Thee
> when Thy will's mine and mine is Thine?
>
> My folded hands just rested in Thy grip.
> My heart just beat by power from Thy lip.
> My eyes just see the greatness of Thy might.
> When weak, Thy strength was always just in sight.

Then came the knock . . . such shock. . . .
*   when I was called for that last walk!*
Within me all so calm. . . .
*   Thy heavn'ly music my eternal balm.*

For one can go in peace when trusting in Thy Word
*   raised hands in blessing, inward courage heard.*
Since I belong to Thee in body and in soul
*   Death is Life! I've reached my goal!*

BASTIAN JOHAN ADER
(translated by Johanna Ruth Dobschiner from the original)

Yes, he knew when Sundays came round. He encouraged his cellmates, wrote sermons on endless rolls of toilet paper and sent them tightly rolled up, through cracks in the walls, to the adjoining cells. Once a teenage boy had been informed that soon the call would sound for his last walk to the exercise ground. There he would be executed with others of his 'Crime-calibre'. The young lad was frantic and became hysterical as the afternoon wore on. Every studded boot on that concrete corridor shook him to the core, tearing his nervous system rapidly to pieces.

Gently Domie took over. He calmed the lad, as only he could do. He strengthened and assured him with the source of assurance from which he himself knew to draw.

Domie used not only his Sundays, but all his days and nights to portray the hope of this world in Jesus Christ, the only mediator and Saviour of mankind.

This Sunday I would enter a Church building for the very first time. A great moment indeed. My heart and my mind would be crammed full with memories and thankfulness, with prayers and sincere pleadings, but above all with a certainty that the invisible God would approve of my first entry into His earthly temple.

With sincere thanks I left my last hiding-place and said a casual cheerio to Mary and her husband, assuring them that I would visit them often, which I did!

Entering the Heemskerk's house I felt as if I was a long lost relative returning home. I had arrived! Now in a position to assess my situation I could think about the future. A job had to be found, most probably nursing.

On Saturday afternoon we were surprised by a visit from an

American Sergeant Major. A kindly rather plump type of man. After he had sampled our cup of tea he stated his mission. Would we be able to billet one of his men—the divisional cook? The kitchen tent would be erected on the green across from the house, and his men would eat inside the adjoining marquee. He was looking for billets all around this district.

Once more it was Mother, encouraged by Father who gave him their generous 'yes'. That selfsame night two new people slept in the Heemskerk's home, the liberator and the liberated.

Billy and I became close friends; he and I, both far from home, had much in common. Our greatest unity however we discovered the very next day, when all the family plus Bill and myself walked to the village Church. We all gave thanks together!

On the first Sunday of our freedom, the village Church was crowded with men, women, children and American soldiers. There were few dry eyes that morning. The worship and thanksgiving came from all our hearts. Later I learned that many boys of this parish had been lost in the fighting some four years before. Tribute was paid to them and to 'all bereaved'. It was impressive to join a service where prayers and singing were conducted in Dutch. I followed every word, praising my Lord and theirs, and then I suddenly realised that He was actually OUR Lord.

When Bill came off-duty late that Sunday night he entered the house with the most delicious smell of roast chicken coming from a dish in his hands. "This is for your supper," he grinned. The 'ohs' and ahs' mingled with two juicy kisses which Mother deposited on Bill's cheeks. Father put on the kettle once more while Mother placed the dish in the oven. We girls bustled around, setting the table, cutting some flowers to decorate it for this special occasion and fussing around Bill who seemed to have endless surprises in his pockets. We stretched this happy evening to capacity, even the youngest staying up until her eyes wouldn't keep open any longer.

Monday morning and duty called us all. Jeantje was out early and Father had left at the crack of dawn. Bill's divan was back to normal, his blankets neatly folded in a pile. The little one played with her dolls and Betty had left for school. After I had helped Mother with the dishes and the general housework, I, too, set off to attend to my 'business'.

First of all, the Red Cross. I left my name and present address, should anyone be looking for me. They enquired about my family and relatives and I supplied all known details. My occupation? Well, I supposed I could call myself nurse. And nurse it has been ever since. Where did I work? Well, nowhere just yet. Almost pleadingly they asked if I could not spare some weeks for their emergency hospital. I was as relieved as they were when we parted that morning. A job already! Almost jubilant I made for home and late lunch. Mother hugged me tightly. We danced around the room. A job! Now I would earn some money. Earn it by working well and hard in the profession of my choice. Too good to be true!

The next few happy months made me feel 'young' once more. I learned to laugh again, laugh out loud, a forbidden act during the past year. It was fun to mix with girls of my own age and be teased by the orderlies in the hospital. We worked well and I cannot recall any selfishness among the staff. There was an understanding beyond the usual interest in one another. There was an eagerness to be helpful, to comfort, to 'share each other's burdens'.

It was a real emergency hospital. We made do with a great deal of improvised material. Most beds were camp-beds. The patients stayed with us as short a time as possible. When the treatment was completed, convalescence continued at home. There were the odd cases, patients who found themselves 'displaced' because of the partial liberation, those who were wounded by stray shells or debris flying around. There were the orphaned children awaiting admission into some home. They, too, stayed with us simply awaiting a vacancy. The elderly were our main concern. They needed constant care and nursing, but above all, love and understanding.

Off duty in the staff room was a rich experience. We talked about everything, sympathised and advised. Our religions were as varied as our ages. With perfect freedom we observed the prompting of our conscience. It was quite common to see a nurse or orderly go to a corner of the room, draw a rosary from their pocket and begin a devout session of prayer.

The priest came each morning to the ward accompanied by a young choir boy or altar servant. He swung a bell backwards and forwards, or from left to right. Most patients, being Roman Catholics, appreciated this extra luxury. While Mass was celebrated in a ward, attended by all Catholic staff, I slipped to the staff room and knelt humbly before the Lord, telling Him all 'He needed to know'. I could worship him quite well in many of the Psalms, which came easily to me, after having read them for months.

The Emergency Red Cross Hospital had served its purpose during these early days after the liberation. A reshuffle of staff and patients was contemplated to allow proper nursing care and administrative reorganisation. I was among several who became redundant. It was inevitable. There had been good money in it while it lasted. Mother had taken only the absolutely necessary amount from me, and encouraged me to save the rest. I had taken her advice and treasured a small nest egg.

When I had attended the local Church for almost six weeks I thought it was time for me to become a member. The minister agreed to see me by appointment. As it was the first time I had spoken to him personally he was rather startled by my request. Had I the time for a long talk? I had all the time in the world! Mrs. Furnee made some coffee while her husband cross-examined me. He explained I could not possibly join his Church without Catechisatie.* I wondered what he meant. It was a collection of lessons one had to know before being admitted to Church membership and holy communion. Questions to be answered? I would gladly try to answer any questions, I assured him. At this point I must have startled him. He wanted to know where I had learned 'my lessons' and who had been my teacher. Eagerly I told him that I'd read the New Testament over and over again and was almost sure I knew all Christ required of me. Christ had taught me Himself. "All right," he smiled. "Come on Friday night to the vestry. I'll try to contact the elders and ask them to come just a little earlier to meet you. It may be possible that you could join the Church on Sunday, be baptised, make your public confession of faith, and be admitted to the Holy Communion Table, we'll see."

It was difficult to restrain my enthusiasm and delight in such dignified company. Politely I shook hands and promised that I would do my best not to let him down on Friday night. I would study the New Testament once more.

When I told mother she treated me almost like a Birthday child. Special week-end preparations were made at once. I would require to get a new costume. One of Jeantje's would do with a bit of

* Confirmation classes.

alteration. She insisted I should go and tell 'all my friends'. This was easy. It just meant Mary and her family, including poor Mr. Metzger who felt very small and behaved like that as well. Too bad for him that the war had ended thus! Also Mr. Keunings, our Church Officer. I liked him and his family. They had a tremendous worry as he was troubled with asthma, but he worked hard, supported by his wife and children. He was not only the beadle, but also the school janitor. I'd spent many a happy afternoon with his children playing football in the large playground. Here, too, I was always assured of a sincere welcome. They had to know. What about the neighbours? No need to tell them, Betty and Fientje had done their work. Glad to have some *real* news they told everyone they met during the next few days.

On Friday night I was surrounded by many elderly gentlemen in black suits and black ties. All managed to smile a little while shaking my hand. Utter silence reigned for some moments after each one had taken their seat. Then Mr. Furnee made his speech of introduction before asking me many questions. Personally I felt he enjoyed it and so did the others. As he continued the atmosphere relaxed and others indicated that they, too, would like to ask 'some questions'. I enjoyed my evening immensely and wished it could have continued a little longer.

By Saturday lunchtime I complained that Sunday would never come. Mother suggested I should rest a little and 'collect my thoughts with prayer'. Sound advice, which I gladly accepted as I was truly tensed up.

As always when alone, my thoughts travelled back sadly many, many miles into the unknown. Where were my parents? Did I have any? Were my brothers still alive? Could they have escaped? How would my people have looked on tomorrow's act of personal decision? Many condemn a baptised Jew. I, too, had thought about such people with disgust, in days gone by. Traitors, apostates, turning one's back on their own folk. Ridiculous! I determined to show my people that this was the most irresponsible statement anyone could make. In turning to Christ, a Jew becomes complete! It was not a case of being converted to a new religion. The old one had become full of meaning. Christ Jesus did not create a new road, He cleansed and revived the old. He and His disciples were my Jewish brothers among whom I felt perfectly at home. Granted, since these early days many Gentiles had flocked to His feet. People of different nations and nationalities had found their way to God through Christ, but that did not change the fact that He came 'to the Jew first', although 'also to the Gentile'.

No, I had no qualms about my baptism tomorrow. I joyously looked forward to this high honour and privilege to confess Him openly as my Lord and my Master; God Almighty!

That night I slept as sound as a bell. Early on Sunday I had a glorious bath and a gift of brand new underwear. I seemed to be new all over. Jeantje told me that Mother had agreed that I should keep the costume; a confirmation present. The little ones had put flowers on the breakfast table, their personal gift. Father looked very smart in a black suit. I had never seen him in it before. It was in my honour, he assured me. I belonged to them, didn't I? They were proud to walk me to Church, and I? I felt protected and loved among them.

At ten minutes to ten I presented myself in the vestry. I was the first one to arrive. The Church Officer welcomed me gladly. In a little while the elders arrived one by one and shook hands solemnly. At last the Rev. Furnee arrived. He, too, shook hands with everyone and then disappeared to return a few minutes later in his black robe. He appeared very awesome. Domie had never looked so severe in his gown, I thought. Majestic, yes, but not frightening. After all he was my Domie. The Rev. Furnee asked which of the elders would be willing to bring me into the church accompanying me to the pew. One nice man stepped forward. He was the local butcher, the Sunday School Superintendent, Mr. Volbeda. I still have contact with him today.

We all bowed our heads in reverent silence while an elder asked the Almighty to strengthen the minister to speak His word to those who wanted to hear. At last the minister led the way walking slowly down the aisle and towards his pulpit. Mr. Volbeda and I followed behind, then came the other 24 elders who went towards their respective pews. I was led to the front seat beside the minister's wife. Behind me I noticed Mother and Father Heemskerk who smiled encouragingly. Did I need encouragement? No, I felt so wonderfully happy and privileged as if I was walking through the gates of Heaven itself.

In front of me lay a beautiful new hymn book opened at Psalm 95. We all rose to sing, verses 1-6. It was great to start worship like that! We remained standing while everyone repeated the creed. I knew it and joined in. We concluded by singing the doxology, 'Praise God from whom all blessings flow'. It acted as a crescendo after the creed.

Silence settled on the congregation when the minister opened the Bible. Mark, chapter 10, verses 46 to 52. Blind Bartimaeus with a desperate plight. Jesus asked simply, 'What would you like? What would you like *ME* to do to *you*?' 'Lord, I want to see'. Simple and straightforward. A discussion between a desperate man who *knew* that no one else could be of real help to him, and the One who was Bartimaeus's last straw. He just *HAD* to try this Jesus! The Christ was here to help such that turn to Him and *EXPECT* results. Gladly, therefore, the Lord replied 'Go your way, your faith has healed you'. Immediately he received sight and . . . followed Jesus.

Bartimaeus did not go his own way any longer, he was ready to follow Jesus who had made him to see light and life in a new way. A wonderful story! I, too, had received sight. I, too, saw the world with different eyes. My heart motivations, my intentions, my aims were all new.

> *'Heaven above is brighter blue*
> *Earth beneath is sweeter green,*
> *Something lives in every hue*
> *Christless eyes have never seen.*
> *Birds with gladder songs o'er-flow*
> *Flowers with deeper beauties shine*
> *Since I know, as now I know*
> *I am His, and He is mine.'*

An unforgettable sermon! When the organ had sounded the last note, I heard the minister call me by name, indicating that I should come forward. This I did very slowly. Suddenly I felt so alone, yet so uplifted and strangely drawn to the Christ who had met me at Easter among the attic beams in the North, while Sister Moony continued to peel the potatoes.

Humbly I knelt on the special stool provided for that purpose. Folding my hands, and closing my eyes I experienced a high and holy moment indeed. It seemed that God had come to place His hand upon me. A moment to be sealed in holy baptism. He was my Father, I had proved it so often, but now He seemed to assure me 'I shall not leave you comfortless, I will come to you' (John 14.18). He, the Father of the fatherless. My earthly father was with me no longer. Now *He* had come so that I would *always* have a father. Till this very day He has acted as such!

While kneeling there, I identified myself with Bartimaeus. 'Lord, let me see, *ALWAYS*'. I was determined to receive all there was of the Holy Spirit of Christ. A voice broke through my thoughts and intentions. It was the minister's voice, "Johanna-Ruth Dobschiner, I baptise you in the Name of the Father, the Son and the Holy Spirit. Amen."

During the words 'Father, Son and Holy Spirit' I felt the cold water touch my forehead in the shape of a cross. When I opened my eyes at last I noticed the minister beside me. His arms were outstretched above me in blessing while the congregation sang the Aaronic blessing from Numbers 6, verses 24 to 26. 'The Lord bless thee and keep thee, the Lord make His face to shine upon thee and be gracious unto thee, the Lord lift up His countenance upon thee and give thee peace. Amen.'

I too said 'Amen', rose and walked thankfully towards my seat. The water on my forehead was still wet, I could feel the *everlasting mark* which no one else would ever see. I had been marked! Back in my pew, I remained standing while making official profession of my faith. I answered all the questions with the 'I do' of the ceremony.

On the last 'I do' the congregation sang my favourite hymn. 'Whatever the future may hold for me, I know that I walk in God's hand; therefore with courage I lift my eyes to all in the unknown land. Allow me to follow without all those "why's", I'll know that your doings are good, teach me just to walk each day with calm serenity and faith.' The second verse ran something like this. 'Lord, I will praise your love at all times although my soul doesn't understand Thee continually. Blessed is he who *dares* to believe, even when the eye sees nothing worth trusting. If Thy ways seem dark, I shan't ask "why", one day I shall see Thy plan and purpose in all its brilliance, the day when I reach Thy kingdom!' GEZANG 300A.

What a beautiful hymn, a hymn of trust in Him who never fails no matter what may happen!

Everyone settled back in their seats, hymnbooks and Bibles were shut. The minister then addressed me: "Johanna-Ruth, may I assure you that the Church, as represented here, is thankful to be a witness of the fact that this morning you are joining her as a proper member.

"In her name do I congratulate you most heartily on this very special event in your life! We wish you most sincerely God's richest blessing. It will be difficult to put into words what must have gone on in your heart during the last few weeks and days and especially during this hour. This is something between you and Christ! It must be very much!

"What we do know is that a period of life lies behind you and a completely unknown future before. I don't dare to suggest that you start an entirely new life of faith. In your relationship to God you have always known yourself bound to the God of Abraham, Isaac and Jacob, Who is the God and Father of our Lord Jesus Christ: Who will guide you also in the future with His trusted, indestructible faithfulness!

"The new part for you is the fact that you are now privileged to believe in the full revelation of the God of your fathers: in His Son Jesus Christ! The new part for you is that God has revealed to you that Jesus is Messiah, the Christ! The Prophet, the Priest, the King for whom Abraham, Solomon, Isaiah longingly craved.

"And what must you do now with this new found faith? You'll experience a marvellously rich blessing! For the Christian faith makes you glad, it comforts you and gives you strength in all circumstances. It gives you inward assurance that, thanks to Christ's suffering and His death, nothing will ever be able to separate you from God's love, and that all things will eventually work together for good.

"On the other hand you won't always find things easy in this new found faith. Neither outwardly or inwardly. Many of your former Jewish friends will be angry with you and look on you as a lost soul and a traitor! Others may even turn their backs on you and hate you! But these are only some of the outward difficulties. Inwardly you will be plagued by doubt and questions like, 'Haven't I done wrong after all, perhaps the old learned Rabbis were right?'

Or, 'What do I feel of Christ's presence? I've lost it all, does He really still exist?' And what will you do then?

"Take the apostle Paul as an example. Paul, too, faced many battles after his surrender to Christ. How did he manage? How did he conquer? In Philippians 3.12-14 he said, 'Not as though I had already attained, either were already perfect: but I follow after, if that I may apprehend that for which also I am apprehended of Christ Jesus. This one thing I do, forgetting those things which are behind, and reaching forth unto those things which are before, I press towards the mark for the prize of the high calling of God in Christ Jesus.'

"Because I am apprehended! *That* was his greatest certainty and assurance and that also will be your greatest certainty and assurance. The old Church teaching regarding predestination does not exist to frighten us, on the contrary it exists for our comfort in life and in death. The fact that you have come in faith to Jesus Christ as your only Mediator and Saviour is no human work, it is God's Work! God's Holy Spirit has begun the Christian life of faith within you! Wherever God begins a good work, He also develops, and completes it.

"The God of Abraham, Isaac and Jacob, the God and Father of our Lord Jesus Christ has given you, Johanna-Ruth, the same promise as He gave to Joshua when he entered the promised land 'I will not leave you nor forsake you!' This God keeps His promises. He is The Way, The Truth and The Life. Hold on to that! Amen!"

We joined in singing another Dutch hymn to close this memorable service.

Quietly we left after the Benediction. To my ears, the bells pealed on and on for a much longer time than usual. Outside we stood in brilliant sunshine while many people nodded with smiling faces in my direction. Some stopped to shake hands, others invited me to come and visit them 'any time'.

Happily, we made our way homewards. An atmosphere of festivity settled on the family and Bill brought some delicacies when he came off duty.

That evening I wanted to walk on my own. I wanted to think and taste the feeling of freedom to do what I liked. Just one week between today's impressive service and next week's Holy Communion. I had been happy during today's service, but I was scared of next week's—the Holy Communion between Christ and those who seek His coveted indwelling, to cleanse and purify one's life, to accept His death and forgiveness, to experience His patience and love. I expected much of next week and was willing to humble myself entirely before Him who is the Alpha and Omega, my Lord and my God.

I travelled back the road we had taken this morning, but now the Church was strangely silent. It stood there all alone, surrounded by fields on three sides. Opposite were a few country houses. There were no people in sight. This was the borderline between Hoensbroek and Treebeek. I walked on, desirous to visit the Lenssens on this special day, since they too ought to know. It would make them glad, even though I had not joined their Roman Catholic Church.

It amazes me just how many houses I passed on my evening walk, houses which I could call 'my ever open door'. As I now look over photographs and letters of all those fine people with true hearts of gold, I marvel when folks grumble and point to discord, friction and unhappiness. True harmony is created by giving, the giving of oneself, everywhere. It resulted in harmony, kindness and peace.

My friends were at home and we enjoyed recalling war memories. I told them my 'big news' and they were delighted. The little ones went straight to their room to look for picture text cards as a 'special present'. I've kept them till this day. Some portrayed a guardian angel, encircled by a halo, looking after children about to engage in some dangerous escapade, the angel was holding them back.

Whoever my guardian angel is I do not know, but there must be one around somewhere, for even Jesus mentions them. I thanked the children for their pictures, thoughtfully contemplating their meaning.

We talked about jobs, and I told them all about the Red Cross Hospital. Amazed that this had already come to an end, they enquired what I intended to do next. I explained I did not know. I had to earn my living but knew so little about jobs and life in this part of the country. Hesitantly I asked Jo and Wiel if they knew of anything or had any suggestions.

218

With a broad grin, Wiel nodded. Oh yes, he knew of a job, but would I like it? Would it not be too heavy for me or too tiring? What on earth could this mysterious job be? Why was he so long-winded? When he told me, I understood his hesitation. How unnecessary. They needed a few more office cleaners at the coal mine. "Quite a modern place," he assured me. Glass panelled cubicles, lino floors, spacious layouts: it was a proper modern office block. The only trouble was that I'd have to start at 4.30 a.m. I would not get transport from Treebeck. Would I consider living with them once more? I was delighted, but had to tell Mother Heemskerk first. Furthermore, it could not be till the Monday after my first Holy Communion.

Meantime he agreed to make enquiries at the mine, and he would ask if I could travel in the miners' bus if I was going to live with them. We had lots of fun and laughter about the possibility of this job. Doesn't the old saying hold true, 'Rolled up sleeves and a willing heart have never seen anyone starving yet'.

The Heemskerks heard about my new venture in between fits of laughter. Fransje down a coal mine! It was too funny for words. Personally, I looked on this as just another adventure to add to the many escapades of the past.

We planned a lovely holiday week together. I would meet many of their relatives, travelling by train, bus and tram, just as 'in the days of old'.

The final crescendo, Sunday's Communion! The Church looked more awesome than usual. The men's suits were almost all black, and so were the ladies' hats. Most extraordinary, I thought. It really looked more like a funeral than a glad get-together to meet our Lord and Saviour in Communion. I just couldn't understand it. The pews were packed, just like last week at my own service. At the front, however, was a long table covered with a white table-cloth. Something was on that table, in the very centre, but it was covered with a large napkin. I decided it was the bread and wine, just as on a Sabbath day at home. Here, however, they represented a deeper meaning.

The service began as usual, but the hymns were more solemn and about communion. Quite soon, the minister took his place at the centre of the table, Mrs. Furnee led me towards a seat and other people followed. The Church Officer stopped the people coming for the first sitting when all seats were occupied. Carefully I listened to all the minister had to say. Lifting the communion cup with the wine he blessed it, and explained that it reminded us of Christ's blood which was shed for our sins. When he broke the bread, he said it was to remind us of Christ's body, broken for us for the remission of our sins.

Christ's body, Christ's blood! It was cruel that He had to endure all that for us. What hardship and loneliness He must have experienced! The physical pain, these rusty nails and a crown made of thorns, must have been terrible. How could the people have been so cruel to One who was only love, goodness, kindness, gentleness and purity? Probably because the light of His life showed up the black evil in their lives. That must have been why they put Him to death. Evil hates kindness. Darkness hates light. It has been so from time immemorial. It will always be like that until Christ returns, to reign for ever.

The plate with bread cubes came my way. I watched the others. They put a cube in their mouth and ate it. I could see them swallowing. Oh dear, I fumbled a bit with my cube and then I too put it gently in my mouth. Poor Christ, His body broken, broken for us, for me. Now His risen presence came to feed us all. Once the cubes had been a whole loaf, someone had cut it into cubes. Divided for us all. Christ had done that. He came to enter into us all individually . . . by His Spirit. He surely had done that. Dear Lord! I swallowed it gently and bowed my head. Thank you, Lord! Abide in me for ever, I prayed.

We filed from the table and others took our place. This went on until all had been served, and the minister repeated his statements for every new company. I heard it many times that morning and even today whenever communion time comes round, when in a special way we meet Christ Jesus in this sacrament, I experience the same depth of His presence as on that first communion on Sunday the 19th November, 1944.

Late that afternoon it was time to move house and get settled once more at the Lenssens. I really hated leaving Mother and Father, for theirs had been my first real warmhearted home since freedom had come. We were sad, but life had to go on and my travels were only beginning.

As I left, Mother, suppressing her tears, gave me an envelope and said, "Keep it my dear and read it in years to come. We won't forget you."

Naturally I read it in bed at the Lenssens.

'Dear Fransje', it read, 'I would like to give you a few words now that you leave our homely family circle:

God will protect you!

'Dear Fransje, we all hope that it will go well with you on your life's road and that your future may contain much sunshine and give you back all that was once dear to you, but above all a warm-hearted home life. May God grant peace very soon and that everyone may come back home again.

These are a few short lines, lovingly written by your foster mother, father, and your sisters Jeantje, Betty and Fientje'.

Of course I read it often. I read into it all the good wishes of the host of people all over the country whom I will probably never see again. I've kept their wishes, their photographs, their love and their prayers and will always remember them. To them I owe my life, my health, my soundness of mind, my hope when, at times, all seemed lost.

In memory I salute them all—men, women and children—from up in the North to the low South, each one did their part to create within me a truly thankful heart.

It was fun, great fun to go to work at 4 a.m. Each miner in that lorry, as soon as he was picked up, went straight back to sleep leaning on each other's shoulders. Momentarily their eyes opened slightly as a sudden stop would be made to collect another batch of their mates. When Wiel and I climbed up the high step and took our places, a sleepy grin could be seen here and there. I grinned almost the whole road to the coal mine. All kinds of funny thoughts crowded into my mind. If my parents or brothers could have seen me shuffling along the road among these great miners! Well, there was no other transport at that time of morning, and one had to work. It was good pay and I needed every single penny to get back to Aunt Jo once the war was over in the North. To find out about Uncle Bas was the most important aim before me. In the meantime, all contact with central Holland was cut. There was bitter fighting on all fronts. How long would it last?

The lorry dropped me at the central building. Wiel assured me

I would find my way back to Hoemsbroek by normal transport at 8 a.m. I was left alone. I decided the best thing was just to start walking, and I would surely find somebody. It seemed the most sensible thing to go downstairs and keep going. Somewhere there was bound to be a cellar for the 'underworld'. I met a woman coming upstairs with a pail, mop, dusters and a chamois hanging out of her overall pocket. It seemed natural to ask her the way. "The boss is down there," she nodded, and asked the obvious question: "Are you new?"

"Very new," I assured her. To me it was like the mineshaft itself. The going down took too long a time for my liking.

At last I reached the 'place', where the noise was a mingling of tin pails, splashing of water and a mixture of dialects.

Certain that I was on time, it startled me when the boss indicated in no uncertain tone of voice. "Check all your gear and return it immaculate at eight o'clock."

"O.K.," I nodded seriously, as if I had been given the most responsible job in the secret service. As I turned to seek the unknown, she called after me "Office No. 9." "Right!" I replied once more, turning politely in her direction. It seemed that we, too, like the offices we were about to clean, were mere numbers to our boss.

Office 9 was fun to me. It was modern, roomy, and easy to dust and mop. When it came to chamois the large high glass partitions, the women arranged to help each other. Since my office adjoined No. 10 the cleaner there held my ladder and I hers. It just wasn't safe to tackle that job alone.

Long before 8 o'clock I returned with my gear to the basement. The boss still looked as grim. With a forced smile I counted out my 'tools' before her. "Thanks," she sniffed, "Will you be back in the morning?"

Amazed, I answered, "Sure I will." It seemed that many of the staff were casual workers, one day here, the next somewhere else. "Oh no, this place suited me fine, just fine! I'll be back."

Jo enjoyed every minute of my long drawn out account, and we laughed heartily over our coffee and rolls, and then I was ordered to bed till lunch time. I did enjoy stretching out after that morning's work, assuring myself that it was a well deserved rest.

Once more I was able to save and pay my way as well. A grand feeling indeed!

17

THOSE HAPPY WEEKS AT THE COALMINE'S OFFICES WERE interrupted by shattering news from Aunt Jo in the North. A letter giving all the details, readdressed, had eventually reached me at the Lenssens. I was dumbfounded. It just couldn't have happened. But the words were before me in black and white. Aunt Jo's own handwriting:

'Dear Fransje,

'Yes, dear child, the rumours you have heard are really true. They have shot our dear Uncle Bas. And I just wish they had done the same to me. It happened on the 20th of November, one day after your first Holy Communion in which you remembered how the Saviour gave His life for you. Now Uncle Bas has given his life for you, as well as others. Have a look and read what it says in John, chapter 15, verse 13. That's what they printed on the little cards which were distributed in Driebergen when Uncle Bas' body was taken there from Veenendaal where it had been buried illegally. Now it rests in the family grave.

'That body of Uncle Bas! What wear and tear it had endured! At last it is at rest. But his burning spirit is alive. I believe that he is very close, inspiring me to continue his work. I really find in doing so my fulfilment in life. Bas-Janneke talks much about his Daddy. Little Erik (his brother) was only sixteen days old when his father was called for his last walk. During that walk he folded a page in his hymnbook at hymn 139, verses 10 and 11, I suppose for us who were left behind. (A Dutch hymn which speaks about the Father's true care; that really nothing can happen to us which is not tolerated by Him. He has promised to be with us in all circumstances and situations, and see us through.)

'They took him from prison in Amsterdam for something he knew nothing about. There had been an attempted assassination on a high ranking German official in Veenendaal. First of all it had been decided that Veenendaal people would have to suffer. The

223

Lord Mayor, however, pleaded for his townsfolk, so an agreement was reached to extradite six prisoners from Amsterdam in alphabetical order. Ader was the first. Some have never been identified, but Uncle Bas had his hymnbook with his name. This was found on his body.

'If you can, and when you can, travel up North my dear, we'll be able to talk about your future. And remember always, that we are surrounded on all sides by the world of spiritual values. Much love from Aunt Jo.'

Numb and cold, with my heart thumping heavily, I sat for a long, long time holding that letter. Uncle Bas dead, shot dead. Our Uncle Bas! How *could* they have done it? Not anger, but utter astonishment filled my being.

He died to secure my life in this world.

Christ died to secure it in the next.

Life here and life eternal by the shedding of blood.

'Greater love hath no man than this, that a man lays down his life for his friends.'

There is no greater love available than this. The highest degree of love is sacrifice.

Would I ever be capable of true love, selfless love which entails true sacrifice? I was convinced that sacrifice like this would be possible in times of peace. Sacrifice does not involve big heroic acts only, but can be called for in day to day living. 'Lord make me worthy of such sacrifice, privileged to live at such cost—Domie and Christ.' This was my prayer.

The sleepless nights before me were usefully employed planning the next step. I just had to get up North. It was a long journey and I could only travel as fast as the troops, for not all Holland was liberated. From city to city I would make my way, mainly by troop transport, thumbing lifts. I could work wherever I liked and save all I was able to. Meanwhile, I planned to stay on at the coalmine and leave after Christmas.

Ministers of three different Churches in the area wrote most beautiful and encouraging sermons in my autograph book. When I left, I finally took with me two such books, filled from cover to cover and illustrated by photographs which I treasure till this very day.

Once more an unknown future lay before me and a long trail of love and security behind.

As usual, in each large city, I registered at the Red Cross Headquarters. Would I have to change course? Had my people been found? "Sorry, not yet, we will keep trying, never lose hope." Those and similar replies rang in my ears more often than I care to remember.

One particular Red Cross Headquarters had a very human army officer . . . a lady. She was connected with the American Section of the Red Cross. In charge of repatriation of Polish soldiers, she was looking for staff to help with the disinfecting of verminous, neglected men. They had to be reclothed, fed and provided with fresh sleeping quarters. "Was I interested in joining the U.S. Army Red Cross?" she asked. I wanted nothing better than that! It brought me back to nursing, my first love.

Here I was truly in the thick of it. It was hectic all day long. Provided with long high wellingtons and even longer white coats, caps and huge doses of D.D.T. we set to work. One did not care about hours of work or off duty, although it was most welcome when one was told to 'go'.

In our off time we wore the U.S. Army uniform—boots, trousers, army jackets (double pockets at top and waist), shirt, beret, belt, the lot. It was a comfortable gear and there were always clean replacements when needed. I can't remember ever wearing more comfortable footwear than these soft, flexible boots. There were hundreds and hundreds of men to attend to, day in and day out. It became child's play, inserting these rubber tubes down their backs and into their vest at the neck opening, then squirting hard on the rubber bulbs. Great clouds of D.D.T. found their way to the unwanted little creatures who plagued these poor men.

At night socials were organised, when clean Polish and American soldiers freely mixed and invited the lady members of staff to dance. Here I just couldn't oblige. This was an art I had never acquired. To me, the orangeade, peanuts, chewing gum and tins of biscuits were as great a delight, as dancing was to the others swaying around the large assembly hall.

One link with these colourful days has never died. The U.S. Officer in charge still keeps in touch with me each Christmas. The arm of love, thoughtfulness and memory reaches over years and continents.

This assignment came to an end, as, strangely enough, there were no more soldiers to disinfect!!

A chance came my way to make a break to the North. A lorry load would be leaving on Friday. "Could I be ready by then?" my Officer friend wanted to know. "Of course, I was always ready." "The journey would be safer if taken in U.S. uniform," she assured me, just in case some officious person might take me for a civilian and tell me to get out. As long as I wore my uniform as a credit to the U.S. Forces I could keep it. When I had no further need of it I was asked to hand it in at any U.S. Base.

On the journey I wore it proudly and well! Hadn't my hospital Matron once told me 'Your uniform is the flag of your training school, wear it to our honour!'

The journey North developed into a pleasant holiday. The weather was perfect for the time of year, with not a drop of rain to mar my memories! Motorways everywhere carried soldiers in all kinds of vehicles. Nationalities mingled freely. I met the Scots, the American Negroes, the Canadians, the English and, seeing that I had had hundreds of Polish soldiers all to myself for many weeks, only a handful of that nation.

Eventually I arrived in the capital of the North. My girl friend, now a staff nurse in the large Diaconess Hospital there, would surely be able to put me up for a short period. One was not conscious of all the red-tape which enfolds our profession today.

It caused a pleasant commotion when a U.S. Army Red Cross Officer, speaking perfect Dutch, entered the hospital asking for Nurse Kroese. I wasn't expected and the welcome was definitely overpowering. She made me comfortable in her room and emphasised that she would be back in a minute. The hour and a half which followed was pleasantly occupied with forty-winks and the sensation of sheer luxury and attainment.

A harassed Ida arrived at last. She had been *so* busy in the ward, two admissions and everything had gone wrong! She had also to wait to see Matron to ask permission for me to stay in the hospital. There was no difficulty about that. I could stay, eat with the nurses in the dining-room and have the freedom of the nurses' home.

Matron wanted to meet me later, once I was fully rested. This warm reception was experienced in all the hospitals which I visited during my travels.

During Ida's spells of off-duty we hiked into the country or lakeland with her Guide troop.

On the first Saturday night I was introduced to her United Christian Fellowship across the road. It was a social get-together of boys from the different Forces who wished 'Christian Fellowship'. The conversations were carried on in English, absolute double-Dutch to me! The American Chaplain in charge was most generous. During that first night he presented me with an interdenominational Hymn and Prayer Book which I treasure to this day.

Nurses and other local girls gathered on such evenings with the soldiers, learning snatches of English phrases and simple conversation. Everyone wanted to try out their school-English, of which I had none.

When it came to singing, all the company joined in. We had duplicated chorus sheets, and plenty to spare.

This was also the place we chose for Sunday worship during those two week-ends which I was able to spend in the hospital.

I began to feel conspicuous in my Army uniform and changed it for one of Ida's uniforms. Matron had no objections as she knew I had no other clothes in the meantime. It was a 'Dutch *Diaconess' which arrived one fine day at the manse in Domie's village. This time I'd come alone, very hesitant to face the meeting with Aunt Jo and yet eager to enter that manse, my manse, my haven of security. As I walked the long road towards the village and the Church, I realised why on previous occasions a bicycle had been necessary to shorten our trip. Such a long walk would have been far too risky. I did not recognise any passers-by, but they must have wondered about the strange nurse, yet every single one called out a polite 'hello'.

There was the house! Our manse, that strange building whose walls could tell stories, a proud heritage for all who in future years would be privileged to serve there.

There was a deadly silence. If only I could run away, never to come back again, but then, hadn't I been drawn? Aunt Jo met me, kindly as always and calling her cheery "come along in". But, alas, our reunion was like nothing more than a get together after a

* European Christian Nursing Order.

morning's shopping trip. If only the floor could have opened up and swallowed me, but such miracles do not happen. I accepted the invitation to go into the room on the left, and heard Aunt Jo say she would be with me at once.

The conversation was polite and superficial which made me most uncomfortable. Aunt Jo had not much to say. Of course, my presence must have aroused a great many memories. I decided it would be best to ask as many questions as possible until we reached a common denominator. How was she keeping? Where were the children? How long had she been back in the manse? She, however, did not follow my lead but guided the conversation into other channels by stating that she would soon have to leave. A new minister would be coming to take over the parish.

We had come to a dead end. She was having to leave this trusted place. Domie was gone but I live to tell the tale.

I had so hoped to stay there for weeks, to have deep fellowship with her to whom I owed so much. Instead I announced that it was a great pity that I had to leave again first thing in the morning. There was a lot to be attended too and I was expected in Amsterdam. No objections were raised, it made me glad that I had acted thus. Feingefühlichkeit, the Germans call it. One must 'sense' the right attitude for the right occasion. Tact!

The night was still as I lay in my familiar room. No one beside me in bed, no boys next door, no mice in the loft and . . . no one to fear. No sudden buzzes, no whispering voices, no one but Aunt Jo and myself, both with personal thoughts, unspoken statements.

It was true that Domie had died for such as me, but hadn't he been spurred on by deep convictions because he just 'couldn't do otherwise'. The job had to be done and so few to do it! There would never be peace on earth, he had assured us, even in normal times. The battle against evil had to continue, until the day dawned and the star would arise in the hearts of men.

Why had he, a man of his calibre, been taken, withdrawn from the battlefront? His view had been that no one really was ever 'withdrawn'. Had Stephen, belonging to the first Christian fellowship, ever been 'withdrawn'? What often can't be accomplished during our life-time, will find fulfilment when our body is at rest. This had been Domie's attitude. He had reached more people since his death than during his life-time. Even the one who shot him twice, through the head and the heart, had been touched to the core by Domie before the act was completed. He assured Aunt Jo that his life has 'never been the same'.

Had it all been worth it, had he died for nothing?

He didn't consider if it would be worth the price, the price of his life. If one is constrained by the love of Christ one doesn't question the price. Once Somebody hung on a Cross. He was a Jew. He died there for the whole world, Jews and Gentiles, for you and for me. Were we worth it? Worthy enough that He died for us?

That night my heart bled for Aunt Jo. She had to face life alone, still too bewildered to get her views into perspective and accept the facts. My presence had caused her more distress than the re-union was worth. It was a certainty that she would rise again, rise above her heartbreak and be father and mother to her boys as much as it lay within her power. Our Heavenly Father would provide the wisdom and guidance needed for each step, of that I was sure.

It was an embarrassed, shy and very humble Francisca who left next morning. I felt as if I had left a slice of my life there, never to be touched again. Uncle Bas hadn't been there, the place lay cold and silent.

Ida wanted to know 'all that had happened' and if I had enjoyed a happy time at the manse. Why hadn't I stayed a little longer when all the time in the world was mine?

Couldn't she understand, not even a little bit? Seriously I told her that Amsterdam was beckoning me. I just had to try to get there. I had to visit all the old places, and especially the central office of the Board of Guardians. They were bound to have lists of camp inmates and their fate. Yes, I had to go to Amsterdam! The manse and my experience there must now be only in my memory.

How was I to travel 'home'? The U.S. Army Uniform phase lay behind me and this diaconess uniform . . . well, I just wasn't ready for it. Ida gladly parted with one of her black gaberdine coats. A dark, plain dress was found in her wardrobe which we brightened with a white collar, made of a rubber plastic substance. It just needed a scrubbing each night, then dried with a towel; it lasted me many months. Indeed it was many months, nearly a year, before I was able to purchase another outfit.

Ida and many of my friends pleaded with me to stay just a little longer, and I agreed. Could it be that I, myself, evaded an issue which just had to be faced? During the next two weeks I prepared for the journey. If it proved as pleasant as the journey North, it would be a holiday. I had very little money to spend but an enormous supply of food and fruit was packed in my holdall. It would be sufficient if used carefully. The money could be kept for drinks and emergencies.

On a Monday morning I set off on the last lap. The last lap? This proved to be a joke. The last lap was to continue from 1945 until the summer of 1953!

To arrive in a large capital, knowing no one and having nothing but one's memories can be a very eerie experience.

Where had all the happiness gone? Why did no one smile, surely we had been liberated? Everyone went their own way. I couldn't see the little groups of people to which one had grown so accustomed. It was so cold here although the sun shone brightly on my arrival. Were people more warmhearted in the South? Had the streets less people? Sheer imagination! Yet it must be true. There had been a war! Five long years! No city can survive without scratches. Scratches! Who mentioned scratches?

My city, my home, the place of my schooldays, the place where true love had been experienced; the security of home life.

As I walked slowly towards the city centre it was hard to believe that reality lay before me. Incredible, I was now nineteen years of age. I used to be so happy around these streets during my school-days. Could it possibly have been a long bad nightmare? Had life to go on, just like this? But I had changed too. Changed very much indeed. True, I was older, but more than that, I had become a dedicated person. I had asked the King of Kings to accept me as His disciple. Ridiculous! Had it all been a dream? Would I waken up soon?

> 'The King of love my Shepherd is,
> Whose goodness faileth never.
> I nothing lack if I am His,
> And He is mine forever.'

Yes, I'd sing this, at present its melody and theme crept through the turmoil of thinking. The King of love! Why, oh why, this endless tragedy? The hatred of man. The greed of nations. The power of ideology. The desire by so many to be a Fuhrer. A Fuhrer in politics; a Fuhrer in home rule; A Fuhrer in Church dogmas and modes of worship; a Fuhrer in clubs and discussion groups; a Fuhrer in your own home.

The King of LOVE my Shepherd is.

If only all mankind were willing to pay homage to the greatest Fuhrer in this life and the next: Jesus Christ, the son of the living God. Then, and only then, will love well up in our hearts and spill over, more and more, to all who are willing to be infected by this flow of love.

Not yet do our lives experience this bliss. We've got to toil, to endure, to cope with the cold shoulders of men, women and youth who are a law unto themselves, who have no desire to bow before a Higher Being; the Almighty, the King of Creation. He who decided to reveal Himself through Jesus Christ centuries ago in Palestine, His spirit is still alive today and I had returned to Amsterdam with Him as my Master.

My Master? Yes, and more than that. Throughout the journey He was my Comforter, Guide, Counsellor, my Prophet, Priest, Mighty God, Everlasting Father and Prince of Peace.

It could have been a tourist excursion. What to view first? Our house! On the way I walked across the large square on which thousands of our boys, including my brothers, had been herded. Here they had had to kneel on those cobbled stones for close on one hour. It was as sacred ground. Slowly and gently I walked backwards and forwards. Were there others in the crowd like me, on a pilgrimage? Looking around I saw no face whose expression betrayed a glimpse of their mission. What I did see was a monument. Reverently I drew nearer. Yes, a sculpture in memory of our boys. How generous. Who could have thought of that? 'Dear Werner and Manfred, I have no words, I shake my head, I mourn for you both and admire your courage. You have gone. You had no choice, you endured in your body the pangs of loneliness, hunger, torture and death.' As I turned away I affirmed quietly, 'We shall meet again, boys, we will meet. No one can deprive us of that certainty'.

Around the corner, the canal! Our canal! There was the turf

barge. The plank from street to ship. It bobbed up and down as usual when another boat passed alongside. I walked more quickly, I was now almost opposite. Here it was, my home. . . . I stood long and silently, with all my memories before me. My eyes saw Father, Mother, the boys, Uncle Michael, Edith, Ruth. . . . I wasn't among them, I was only an onlooker. I saw them going up and down those terraced steps. Would anyone lift those curtains? Who would look down? I'd often been called for dinner while playing here on my bicycle or with conkers. But these weren't our curtains? 'Oh, Fransje, don't give in', I encouraged myself, 'look up, not just to those windows, look higher, higher, higher! "I *will* lift up mine eyes unto the hills from whence cometh my help" (Psa. 121. 1)'.

> 'My times are in Thy hand,
> Why should I doubt or fear,
> My Father's hand will never cause
> His child a needless tear.'

My times are in Thy hand! Let it be so! I'll get nowhere without Thee, oh Lord, and life isn't worth living without Thee either. I've put my hand to the plough, I won't look back! I am determined to trust Thee implicitly. I've proved Thee faithful, Lord, and believe entirely that Thou art the Immanuel, God with us! In life, with all its ups and downs. Only eternity will reveal the complete truth to us, but I do believe. Thou art Immanuel!

"Hello, Miss Dobschiner, it's you. It's good to see you!" The son of the owner of the barge had come over the plank. He, too, looked up, and then at me, hesitant to ask the question. "No," I said, "I haven't heard anything yet, I'll let you know, it will take some time though." He just nodded and shook his head slowly.

"Who's up there?" I was eager to know. He explained that it was a poor family. There were several children, and the mother was expecting another one any day. The father was off work with T.B. He encouraged me to make myself known to them.

We hoped to meet again, but never did. Here was our wooden staircase, clean and brightly scrubbed by every tenant on the landing. Plain, white clean wood. There on the right was the long thick cord, allowing even the top floor tenant to open this door. Gently I closed it behind me and climbed the narrow stairs. Pausing for a while on the first floor landing I knew that any second now my own room door would be visible. My room, the only one with a separate entrance, faced me as soon as I came round the bend of the stairs. It was made of coloured glass, allowing the sun to cast her bright beams in a kaleidoscope of colours across the landing. None of my friends had a separate entry. It made me feel grown-up, adding attraction to the already old, quaint building, dating back to the former Dutch export merchants. We had all loved this house. It had character, our boys used to say. It could speak, it was built for living, living to the full. The barges could be seen cruising along the canal waiting patiently for their turn to pass the bridges. Slowly the bridges opened up, raised their parts left and right, as giant arms heavenward, saluting each ship as it slid through the gap. Each one paid their dues into a wooden clog, dangling down from a fishing rod. It used to be fun watching all the activities on the canal. The children of the barges always looked up for people behind the windows who would take time to wave. . . .

Well, how long did I stand dreaming on this landing? I had to knock. Which door to choose? There were three entries to our flat. My door, the living-room door and the main hall. From the inside the lay-out almost resembled a ruler, with connecting-doors between all the apartments. The kitchen was the exception; it, and a very large coal bunker cupboard, practically faced one another in that long trail. Our kitchen was raised some steps upwards. Behind that lay the room of memories, the large divided room which was occupied first by my brothers and later by our foster children and myself. A quaint architectural lay-out, but very, very homely and airy.

Hearing voices behind our living-room door I chose it determinedly. A very thin, tired looking young man asked what he could do for me. When he heard my name, he pulled me inside and secured the door. I was in! While tactfully glancing around me I had to answer his eager questions about my parents and brothers. But I knew nothing. All this, while still standing behind the closed door. He hadn't given himself or me a chance to sit. There was no doubt that something pressed heavily on his mind. Someone, having heard our voices in the living-room, came down the kitchen steps towards us. His wife, heavy with child, raised her eyebrows questioningly.

"It's Miss Dobschiner herself," he informed her.

It was Mrs. Huigen who suggested that we should sit down before we went any further. Went any further? It underlined my suspicion that something was going on.

Interrupting each other they told me a remarkable story, producing evidence within seconds. Spread out before me on that plain wooden table I recognised my father's and my mother's watches. Her ring, earrings and a bracelet. More; from a kitchen towel he pulled a few sets of silver cutlery and my brother's silver propelling pencil. There was an old coin which my mother had kept in memory of the twins' birth. There was also a silver replica of the ten commandment tables.

Astonished I looked from one to the other, that moment of silence spoke of years of hardship, years of strong and honest character of these two obviously poor people before me.

How on earth had they come by these?

It was Mrs. Huigen, who began the story. They had been offered the flat when the Germans had confiscated all our earthly goods. The coal bunker had been left intact, but that was about all. Even the linoleum was stripped off the floors and not one curtain was left hanging.

"When the cold days came along, coal and turf was ordered and heaped on top of that already in the bunker. It had lasted all winter and one was glad that a good summer had been forecast. The next winter 1944/45 food and fuel were in very short supply and money even shorter," he added with a wry smile. "It was the toughest winter in my life. We literally 'scraped' to keep going. It was for this reason that we dug deeper and deeper into the coal your parents had to leave. We used it all, till the last lump and then . . . then we heard some rattling and found this cutlery. We were dumbfounded, and eagerly began to search for more, but nothing was visible. Not till many weeks after, when cleaning our hall with a good stiff brush, we happened to press against the ventilation holes within the bunker door. Something fell into the dross, and when reaching down I noticed a small ray of sunlight. It came through the now open ventilation hole. Only then did I realise that all holes were blocked with black paper. Carefully we unplugged each hole and found hard objects within all the papers. While the children were out playing, we completed the treasure hunt. So here you are,

Miss Dobschiner: your parents cared for the future, it's all yours."

What could anyone say or do to repay such faithfulness? Poor people who undoubtedly knew like thousands of others the pangs of hunger. They had in their possession gold and silver which could have provided them much good food on the black market. A gold watch would have fetched a loaf or two of almost fresh bread . . . unbelievable. . . .

It was with great humility that I accepted these well-known treasured items. I'm sure they realised just how I felt, and how great my gratitude to them was and always would be.

I promised to visit the Huigens often as long as I stayed in the city, and even afterwards I have and always will keep in touch.

One day, a letter forwarded from a previous address, reached me. It was from the Huigens. She had borne another baby boy and decided to call him after me, using the equivalent of my name. Hans, but Hansje while small. That gave me a real thrill and bound me afresh to the house of my youth.

18

IT WAS STILL EARLY IN THE DAY AND ENQUIRING FOR AND finding the city's Red Cross H.Q. was an easy job. I walked. Something was strange about Amsterdam. It took me quite some time to realise just what that 'something' was. The strangeness, came from the sight of the many empty and neglected houses throughout the city centre. People were missing. Familiar faces one expected to see at this time of day were nowhere to be seen. They were gone! Shops were unopened or deserted with dirty smashed windows, boarded up with wooden planks. Where were those homely merchants shouting aloud, advertising their wares while pushing a shaky barrow? And the children? Toddlers below school age? They had always played 'houses' around here, using a close-opening for play. One used to push one's way along these pavements, waiting for a gap to press ahead. Now the narrow pavements were deserted.

At last I reached the H.Q. but their non-committal answer sent me on my way in the same frame of mind in which I had entered those swing doors.

These hours in my city had to be digested. I set off towards the main Autobahn! Hilversum had been in my mind since the visit to the hospital up North where I had stayed with Ida. During several interviews with the Matron, she had advised me to get in touch with their hospital near Amsterdam if I felt inclined to do so. It would be quite in order to mention her name and my stay in her hospital.

Soon I stood before the main gate of the Infirmary which was to be my home and training centre for close to a year. I received a thorough training there, special attention being given to the ethical aspect of nursing, its 'high calling' and the care of a human being as a whole: body, soul and spirit. Plenty of time was devoted to testing a new recruit regarding her personal integrity, her dedication and health.

At last I was accepted and permitted to peel countless stones of potatoes in the hospital kitchen. Soon promotion was given: I could clean the large pots and pans, but the job had to be scrupulously done! Proudly I wore my black stockings and apron for this task. At last the big day came when the ward kitchen opened its door to me. Here I was closer to the people I wanted to nurse, the patients, but . . . I still was not allowed to draw near or to touch. Evidently I still wasn't ready. Happily I washed dishes, morning, noon and night. Dishes, dishes, dishes. No small wonder that household wash-ups do not present the slightest problem now!

At Christmas I performed my first official duty watched by all the staff. Each novice took part in the lighting of the candles on the large Christmas Tree. Our little group had been provided with one candle each. We found it beside our place at the table. After the minister had given his special address, our group came forward in alphabetical order. Before the tree we recited our well learned text, in a loud, clear voice, then lit the candle and placed it in its holder.

Carefully I watched the other 'novices'. When I rose I did as they had done, but recited my own text:

'Ho, everyone that thirsteth, come ye to the waters, and he that hath no money, come ye, buy, and eat; yea, come, buy wine and milk without money and without price. Wherefore do ye spend money for that which is not bread? and your labour for that which satisfieth not? hearken diligently unto me and eat ye that which is good, and let your soul delight itself in fatness. Incline your ear, and come unto me: hear, and your soul shall live; and I will make an everlasting covenant with you. . . ." (Isaiah 55. 1-3).

One of the finest outbursts of wisdom, advice and sincere pleading for foolish, misled humanity. A text which could find its place at the commencement of every service, every convention, every new venture. A text which is appropriate for each generation. Old and yet ever up to date for all nations.

Earlier in the day we had sung to the patients. Down in the main vestibule a Diaconess played the organ, some sisters had gathered there, while all the others spread themselves over the broad spiral staircase right to the top of the building. The ward doors were wide open and our carols resounded throughout the hospital. It was very impressive! Patients and staff voiced their delight with the bright beginning of this Christmas Day.

A month later yet another ceremony interrupted the 'normal' routine, if anything can be called normal in a hospital. We novices were 'headed' not *be*headed as some insisted on calling this important moment. To be 'headed', we at last received our 'hat', our cap, to be precise. This made us proper nurses, having arrived, at last, at the stage of giving bedpans and cleaning the ward. . . .

It was an official ceremony to which all the staff were obliged to attend. The minister addressed us on the importance of our calling to this Christian Hospital. All present then bowed their heads while we were 'sworn in' by prayer.

The senior administrative staff filed past us and shook hands, while congratulations sounded all round. At last we were called forward, one by one for the official 'capping'. I felt like a knight when I walked with uplifted head from the hall, with that cap pinned firmly on my head by pins which I'd bought some months previous, just in case I'd forget, and under my arm, a prize book.

If Ida could have seen me that day, I thought. We were truly sisters, dressed alike, serving the same hospitals and the same Master. That week-end I wore my own out-door uniform to Church. I had become a Diaconess.

I still can picture the layout of our hospital, remember some patient, and many of my fellow sisters. One novice contracted typhoid from a patient and to this day she is incapacitated.

Our training was stringent, the discipline tough. It is for the good of the patients and the forming of our personality, we were told. We had our own room. Study, devotion and relaxation when off-duty filled the day. Our free time was short, but the general atmosphere pleasant and happy. It did not worry us to serve long hours in the wards. We loved it, as we had given careful thought to the choice of profession.

Through my work I made many good friends. I visited homes and was invited to spend days in the Veluwe, the heather fields between the cities.

The salary, although not extravagant, allowed me to save a little. Britain still exercised its magnetic power and Scotland in particular.

Towards the close of my first year I made preparations to leave my country for good. When I left that hospital, many of the sisters impressed on me 'Sister Hansje never forget, once a Diaconess always a Diaconess. The uniform is not needed to continue this service to mankind. Remember your consecration: Ancilla Domini'.

And so I left Hilversum, left my friends and my post, reminded that duty would be everywhere, at all times.

As usual the first part of my journey took me back to Amsterdam. I made this a point of prime importance before the commencement of any other step towards . . . towards . . . what? No, I didn't know. The future was unknown. One step at a time: Amsterdam.

This time I travelled respectably: by train.

I wondered if I should call on my girl friend? True, we had been close before the war, but . . . so much had happened and she, too, might have been bereaved. I wondered if she would still be at the old address. Ridiculous! No one could get their homes back, unless, of course, it was just empty at the time.

Not being able to decide what else to do, I made my way to Amsterdam South.

There was the house. Neat curtains. Clean! It could be true. The milkman next door continued polishing his cans. Observing him and the ground floor flat next door, I made up my mind to take the risk. . . .

On the door, the usual nameplate, the parents' name: Hakker. Now then. . . . The bell rang loud and clear. Quick steps and a voice—Moeke's voice. It was Moeke's indeed! In her usual quick way she opened the door wide. She gasped in astonishment, her eyes filled with tears while a delighted smile spread over her lovely face. . . . Loudly she exclaimed: "Han n n n n s s s s je. . . .!!!"

We fell into each other's arms embracing one another long and warmheartedly until the open door brought the realisation it would be better to continue our demonstrations indoors!

While drawing me into the living-room she continued shaking her head, pronouncing only my name. Unashamedly wiping her tears, she asked me question upon question. Where had I been? Was there any news from my people? When did I come back. Each question I reciprocated with an enquiry about her and her family.

Mr. Hakker hadn't come back and neither had her only son. It grieved her to talk about these facts of stark reality. The loss of her only sister, even closer than a twin, had left her almost broken. But Sonny, the youngest daughter, was with her.

Knowing Sonny as I had, I was sure she'd make up for everything. While diffusing around her an air of carefree enjoyment, she was as sensible and understandingly tender as any mature adult. Always a close friend of my family as well as myself, we knew each other intimately.

A persistent ring of the bell announced her arrival. Moeke pressed her finger over her lips for silence. No, I wouldn't say a word. "Sorry for all the noise," I heard her shout. "Could only press with my little finger, oh dear, I'm laden, I should have taken a shopping bag." Once Moeke and Sonny had disappeared to the kitchen, the clatter bang indicated that her load had been dropped on the table. Discussion followed about prices and people, and Moeke's voice interrupting her daughter: "Come to the room, I've got a surprise."

"Ha, blanus!" she replied, as much as to say 'who are you kidding?'

Briskly I heard her come towards the room where I was hidden, the door flew open and ... "Han...n..n..n...sje!" she ejaculated "What a lovely surprise, you've come back, good for you! What have you done with yourself? Your hair is a mess and where on earth did you pick up these 'fashionable' clothes?"

Typical of Sonny, her own sweet self! Oh, it was good to be there. Almost instinctively I knew they would ask me to stay.

Anyhow, I hoped so, for where else had I to go that night?

"Where are you living?" she continued. "Anywhere near?"

This had given me plenty of time to phrase my answer.

"Well," I began, "the truth is that I don't have an address as yet, I just arrived in town this morning intent on finding a job somewhere. Nursing or with children."

"Ah," they nodded, and then almost as with one breath, "Why not stay here meanwhile?" They burst out laughing, and I could only join in and be thankful.

"Anyhow," Sonny resolutely continued, "never mind where you'll sleep, I'm starving so I will set the table right now." She had taken over as usual. "We'll eat first and talk later. Do you still love Vienna sausages with mustard, Hansje?" Did I still love them? I hadn't tasted them since that day in the Weesperstreet, after leaving the Creche.

"I love anything," I assured her.

"Good!"

Systematically she pulled out the table leaves, arranged chairs, tablecloth, dishes, cutlery, all in a jiffy.

"You can relax a while and just watch and see if you still remember our delicacies."

The trolley squeaked through the open door, and Moeke, still with that happy grin on her face, pushed it in front of me.

I stretched my neck to admire, when Sonny decided: "Later."

One by one glass and earthenware dishes arranged between bottles of sauces found their position on to the white, starched tablecloth. There was fresh herring with little cubes of raw onions, the country's appetiser. The hot Viennas steamed in the centre, surrounded by Salami, potato salad, tomatoes, cucumbers, olives, peanut spread and an elegant cut glass plate with slices of lemons for our tea.

All this had appeared in no time at all, due to Sonny's speed and capability; a girl in a thousand!

Over this leisurely meal we discussed our past, present and future. I learned that Sonny was to be married next month; her husband-to-be had also lost most of his family. They had found each other and love and had decided that life for them meant marriage. There and then I was invited to their wedding but . . . "not in that dress!" Sonny emphasised. With a hearty laugh Moeke assured me that we would find a 'dream' for me. There was no time to wonder what that dream would be, as we moved to the next subject.

A job. The Jewish hospital could do with a great deal more staff. What about going there next morning?

It was my turn to enlighten them, and on an occasion like this, it was the most difficult task. I knew how they'd feel. It would have affected me in exactly the same way. It just did not make sense and would sound like one big, silly joke. How was I to begin? It had to be told.

Seeing my hesitation, Sonny impatiently shuffled around on her chair, wanting to know if I wasn't fit enough yet. I could spend a little time with them, it would do me good.

It was time to speak, but how to begin?

"Moeke, Sonny, you may think I have done something terrible, but if you allow me to explain, you may understand and not judge me too harshly."

Raising their eyebrows, they must have wondered just what was coming.

"I'll make it as short as I can," I said, "and then you can say just what you wish! You may think me rather odd or old-fashioned, Moeke, but although I am young, I do believe in God. Not because of all I've learned at Cheder (Jewish School), not even because of my strict religious upbringing, our family observances of diet laws and other religious practices. Not only because of the happy, harmonious family atmosphere it created, but because I've thought this out for myself, Sonny. Please bear with me as I try to explain. Although God is invisible I trusted Him, because His was the only Being one could rely on. Even when my family and all these other millions were killed after the most inhuman torture, even then I believed that a God was alive who would receive these suffering souls into some place of relief. Anyhow, I trusted He would. That was all. Then, when I was underground, a lot happened, I'll tell you some day in detail. What matters now is that you understand that it gave me plenty of time for reflective thinking. Probably I 'imagined' for quite some time that our invisible God would act, very suddenly perhaps, like the miracle of Jericho's wall, or the Tower of Babel, or the parting of the Red Sea and the drowning of the pursuers, the Egyptians. I lived happily in that expectation, but gradually realised that this was childish make-believe.

"After a while I read our Tenach (Bible) in Dutch. Only then did I become really acquainted with our history, our good and evil deeds. The promises we made over and over again to Almighty God and then broke. In short, it became plain to me that, although we are God's chosen race, Abraham's seed, Israelites by birthright, from God's point of view we are sinners and Joum Hakipuriem (The Day of Atonement) can't put us straight with God and make us acceptable to Him, for the next day we are just as bad again. We need *daily* cleansing and forgiveness, and that can't be accomplished, because we haven't got a temple any more, where the stipulated sacrifices can be offered."

By this time both looked serious. I could almost detect a trace of real anger in Sonny's face, while Moeke questioned me impatiently. "What on earth are you trying to say? Have you started studying theology or something? You almost sound like a 'Geschmad' (Apostate, a Jewish person baptised into the Christian Faith)."

242

I nearly lost heart; it is difficult to explain a living conviction, when the listener looks at you with eyes of blind anger. Yet, it is so natural. Everything to do with the religion of non-Jews is 'Christian' to the Jewish rank and file.

"There is something queer coming up," Sonny exclaimed, "but you may as well get it over and done with."

"Hans, are you a Geschmad?" Moeke asked bluntly.

I knew I had let them down before I replied, trying to explain my action more fully. It was essential to finish as quickly as possible. Taking another deep breath I tried hard to be kind while hurting them so much.

"Don't call me 'Geschmad'," I begged, "before I've told you all I've done. It isn't as complicated or wicked as you may think. Yes, I have read the New Testament, that part of Holy Scripture which the Christians read, but not before I had thoroughly traced my way through Tenach. It was then I learned a lot that I had never heard at Cheder regarding the birth, life and death of one of our own prophets called Jesus of Nazareth."

It was very difficult to pronounce this good name in their presence, seeing how scorned it was, yet it *had* to be said.

"This Jesus was expected to come into this world by many, and He received a welcome when He was born. During His life He experienced their homage, and their reverence when He died. He was born a Jew, lived a Jew and died a Jew. His whole life's purpose was a task, a task from Almighty God, to act as a Mediator between God and man and finally to become the once-and-for-all-time sacrifice for man's sin. Having achieved all this, He accomplished a climax, obtainable by every human being who accepts Him as Master and Saviour—eternal life! Avoiding the terror and loneliness which death holds in its apparent finality, one can view this departing as re-birth into LIFE-PROPER. There is sorrow for those who have to be left behind. Sorrow in the separation for a while, but sorrow which is surrounded by an eager anticipation of the re-union there, where no death can part again."

"A beautiful sermon, Hansje," Sonny interrupted, "and so you believe all this . . . this . . . story."

"I believe, Sonny, that this Jesus is the Messiah promised to us throughout history. I believe that He lives and reigns and is willing by His Ruach-Hakoudesh (His Holy Spirit) to enter the lives of any

243

human being who is willing to let Him in. I believe that He is God. God Almighty came to us in human form for a while, to explain to us what He is really like. Somehow, we, His people, have lost all contact with Him, have looked on Him more like a religious figurehead, rather than a living friend who is also King of the Universe. Because of His Godly, unexplainable love, He thought of a way to show Himself as He really is, to create a way for the cleansing of our selfish sinful nature. He came as a human being, born into this world in an unbelievable way, as some of His actions may be unexplainable and unbelievable, but to those who accept Him and His ways IN FAITH, they are power and salvation. He allowed evil to kill good and showed them that in its last instance evil is always the loser."

"All right, all right, you've said enough," both of them exclaimed. "We understand. You *are* a Geschmad!"

"I wish you wouldn't call me that," I begged once more. "I only accept in a most natural way what's been promised to us. There's nothing wrong with accepting the fulfilment of God's plan."

Quietly I added, "I know how you feel and think; you can't see any God who is interested in us with all this horror around us, with all the death and cruelty to innocent people. To me it's puzzling too, but then it is not God who hurts mankind, but we who hurt each other because of our sinful nature. The people who have done all this to us are not doing God's will. They obey the commandments of men. They do their superior's will, or their own, but NOT GOD'S WILL. Don't let's blame God. He seeks continually to change men so that they will listen to Him and do His will. He approaches Jew and Gentile, rich and poor, old and young, black and white, any nationality and . . . He approached me. I really want to do His will and obey Him and that's why I follow Jesus Christ. He enables me to lead a life which can be of use to Him among my fellowmen. How? I must leave that to Him. All I am privileged to do is to follow.

"So, Geschmad or no Geschmad, I'm the same Hansje as ever, just under-new-management, that's all!"

A wry smile from Moeke, but not a word from Sonny, only silence which seemed like eternity. She nibbled a biscuit. I wished I could drop into a hole in the floor. Moeke just sat there. At last Sonny rescued us all, including herself: "Come on 'schmattie', with

244

all your beautiful butterflies, the dishes still have to be washed."
Silently, we cleared the table, tidied the room, went into the kitchen
and washed the tea dishes.

"I'm sorry if I've spoiled your evening," I ventured. "Don't be too
upset, I know it's been a shock to you, but in time you will realise
that this doesn't change a person for the worse, or make them
deny their birth and upbringing. I'm proud of it, every bit of it."

"Hmm, we'll see. Let's get cleared up for the evening," was the
only answer.

The kitchen was immaculate in no time, due to six willing hands.
Sonny warmed up: the cooling effect of our discourse set aside,
she made an attempt to create a worthwhile subject for the evening.

We had a homely and harmonious time exchanging news of
friends and relations. We grew closer once more, closer in our
loss and closer in our aspirations for the future.

They were genuinely interested to see me settled, earning my
living and making new friends with a view to a happy and successful marriage. True to tradition, they insisted on filling the role of
my parents and creating a situation for matrimony. We had many
a hearty laugh. Money didn't stop them playing a make-belief
game. 'To your forthcoming engagement, with love from Moeke
and Sonny'. This pretty card attached to a large bunch of dark red
roses! Oh, such rascals!

During the week-end I met Sonny's fiancé. A handsome young
man, slightly older than herself, but evidently deeply in love. I
could see he had been told about my doings and that he took the
matter very seriously, showing his disgust.

I wondered where I would go after their wedding. This question
kept me occupied. Needless worry! 'Your Father knoweth that you
have need of all those things'. For the time being I slept in Moeke's
bed. She had offered it to me, and she herself, slept with her
daughter on the large lits-jumeaux. These Dutch beds were my
delight, 'I'd love to possess one myself someday', I often thought.
The complete made-up bed, kept in place by three rubber straps,
could be folded right up against the wall, underneath a modern
bookshelf. Curtains were drawn across, and it looked like a stream-
lined wall fixture. As her future son-in-law was the manufacturer
of the beds, Moeke had extra fitments added. This particular bed
had a smart bookcase with glass sliding doors right along its shelf.

On each side of the curtains, Moeke had planned special fitted cupboards, one for hanging suits and dresses, the other with pull-out drawers for linen and underwear. Once Sonny was married, the young couple would stay with Moeke and she would have to go back to her own bed as Sonny and her husband would move into the large bedroom with the lits-lumeaux.

Sensing my apprehension regarding the future, Moeke had assured me that the young couple would not mind my presence, but I would have to look for a job. This had been my primary concern. Work—where I could eat, live and spend my off duty hours. Only sleeping accommodation was of immediate concern.

Sonny had been able to interest me in the nearby orphanage. 'It is a large modern building, and "A Christian place, too",' she added, slyly.

To the Superintendent it was as if 'I'd been sent'! They were one lady short in the boys section which consisted of 12 to 14 year-olds. Illness always cuts staff in any community and no replacements are quickly available; so when could I start?

"Tomorrow," I announced bravely. At home we toasted this quick success.

My section had twenty-two boys: Corrie and I managed all the work between us once our gang was off to school. Some came home for dinner, others descended as ravenous wolves on their meal at night. We mended torn trousers, socks, and worn jumpers; we played games during rainy week-ends and took them to the country on public holidays. We humoured quarrels and listened to their difficulties. In short we were a substitute mother and father, and I loved my work.

If only I could have settled down again, then this orphanage would have been a devoted task to accept. But there was a restlessness within me, and I realised the truth of the saying, 'The heart is restless until it finds its rest in Thee'. 'If only,' I thought, 'I could be in-the-way-of-the-Lord, know it, and follow it, my restlessness would cease.' I was determined to search and pursue His will, then and only then would this striving end.

'Teach me thy way, oh Lord', was my prayer as well as the Psalmist's. Having asked for guidance I left it at that and continued my daily work in the orphanage. On Sundays I made my way to the Begijnehofje in the centre of Amsterdam, where the Church of

Scotland held weekly services in English. The minister came all the way from Scotland, and the worshippers consisted of tourists, students, school children and genuine British people living in Amsterdam, seeking to worship in their mother tongue. I loved to worship there. I learned new words in a strange and beautiful language. Up till that time my vocabulary had only consisted of a phrase so frequently overheard of American soldiers, 'It's raining cats and dogs'.

Although I could not follow the service, the atmosphere was charged with the presence of the living Christ. Him, I was able to adore from the depth of my being. The language barrier didn't exist. On the contrary, I began to learn a new language. Following the lessons in my Dutch Bible, I carefully listened to the English Text. It was fun. Soon I boasted, I could speak a little English when sentences flowed from my tongue. People must have been very polite when they did not laugh at my 'Art thou hungry' and 'I thank thee' to a child. It wasn't till much later that the phraseology sorted itself out. During the singing of the hymns I got hold of the pronunciation, but the general benefit lay in the 'feel' of the language and the longing to see Scotland one day.

In the Begijnehofje, this longing was conceived. But how, how was I ever to get so far. No language, no money, no prospects: ridiculous! Yet, just nine months later, I arrived at the Central Station, Glasgow, Scotland.

During these nine months I had to travel another long, long road. A road which took me from home to home, from country to city, from village to town. A zig-zag of a journey, aiming all the time for Scotland. Once more I had to meet dozens of new people, had to tell my story over and over again, yet in the framework of these simple accounts I decided to cross the border.

19

ALLOW ME TO INVITE YOU TO A FAREWELL PARTY. COME with me to see how I celebrated my first and last Christmas in the city of my youth. Here in Amsterdam we worshipped the babe born in Bethlehem.

I celebrated it in a cellar, with other young Jewish teenagers. The cellar was in Moeke's house. She and Sonny were fast asleep, but they had given permission to let me have my friends here. "After all, it's your home," they had emphasised.

There were seven of us there. We all lived in Jewish homes, yet all had experienced the presence of the living Christ, and were drawn together by a desire to honour Him very specially, because our people had denied His living existence.

At intervals, a tap on the gutter window announced the arrival of yet another believer!

Since Sonny's wedding, I had taken up residence in the cellar below Moeke's bedroom. I loved the privacy of this place in the security of a home where true love was shared. Did they worry about my presence down there? I assured them I would not want to exchange it for the finest villa in the world.

Each night after duty in the orphanage, I would lift the hatch and descend to my own private domain. Just now it was decorated like a garden party in midwinter. All boxes and crates had been pushed to one side and covered with gaily printed materials, old curtains and rugs. My bed had a special, clean counterpane and Moeke almost buried me with gifts of fruit, chocolates and sweets.

Our number was complete by 11 p.m. and we made final arrangements for our united departure to the midnight service. My guests informed me that it was 'freezing' and they had all come supplied with woollen socks to pull over their shoes to prevent a broken limb. Did I have any socks? Of course I didn't, where would I get them? Yet when we were ready to leave at 11.30 p.m. a pair lay right across the inside front door. 'For Hansje, from Moeke with love. Be careful!'

Trust Moeke! she thought of everything.

Avoiding the noise of a slamming door I placed my key carefully in the lock and quietly closed the door. After retrieving the key of this, my kingdom, we went our way.

The sky was alive with stars, the air cutting our ears with its iciness, our hearts just thrilling with happiness and expectation. This was the night in which our Saviour's birth would be commemorated. *Our* Saviour. To feel part of such union, to belong to such company, to know yourself a beneficiary of such divine security. Words can never express what a soul experiences.

One of the boys in our group, wrote and composed a hymn for this night.

> 'Royal child,
> with a crown
> Brilliant is Thy world renown. . . .'

He sang it quietly while we made our way to Church. We avoided the pavement, walking along the grassy footpath in the centre of this large boulevard, and thus we were able to join him in his hymn of adoration. It didn't take long before we had caught the tune and all the words. We sang it over and over again. A group of young disciples as in days gone by. Secret believers. None of our group were secret! On the contrary, a fierce and determined flame burned at all times on the altar of each heart. They were ready to testify of Him to Whom they belonged. Their testimony was a glad, definite affirmation of the privilege a disciple of Christ may enjoy. We knew ourselves called, chosen, loved and guided. Each with our separate backgrounds; each with our separate disposition and characters: each with our different jobs and trainings; our aim was a common desire to love and serve Almighty God, who, as the Babe of Bethlehem, chose to enter the realm of humanity for a while.

The midnight service was impressive. We worshipped, but far greater was the worship during our journey back to my cellar. No words were exchanged: no hymns sung: many of us held hands and our heads high: The King of Glory within, had been honoured!

When at last I followed the others in their descent, I could scarcely keep my tears back. What a spread met our eyes. Moeke must have read Matthew's gospel, chapter 25 verses 31-40. Was she a secret believer? This is something between her and her Lord, but oh, how very kind. Thermos flasks with hot chocolate, nuts, cakes, biscuits, a complete welcome for the cold troop of Hebrew Christians.

Around 3.30 a.m. we were eager to leave again. Local carol singers from the Salvation Army had invited us to join their company. It was a good opportunity to air our views in music and song. To forget this 'underground' silence and sing at the top of our voices, 'Glory to the new born King; born, the King of Israel'.

At 7 a.m. we needed more hot chocolate and sandwiches. The whole group were entertained in the local Army Hall. We remained together till the commencement of the early morning Christmas Service where we listened to children's choirs, each taking part to honour Him to whom all honour is due.

During Channuka the little lights of liberty had burned brightly upstairs, but at Christmas the big light of love shone brilliantly through the dense walls of my cellar, and right into our hearts!

A week to spare and then a brand new year to make or mar. 1947 waiting to receive mankind.

The New Year was full of plans. Britain was still high on the list of my desires. Scotland, especially, exerted a strange drawing power. It was to be my 'heavenly Jerusalem' on earth! Had I reason to place such high expectations on any country of which I had no previous knowledge? None whatsoever! Was this the way of God's invisible guidance? I was compelled to accept this as the only possible explanation.

Once my entire attention was turned towards the country of my adoption, all other preparation proceeded without the slightest hitch.

Moeke allowed me to save hard, adding here and there a little extra for the journey. I worked extra hours at the orphanage to make that extra penny. Still more was needed. At last I sold the family silver which I would never use again, also the cutlery, the candlesticks and some ceremonial articles.

A new life was beckoning. My father's only surviving brother lived in London and I longed to see him, and look after him. He, too, had lost all his close family. Could we build up a new life together, looking after each other as our families would have wished? Would he be willing to accept me, a 'geschmad'? Would he, an official among Jewish dignitaries be as understanding as

Sonny and Moeke had been? It could be that my travels were not over yet, even if I found him.

Can an active mind cease to think? Can a living heart cease to beat with love for another? Can a 'saved' soul cease to long for another's salvation? Mind, heart and soul craved deeply to be, to belong and to share that highest, most coveted treasure available for all humanity: the heritage in Christ!

It had become clear to me that nothing else in life could carry a person through thick and thin than the invisible Spirit of the living God, in Christ. I would, therefore, proclaim Him under all circumstances and at all times. No one, rich or poor, can afford to ignore Him. Those who do and insist in doing so engage in a graver risk than the most daring adventurer.

With a heavy heart I viewed the future, as I had not yet begun to understand the freedom which is created by taking Christ's own advice in John chapter 15, 'Without me you can do nothing'.

This year, 1947, I intended to emigrate.

I left little and prepared to take just as little with me. Christ had assured me that He would see me through. Nothing would be lacking, but always and under all circumstances my aim was to be, 'seek ye first the Kingdom of God'. He will do the rest, promised in his words recorded in Mark 10. 29-30.

Countless farewell parties were behind me, but the last and most important one was still to take place at Moeke's house! It was a table fit for a queen. Sonny's wedding silver was out, also her best china, complicated and tasty dishes were prepared, bottles of wine, soda and the inevitable nuts and salty biscuits of all kinds were served. Was this a farewell from people who shunned, hated and despised your faith in the apostate, the false prophet? Those presents, good wishes and warmhearted love, were those gifts from cold indifference?

The Almighty has to bear constantly with our false and incorrect judgement of one another and advised Samuel, and also us, to leave judging to Him who knows best! 'For man looketh on the outward appearance, but the Lord looketh on the heart' (I Samuel 16. 7).

Next day human security would be left behind. The invisible, dependable Godly security lay once more before me. I had to jump. No turning back. The day was awaiting: action!

When Sonny, Moeke and myself arrived at the station I was

flabbergasted to see the many friends who had come to say good-bye. The teenagers, Hebrew Christians, old and young. Those I had dined with on Sundays after Church. Those I had sung with on Saturdays around the organ. My boys from the orphanage and Corrie with her fiancé. It was my day.

Although all emigration papers had been completed and in my pocket for the past few weeks, the act had still to be accomplished. I was leaving my country, my friends, my memories. What did I take with me? My little black case, a larger one too, and a bundle of hopes, faith and many worthwhile lessons learned.

Wherever I went, of one thing I was certain, what I was leaving I would find again, for Christ's ambassadors are scattered throughout the world. A Christian just can't be lonely, can't be alone, can't exist on his own. A Christian, by the very nature of his creation, must have fellowship with others. 'Bear ye one another's burdens, and so fulfil the law of Christ'.

What I was leaving I would find again, What I could no longer give in Holland I would give elsewhere. The same sun, moon and stars which I had observed through the skylight of many a Dutch attic, would shine in the country of my adoption. The heavens envelop us wherever we roam. Over us all reigns the same Creator. All countries and people of every class are alike before Him. He indwells all who invite Him to do so.

Where is the old, and where is the new? All will be alike. People with joys, sorrows, hopes and fears.

People who dare, those who don't care.

> Some who do try, others just lie.
> Few who are sorry, many never worry.
> The gentle and humble
> And those who must grumble,
> Proud and unbending,
> One finds them pretending
> In countries throughout this whole world.
>
> Then why mourn these partings,
> Tomorrow you'll be starting
> To meet the same over again.
> Does language deceive you,
> The heart will believe you
> Certifying: Mankind is alike.

There was little to say as I stood at the window of the compartment; just the usual 'Take care of yourself' and my constant repetition of 'Thanks for all you've been, all you've done'. Already I carried many a little keepsake and others were handed through the window. Someone insisted on the last taste of a Dutch delicacy: fresh herrings with raw onions! A memorable farewell when I kissed each one good-bye with the penetrating smell of raw onions! I couldn't have refused that 'well-meaning' well-wisher!

All too quickly the whistle sounded. I waved and waved till the train swung round the bend.

"Holland myn Holland ik vind je zo mooi" (Holland my Holland how beautiful thou art). Suddenly this school song rang through my mind while the wheels beat the rhythm on the track.

I felt grown up all of a sudden. This time I was emigrating all on my own, seeking the new. I was creating a new life, in a new environment, with a new language and new friends. 'Behold, I have set before thee an open door, and no man can shut it . . .' became the peg on which I dared to hang my young life.

'Lo, I am with you alway.' Countless promises like these from God Almighty hit my mind like laden arrows. Yes I was brave with the good Shepherd beside me. 'Thy rod and Thy staff shall comfort me. Though I walked through the valley of the shadow of death *thou* hast been with me and always will be with me. I believe firmly, Lord, that goodness and mercy shall follow me all the days of my life and then. . . . Then I shall dwell in the house of the Lord for ever.'

Don't dream, Hansje, it's almost Rotterdam. There would be others waiting to shake my hand and kiss me farewell. Look out for Rotterdam. Two more stations. There they were: the whole family Ornstein, their neighbours, friends and the inevitable cup of coffee through the compartment window, a roll with cheese and one with tomato. I'd eat it later. The whistle . . . cheerio, cheerio, God bless you all, each one, cheerio!

Hook van Holland won't be long now, get your two cases down, Hans! The trains drove right to the quayside. What a large ship! Like a child, I could hardly wait to board it. There were formalities to comply with, customs regulations, forms to fill in, questions to be answered. At last I climbed up the gangway, then looked for a space and squarely rested my arms on the railing, staring down into the muddy water.

Don't Hansje, I urged myself, up, up, up! 'I will lift up mine eyes unto the hills' (Psalm 121. 1). The hills: Scotland!

A free agent, I walked with uplifted head to a seat on the deck. There lazing in a chair, I reflected on those years gone by.

One long severe thunderstorm! It was frightening and very dangerous at times. The rumbling thunder of threat and rumour was heard continually, then the crashing thuds coming nearer and nearer. Would the lightning strike this night? The flashes hit right, left and centre, then suddenly hit us as well, burning all that was near and dear. Still the storm continued—frightening, rumbling, striking all over this and other continents.

Thunderstorms hitting continents, nations, countries, cities, villages and homes. But thunderstorms must pass! Of course, they leave devastation, destruction and death.

There raged a thunderstorm when the King of this universe experienced the act of dying for us.

Whenever electric storms hit your home or family life, look at the storm which shook Calvary. Allow it to be the yardstick for the circumstances confronting your storm.

The sky will clear, you will experience the deathly silence of loneliness, or despair, hopelessness, indifference to continuing in this struggle for life and then . . . after that silence, that space of time we need to come to, we shall come to see colours again. Brilliant colours; a rainbow through the rain! It beckons us to continue to lift up our heads, to look at that miracle of nature, that promise of Almighty God in Genesis 9. 13-16. Presently the sun will shine again for you, too.

Calvary, storm, rainbow and then . . . then brilliant sunshine! Resurrection! also for you.

Believe it! Look for it! Lift up your heart, lift it up away from the base and destructive rumblings of doubt and fear.

Hold up your heart, mind, emotions, head and eyes. Up, up, there you will detect colour again, brilliance, and promises with certainty of fulfilment.

While the wounds inflicted by the lightning still hurt and burn and undoubtedly will leave their scars for ever, yet your general health will be bathed by the warmth and radiation of God's sun of love. You will tan and recover, stronger to determine your attitude for future storms.

You, too, will join the millions who quietly, humbly but very sincerely dare to utter:

'We know that *ALL* things work together for good to them that love God, to them who are called according to His purpose' (Romans 8. 28).

The ship had reached mid channel. Surrounded by water and sky I mused on the fundamental barrenness of material possessions. I saw no land, no human dwellings. I knew nothing had been left behind and nothing awaited my arrival.

An undying soul addressed Him whose twenty-four hour service has one, and one aim only, to select *willing* souls to LIVE.

'Praise, my soul, the *King* of Heaven.'

King of heaven, Father of mankind. My father, my *King*. In this royal relationship, no poverty or death can sting.

Be persuaded when you hear His voice:

'Come unto *Me*, all ye that labour and are heavy laden, and *I* will give you rest. Take my yoke upon you, and learn of me; and ye shall find rest unto your souls.'

When you have closed this book, be certain that you, too, are selected to live. Never doubt it. Repeat it often amidst thunderstorms. Repeat it when lost in a maze of worry and fear. Repeat it when baffled by life's problems with its avalanche of daily, homely, petty strains.

You are selected to live, to give, to share, to affirm that Christ Jesus came into this world to kill religion, to instil new life into this artificially breathing world by living according to God's will and enabling you to do the same.

> Selected to live, an undying life.
> Selected to live an attached life, to its source.
> Selected to live under Royal command.
> Selected to live in service for others.
> Selected to live!
>   Go forth then and give. . . .
>   LIVE!

Please join me now in reverent silence,
Salute deep within you those who are gone.
Like me, you'll be baffled and won't know the answer
What really in mankind has gone wrong?

We don't know the answer; pretend we don't!
The wicked, they acted—we passive, permitted;
No mad demonstrations, not anywhere!
Individuals objected. The church was asleeping
And murders continued wholesale.

Prompted to bow our heads in silence,
We contemplate our united guilt.
Yet while we ask for wisdom, action,
'Ne'er tolerate such crime again!'. . . .
Throughout the world, men, women and children
Beg us to notice their plight and pain.

Millions still suffer, they always will
While we are comfy, secure.
Not ours, but Christ's love must conquer that evil
In your labour of love for . . . ONE life.